CHINA'S FOREIGN RELATIONS

Also by Denny Roy

THE NEW SECURITY AGENDA IN THE ASIA–PACIFIC REGION
(*editor*)

China's Foreign Relations

Denny Roy

ROWMAN & LITTLEFIELD PUBLISHERS, INC.
Lanham • New York • Boulder • Oxford

ROWMAN & LITTLEFIELD PUBLISHERS, INC.
Published in the United States of America
by Rowman & Littlefield Publishers, Inc.
4720 Boston Way, Lanham, Maryland 20706

Library of Congress Cataloging-in-Publication Data
Roy, Denny, 1960–
China's foreign relations / Denny Roy.
p. cm.
Includes bibliographical references and index.
ISBN 0–8476–9012–1 (cloth). — ISBN 0–8476–9013–X (pbk.)
1. China—Foreign relations—1976–   I. Title.
JZ1734.R69 1998
327.51'009'045—dc21   97–51889
                                                              CIP

Printed in Malaysia

Contents

Preface

Complementing the more advanced and specialized discussions of particular aspects of the topic in a number of recent articles I have written for academic journals, this book is designed to provide an accessible and general introduction to post-Cold War Chinese foreign policy.

Chinese terms and names used in this book are transliterated according to the Pinyin romanization system. I have made a few exceptions for well-known names traditionally spelled differently, such as Sun Yatsen and Chiang Kaishek, but in these cases I have removed the usual hyphens for greater consistency with the modern practice followed for most other Chinese names that appear in the book.

Readers will note that Chapter 8 is much longer than the other chapters, but the material covered is so closely and organically interrelated that I have decided it is better to keep it together than to divide it artificially for the sake of uniformity.

I am grateful to the Strategic and Defence Studies Centre (SDSC), Australian National University, and to the Department of Education, Employment and Trade (DEET), Government of Australia. DEET provided the funding for my research fellowship at the SDSC, under the auspices of which this book was written. I am indebted to SDSC Director Paul Dibb and Professor Desmond Ball for their support and patronage. SDSC staff Tina Lynam, Karen Smith, Sue Gerrard, Elza Sullivan, Jena Hamilton and Carol Taylor also deserve my gratitude. My publisher Steven Kennedy and an anonymous reviewer gave me excellent advice on revising earlier versions of this project. Finally, I thank my wife and daughter for cooperating willingly when I needed to devote extra time to finishing this book.

DENNY ROY

List of Abbreviations

AMS	Academy of Military Science
APEC	Asia-Pacific Economic Cooperation
ARATS	Associations for Relations Across the Taiwan Straits
ARF	ASEAN Regional Forum
ASEAN	Association of South East Asian Nations
BWC	Biological Weapons Convention
CCP	Chinese Communist Party
CIA	Central Intelligence Agency
CMC	Central Military Commission
COCOM	Coordinating Committee for Multilateral Export Controls
COSTIND	Commission of Science, Technology and Industry for National Defence
CTBT	Comprehensive Test Ban Treaty
DPP	Democratic Progressive Party
GATT	General Agreement on Tariffs and Trade
GLD	General Logistics Department (of the PLA)
GPD	General Political Department (of the PLA)
GSD	General Staff Department (of the PLA)
IAEA	International Atomic Energy Agency
ICBMs	Intercontinental Ballistic Missiles
IOC	International Olympic Committee
JSP	Japan Socialist Party
LDP	Liberal Democratic Party
LOC	Line of Actual Control
MFA	Ministry of Foreign Affairs
MFN	Most Favoured Nation
MIRV	Multiple Independently Targeted Re-entry Vehicle
MOFTEC	Ministry of Foreign Trade and Economic Cooperation
MTCR	Missile Technology Control Regime
NDU	National Defence University

NFU	No First Use
NICs	Newly Industrializing Countries
NPT	Nuclear Nonproliferation Treaty
NSA	Negative Security Assurance
ODA	Overseas Direct Assistance
PAP	People's Armed Police
PECC	Pacific Economic Cooperation Council
PKI	Indonesian Communist Party
PLA	People's Liberation Army
PLAAF	PLA Air Force
PLAN	PLA Navy
PRC	People's Republic of China
RMA	Revolution in Military Affairs
ROC	Republic of China
SAR	Special Administrative Region
SEF	Straits Exchange Foundation
SEZs	Special Economic Zones
SLBMs	Submarine-Launched Ballistic Missiles
SLORC	State Law and Order Restoration Council
TMD	Theatre Anti-Ballistic Missile Defence System
UNCLOS	United Nations Convention on the Law of the Sea
WBG	World Bank Group
WTO	World Trade Organization

1

Introduction

For various reasons, China has always been an important country. It has long been the world's most populous nation, with vast economic potential that is now finally being realized. It is also one of the world's oldest and most influential civilizations, and one that has fascinated foreigners for centuries. During the early phase of the Cold War, the People's Republic of China (PRC) threatened to destabilize the region with its militant, revolutionary ideology. Today its rapid development puts the PRC in line to become the world's largest economy early in the twenty-first century. Accordingly, China's international political influence is steadily increasing as well. China may well become the next superpower. Conversely, China already features so prominently in both the world economy and the global strategic landscape that domestic social or political turmoil would also have dramatic ramifications throughout the world. Indeed, whatever the PRC's fate, all of us will inevitably feel the impact of its external orientation and behaviour wherever we live.

The study of Chinese foreign relations has never been more compelling than in the post-Cold War era, when the key element of PRC foreign policy is a comprehensive national buildup. If the Cold War era saw China attain 'liberation' and consolidate its independence, the PRC now seeks to close the gaps in political, economic and military capabilities separating it from the other great powers and to take what it sees as its rightful place as the preeminent state in Asia. The PRC leadership's emphasis on economic development has entailed two major corollary strategies. The first is active participation in global economic and other regimes to maximize Chinese access to the world's wealth, knowledge and influential institutions. The second is omnidirectional rapprochement, intended to create a favourable political environment for foreign trade and investment and the diffusion of advanced technology and

1

expertise, and to minimize resource-draining military tensions. The success of these strategies has raised the prospect of China supplanting the United States as the reigning Asia-Pacific power, resulting in a period of long-term tensions between Beijing and Washington, which sees the emergence of a dominant regional state as a threat to American interests. While China is willing to abide by many of the aspects of the current international system, its policies and interests challenge some of the norms favoured by other Asia-Pacific countries. Examples are China's lack of transparency in defence affairs and willingness to use force in the resolution of the 'internal' matters of Taiwan and the disputed Spratly Islands.

Accordingly, Chinese foreign policy has attracted the attention of a multitude of analysts. Yet the main conclusion one is likely to draw from this plethora of studies is that a consistent explanation for China's foreign relations is impossible to pin down. According to one assessment, 'What we are dealing with here is less a coherent policy position and more a set of actions and reactions, each reflecting a different mix of interests, domestic pressures and constraints from past policies' (Wilson, 1993, p. 195). It is only the importance of the subject matter that provides enough motivation to tackle such a complex topic as China's foreign relations. To get the most out of this enterprise, we should try to find a manageable number of principles or assumptions to serve as guides in interpreting Chinese foreign policy.

Science seeks to understand, then to predict, and ultimately to control. This process is clear in natural sciences such as physics and chemistry. The agenda underlies the social sciences, including international politics, as well, even if it is rarely spoken of openly. The real motivation for studying the foreign policy of a country such as China is the hope that we can anticipate or even influence its government's external behaviour. (This is not Western arrogance; Chinese analysts take the same approach to studying the United States, and rightly so.) Of course, the social sciences are far behind the natural sciences in predicting and controlling. Presumably this is not because physicists and chemists are more intelligent than political scientists, but because the behaviour of governments is far more complex and variable than the behaviour of asteroids and molecules.

A simple explanation is preferable because the simpler the explanation, the greater the possibility of mastering the more advanced steps of prediction and control. Unfortunately, however,

while some relatively simple explanations for particular PRC policies have found broad acceptance, scholars and analysts have
reached no consensus on a simple model of Chinese foreign policy
in general – i.e., an explanation that covers *all* PRC policies. Some
analysts have proffered relatively simple theories of Chinese foreign
policy, arguing that Beijing has one or two overarching goals that
guide decision-making. A common assertion, for example, is that
the PRC's overwhelming concern is in promoting a peaceful environment for Chinese economic development (Chen, 1993, p. 244; Xu,
1994, p. 6; Cossa, 1994, p. 20). But other theorists have seen the
desires for regional hegemony, improving China's international
status, promoting socialist revolution, and punishing the former
'imperialist' powers as the driving forces of Beijing's foreign policy
(a few examples: Pan, 1993, p. 66; Gurtov and Hwang, 1980, p. 17;
Wei, 1985, p. 142; Elegant, 1996, p. 8).

Many theorists reject the notion that a simple model is feasible.
Kim writes, 'Chinese foreign policy behaviour seems to be in such a
state of ambiguous motion that one can never fully understand what
really makes it tick. . . . Given the complex, involved and multi-
dimensional nature of post-Mao Chinese foreign policy, no single
concept, method, or perspective is adequate to describe and explain
it' (Kim, 1989b, pp. 4, 6). Thomas W. Robinson adds that 'No
integrated "model" of Chinese foreign policy yet exists that meets
the two essential tests of any theory: capability of explaining most
facts and developments on the basis of a small number of carefully
defined variables, each meaningfully related to the others; and
general acceptance by scholars in the field' (Robinson, 1994a, p.
556n).

Therefore, since Chinese foreign policy-making involves many
factors and variables, we should aim for a *simplified* rather than a
simple answer – a set of interpretive guidelines rather than a pithy,
one-sentence formula. A feasible objective is to separate out from a
mass of details those that matter more from those that matter less,
and to identify patterns that will lead to useful interpretations. These
in turn might provide a meaningful and reliable basis for analyzing
present and future Chinese foreign relations. Such is the objective of
this book.

Every book has a point of view, whether consciously or uncon-
sciously. My discussion of Chinese foreign relations is based on
several assumptions. To begin with, I find that China's foreign
policy behaviour is largely consistent with Neo-Realist Theory

(prominent works include Waltz, 1979 and Mearsheimer, 1994/95). In brief, Neo-Realism maintains that since states exist in an anarchic system in which they are constantly and unalterably subject to harm by other states, the chief concern of governments is maintaining or enhancing their relative national power, particularly *vis-à-vis* their most dangerous potential adversaries. Furthermore, the actions of states are generally motivated by narrow self-interest rather than moral principles, although a state may well judge, in Machiavellian fashion, that *appearing* to be moral will serve its interests in the long run. Neo-Realists expect that alliances will be flexible, and that a government will seek security cooperation with its neighbours to offset the power of the state or states it considers most threatening. But since today's ally may be tomorrow's enemy, ultimately a state can rely only on itself for protection; therefore states seek to develop their own capacities to defend their interests, and tend to resist the imposition of restrictions on these capabilities.

Nevertheless, Neo-Realism does not explain the complete picture of China's foreign relations. Three additional theoretical assumptions must be admitted. First, Chinese historical experience strongly influences how Chinese policy-makers perceive the international environment and China's place within it. How Beijing defines its interests and how it assesses the likely consequences of particular policies may be shaped by factors unique to the experience of PRC elites. Unique historical experiences explain some of the distinctive features of Chinese foreign policy: an obsession with Chinese 'sovereignty'; the desire to maintain an international image of China as a principled actor; and the curious mixture of great power and weak power attitudes, with Beijing insisting on the one hand that China be accorded due respect by other politically powerful countries, and demanding on the other hand special privileges due to China's economic underdevelopment and past victimization.

Second, China's internal politics can be a critical factor in foreign policy-making. In China, as in many other states, politics do not stop 'at the water's edge'. The leadership may sometimes select a certain foreign policy option because it is expected to have desirable effects on China's *domestic* political environment, not necessarily because they think it will best enhance China's relative national power. This apparent departure from the Neo-Realist model must take into account the Chinese tendency to view regime security (i.e., keeping members of the Chinese Communist Party in positions of power) and national security (i.e., protecting Chinese citizens, territory and assets from harm) as overlapping, and internal and external security threats as interrelated.

Third, even in China's one-party political system, several disparate groups have important policy-making influence, and the policy-making process involves considerable debate and consensus-building. Organizations or factions within the government often support narrowly self-interested policies, and may occasionally become powerful or persuasive enough to implement their agenda.

These assumptions will resurface throughout the book, which is structured to first examine the Chinese foreign policy-making milieu, then to explore specific Chinese relationships with the outside world, and finally to extrapolate on the observed patterns. The next chapter briefly surveys the evolution of recent Chinese foreign policy, identifying some of the important historical experiences that influence policy-making today. Experience with past foreign relations is one of the major factors that has forged the particular outlook on international politics of PRC elites, which is examined in Chapter 3. This outlook, in turn, is crucial to comprehending contemporary Chinese policies. Chapter 4 expands on the theme of contention among self-interested organizations in the foreign policy-making process, paying particular attention to the roles of the Ministry of Foreign Affairs and the People's Liberation Army (PLA), two of the most influential of these organizations. The PLA's role in executing (as opposed to formulating) policy is examined along with other issues related to China's military defence in Chapter 6.

Chapter 5 focuses on China's relationship with the world economy, including Beijing's struggle to gain the benefits of global economic exchange while maintaining its sovereignty. The same theme recurs in China's position on other global issues, such as arms control, human rights and the proper role of the United Nations, which are discussed in Chapter 7. This book also surveys China's recent relations with specific countries. Since they have directly global ramifications, Beijing's relationship with the former superpower Russia and the current superpower America are covered in Chapter 7. Chapter 8 extends this coverage to China's regional neighbours Japan, India, Korea, and the Association of Southeast Asian Nations. Chapter 9 takes up the momentous question (which is not to say it provides a momentous answer) of the future direction of China's foreign relations, while Chapter 10 summarizes this book's general findings and places them in the larger context of theories of international relations.

2

A Historical Overview of Chinese Foreign Relations

The past two centuries have seen tremendous flux in China's relationship with the outside world. They have also generated attitudes, assumptions and a historiography absorbed by successive generations of Chinese leaders. This historical baggage, including China's own recent foreign policies and their consequences, form a crucial part of the context of China's present-day foreign relations.

Pre-PRC Foreign Relations: The 'Century of Shame'

The depth of Chinese humiliation over what came to be known as the 'Century of Shame' cannot be fathomed without first recognizing that for previous millennia China had seen itself as the political and cultural centre of the earth, the 'Middle Kingdom' (*Zhongguo*, the Chinese name for 'China'). In terms of its physical size and achievements, ancient China certainly deserves to be classed with the great empires of history. In terms of longevity, the Chinese civilization is perhaps in a class by itself.

China indeed boasted a well-developed culture, and for centuries the Chinese had little or no contact with other peoples who might have impressed them. Foreigners were considered inferior; Chinese elites had little interest in studying or trading with them, since foreigners had little to offer the refined culture and civilization of China. The only serious outside military threat came from nomadic tribes in the north, who were numerically relatively small and who

6

would be sinicized, or forced to adopt Chinese habits and customs, even if they succeeded in seizing the monarchy (Adelman and Shih, 1993, p. 30). The dividing line between China and the outside world was less distinct than in the modern world's community of nation-states. In theory, the Chinese emperor was the natural ruler of the civilized world. In accordance with Confucian philosophy, the emperor's real power was thought to derive from his moral and cultural superiority (although with its large population and comparatively advanced science and technology, China also had the more conventional elements of power as well). Thus, the conquest of China by a militarily superior people such as the Mongols or Manchus did not disprove the ultimate superiority of Chinese civilization. For most of their history, the Chinese had little reason to doubt the national ideology that they were the world's pre-eminent civilization.

China proper stretched from the Great Wall in the north to Indochina in the south, and from the east coast to the western plateau. Many of the people close to this Chinese hub were at least partly sinicized – the Koreans, Taiwanese, Mongolians, Tibetans and Annamese (ancient Vietnamese). Beyond these kingdoms, Chinese influence waned. Thus, in the eyes of the Chinese, foreigners were more foreign the further they resided from the Middle Kingdom and its influence.

China's neighbours could find a place, if an inferior one, in the Chinese order through the tribute system. Emissaries from neighbouring states were required to acknowledge the emperor's moral and political authority by visiting the imperial court at the appointed season, performing the 'kowtow' or ritual prostration, and presenting the emperor with lavish gifts. In return, tributary states received from the Chinese trading privileges, instruction, and sometimes military protection. Some peoples, of course, refused to recognize the emperor's authority; the Chinese took this as an indication of irredeemable savagery. The Chinese did not traditionally accept the Westphalian principle of legal equality among nations; in the Chinese scheme of things, China was at the top of a hierarchical international order. In theory, this precluded the Chinese government from making military alliances with other kingdoms or from tolerating the refusal of some powerful neighbours to ritually acknowledge Chinese superiority – a civilized country was supposed to operate strictly on moral principles, not through crude deal-making. In practice, however, Chinese officials sometimes bent these rules out of political expediency.

Internally, China's politics revolved around the struggle to achieve or maintain unified control over a large, populous, and multi-ethnic land. Organized rebellion was a perennial worry of the central government; indeed, several uprisings in the late Qing Dynasty helped hasten the *ancien régime*'s collapse. The most serious of these, the 1850–64 Taiping Rebellion, resulted in millions of deaths. Sometimes the central government had to battle against internal uprisings and foreign invasions simultaneously. It became an aphorism among the ruling elite that internal disorder increased China's vulnerability to foreign attack (*nei luan, wai huan*).

When Westerners began to arrive at China's borders, the government first treated them as just another group of distant barbarians drawn to the splendour of Chinese civilization. In 1793, Lord George Macartney and a large entourage laden with gifts calculated to impress the Chinese called on the emperor to request modest British trading rights in China. Emperor Qianlong responded negatively in a letter to King George III. 'We have never valued ingenious articles, nor do we have the slightest need of your country's manufactures', Qianlong wrote. Macartney later compared Qing Dynasty China to a huge but obsolete warship destined to drift aimlessly until it was 'dashed to pieces on the shore' (Spence, 1990, pp. 122–3). In fact, many Chinese officials soon began to argue that it was essential for China to acquire Western technology and scientific knowledge, if for no other reason than to protect China from vulnerability. Inertia within the Chinese monarchy and bureaucracy, however, would make Macartney's remark prophetic.

The Opium War was the first of the serious 'humiliations' China would endure at the hands of foreigners. By the 1830s, the widespread smoking of opium, brought to China by Western traders, had become a serious drain on China's supply of silver, the traders' preferred currency, not to mention a debilitating social vice. The emperor Daoguang appointed Lin Zexu a special commissioner and in 1838 dispatched him to the thriving port of Guangzhou (Canton) to halt the illegal opium trade. Lin, in many respects the model Confucian administrator, pursued his task with dedication, shutting down the foreign smuggling operations and destroying a massive stockpile of 3 million pounds of unrefined opium in 1839. In retaliation, the British government sent a large fleet to the Chinese east coast, which arrived in June 1840. With their superior military technology, the British forces captured several important cities and blockaded key waterways over the next few months. In August 1842 Chinese authorities accepted the Treaty of Nanjing, under the terms of which China would pay the British $21 million in compensation, permanently cede Hong Kong Island to Britain, and open five more Chinese cities to residency by British traders.

The Treaty of Nanjing was only one of a series of 'unequal treaties' that foreign powers forced upon the increasingly feeble and embattled Qing Dynasty government. When China tried to expel Westerners in the 'Boxer Rebellion' of 1900, the eventual result was another crushing military defeat, accelerated foreign penetration, and demands by the Western powers for massive reparation payments.

The realization by Chinese that their society was not, as they previously thought, the apogee of human civilization was itself a shattering blow to the national psyche. The full implications of Chinese technological and economic inferiority were even worse. By the turn of the century, China was a semi-colony, its regions divided into spheres of influence controlled by various foreign powers. Foreigners secured sweeping legal and economic privileges not only in the coastal provinces, but also in the Chinese interior, where foreign businessmen sought to exploit China's natural resources with the help of cheap local labour. Whole districts of some of China's most important cities were placed under the jurisdiction of foreigners. China was forbidden from levying anything beyond token tariffs, which both ensured favourable terms for foreign traders and undermined the development of Chinese industries. Many Chinese were also resentful that their country was forced to receive foreign missionaries, whose creeds seemed to turn local converts away from Chinese culture and toward Western philosophy. Chinese feelings of humiliation over their subjugation at the hands of foreign colonists coalesced in the oft-invoked myth of a sign at the gate of Huangpu Park in foreign-administered Shanghai that read, 'Chinese and Dogs Not Permitted'. (Chinese were in fact forbidden from entering parks in Shanghai's International Settlement, which were reserved for foreign residents; it is doubtful, however, that the notorious sign ever existed [Bickers and Wasserstrom, 1995, pp. 444–66]).

Even Japan, a former inferior in the traditional Chinese political hierarchy, demonstrated by its victory in the Sino-Japanese War of 1894–5 that through industrialization and political restructuring it had surpassed China as the region's strongest military power. The fruits of Japan's victory included control over Taiwan and Korea, formerly parts of China's sphere of influence.

Sun Yatsen, the most famous Chinese nationalist leader of the pre-Second World War period, wrote bitterly, 'We are the poorest and weakest country in the world, occupying the lowest position in world affairs; people of other countries are the carving knife and the serving dish while we are the fish and the meat' (Sun, 1928, p. 12). Sun, who advocated a republican government, was instrumental in rallying support for an overthrow of the hopelessly feeble Qing monarchy. Years of revolutionary activity and the support of the central government's supreme military commander, Yuan Shikai, allowed the republican movement to force out the Qing regime in October 1911. But Sun's dream went unfulfilled. Yuan, who had assumed leadership of the provisional government, showed little interest in establishing a democratic republic and gradually moved toward reinstituting the monarchy, eventually getting himself appointed as the new emperor on 1 January 1916. His government having proved ineffective, Yuan's final move brought widespread condemnation both within China and abroad. Yuan's death a few months later left China without a central government and inaugurated the 'warlord period', when leadership devolved to provincial strongmen with private armies.

China under the Guomindang

Sun's Guomindang (Nationalist Party, sometimes rendered Kuomintang) named 'national salvation' as one of its key tenets, but in the early 1920s the party was itself in need of salvation. Marginalized and short of funds, Sun accepted an offer of support from agents of the Soviet-sponsored Comintern. The Guomindang was reorganized along the lines of the Soviet Communist Party, and in 1922 it began admitting communists into its ranks. Sun died in 1925 amidst this awkward and short-lived alliance between the Guomindang and the communists. Hence, he has the unusual distinction of being revered today in both the PRC and in the Republic of China on the island of Taiwan, to which the Guomindang fled in 1949 to escape destruction by the armies of the Chinese Communist Party (CCP). Leadership of the party, and the task of national salvation, fell to Sun's deputy, the young military officer Chiang Kaishek (or, more properly, Jiang Jieshi). Himself a fervent nationalist, Chiang in

1926 initiated a military campaign known as the 'Northern Expedition' to conquer or otherwise subdue the warlords and unify China under Guomindang rule. Before completing the campaign, Chiang suddenly turned on the communists. In a surprise operation in April 1927, Chiang's forces slaughtered as many communists as his forces could find in the cities then under Guomindang control. China was nominally unified by 1928, but its hardships were far from finished. The Guomindang was now locked in a fight to the death with the communists that would last another two decades. As the communists would be quick to point out, Chiang's regime was corrupt, frequently brutal, and showed little interest in bringing justice or improved living standards to the majority of China's downtrodden population. Finally, one more great foreign humiliation remained to be endured: the Japanese invasion. The increasingly powerful and assertive Japanese military seized Manchuria in 1931. They formed a new state, 'Manchukuo', which they claimed was an independent country that gave the Manchus their own homeland, but which was actually a Japanese satellite. Chiang did not attempt to expel the Japanese, fearing that his forces could not match those of Japan and that he had to preserve his strength to fight the CCP.

The CCP came close to extinction in 1934, when its main force was surrounded by Guomindang forces in Jiangxi Province. The communists broke out, but to find safety they had to embark on what became known as the 'Long March': a year-long journey over 6,000 miles of rough terrain, carrying meagre provisions, and sometimes under fire, to Yanan in Shanxi Province, where the CCP established a new base. Only half of the 80,000 who began the Long March reached Yanan. Along the way, Mao Tse-tung (Mao Zedong) had established himself as undisputed leader of the Chinese Communist Party. Mao insisted that the CCP maintain autonomy from Moscow, which previously had been highly influential in important CCP decisions, sometimes with disastrous results.

In 1937 Japan invaded China proper, and within a few months captured the major cities of eastern China. The Japanese occupation was cruel, marked by many incidents of systematic murder and torture of civilians and prisoners of war. The most notorious of these incidents was the orgy of barbarism that followed the Japanese capture of Nanjing in December 1937. Estimates of the number of Chinese civilians killed there run as high as 200,000. In addition to the theme of Japanese war crimes, this period is famous in Communist Chinese lore for the Guomindang government's unpatriotic and incompetent defence policies (allegations challenged by some recent scholarship: Hsiung and Levine, 1992, esp. pp. 28, 46–8). The Chinese Communists, by contrast, cultivated an image of themselves as heroic guerrilla warriors who did not hesitate to battle against the superior Japanese forces. This image strengthened the Party's nationalist credentials, and its legacy is visible in the erroneous belief of most mainland Chinese today that CCP forces were the main factor in China's victory over Japan during the Pacific War. According to the Chinese Xinhua News Agency, in a mid-1995 survey of the foreign affairs views of Chinese 'youth' (young adults, including some in their 30s) conducted by the *China Youth Daily*, over three-quarters of the respondents said the leadership of the Chinese Communist Party was the main factor in China's victory over Japan during the Pacific War, while only 2.8 per cent credited the defeat of Japan to 'international support'. Older, less-educated Chinese would be even more likely to credit the CCP with winning the war.

The Guomindang and Chinese Communist forces officially suspended their own power struggle during the Second World War to join forces in a 'united front' against the Japanese. After Japan surrendered in 1945, the Chinese Civil War resumed and ground inevitably toward a violent denouement despite repeated American attempts to mediate a peaceful solution. At the conclusion of the Pacific War, Guomindang troops outnumbered communist troops tenfold, 3.7 million to 320,000. These numbers, however, proved deceptive. The brutality, corruption, and carpet-bagging of Guomindang officials contrasted unfavourably with the discipline, egalitarian spirit and land reform programmes of the communists. The communist message played particularly well in the countryside, enabling Mao's troops to conduct an effective guerrilla warfare campaign. Communist troops saved their attacks for Guomindang supply convoys and smaller, isolated groups of Guomindang soldiers, avoiding the large garrisons based in major cities. The balance of forces shifted as the Communist armies gained new recruits and captured large quantities of weapons and ammunition, while the demoralized Guomindang forces suffered mass surrenders and desertions along with their battlefield casualties. By mid-1948, Chiang's troops had decreased to around two million, while communist forces had grown to over one-and-a-half million and had more artillery guns than the Guomindang armies (Chassin, 1965,

p. 177). Mao was now able to attack and defeat Chiang's armies in conventional pitched battles, and the territory under Guomindang control shrank rapidly.

With victory in hand, the CCP proclaimed the foundation of a new government in Beijing in October 1949. In December, Chiang and about two million of his Guomindang followers fled to Taiwan, which had only been reclaimed from half a century of Japanese rule in late 1945. The Guomindang saw itself as preserving the heritage of the 'Republic of China', proclaimed in 1911, on the last piece of Chinese territory outside the control of communist 'bandits'. (Henceforth, this book will use the names 'Republic of China' and 'Taiwan' interchangeably). For the CCP, Chiang's escape meant that a complete communist victory over the fascist enemy would have to be deferred, and in the meantime the Party's bitterest enemy would control China's most economically developed province.

The founding of the People's Republic officially marked the end of the Century of Shame, and it was undoubtedly with the humiliating events of this recent past in mind that Mao said in one of his first public speeches as his country's new leader, 'Our nation will never again be an insulted nation. We have stood up' (Fan, 1972, p. 91; Camilleri, 1980, p. 6). What John W. Garver terms the 'myth of National Humiliation' (Garver, 1993, p. 7) has become central to the identity of the PRC, and redressing the wrongs done to China by the foreign powers became one of the most important aspects of the PRC's foreign relations. Mao and other CCP figures argued that the Century of Shame was an anomaly in Chinese history, during the great majority of which the Chinese have been an advanced and venerable people, and that China's inability to defend itself was the result of a combination of foreign machinations and poor government at home. The important lessons of the Century of Shame were these: foreign powers want to weaken and exploit China; the Chinese must never again leave themselves vulnerable to abuse at the hands of foreigners; the world has not adequately acknowledged the great injustices done to China nor given China due respect as a traditionally great civilization and a nation of outstanding recent accomplishments; and, finally, the legacy of the Century of Shame will not be completely overcome until Beijing regains control of all historically Chinese territory, especially Taiwan.

The PRC's foreign relations may be divided into three periods: the revolutionary period, beginning in 1949; the 'strategic triangle' period, beginning in the early 1970s; and the 'open door' period, starting roughly with the decade of the 1980s. Although there is some policy overlap between these divisions, this categorization is nonetheless useful, as each period marks the emergence of a distinct and fundamentally new orientation in Chinese foreign policy.

The Revolutionary Period

The CCP regime came to power with a Marxist worldview. A class struggle, a conflict between the 'haves' and the 'have-nots', was thought to be the driving force of history, not only in individual states but also in international relations. World history was moving through stages; it was inevitable that capitalism would give way to socialism and eventually the utopia of communism. Capitalist states would therefore see the rise of socialist states as a mortal threat and strive desperately to repress and destroy them. Imperialism by the capitalist states was considered the principal cause of war.

Mao also emphasized the importance of self-reliance. China should create its own model of nation-building rather than attempt to copy the experience of other nations (Mao had often hotly disagreed with Moscow over CCP political and battle strategy during the Chinese Civil War), and the PRC should rely as much as possible on its own resources for economic and social development. Mao feared the vulnerability that foreign trade and investment would engender; at some point, he believed, foreigners would invariably try to use this influence to weaken China.

Stephen M. Walt argues that states that have recently undergone a social revolution are especially likely to be involved in a war. In a social revolution, not only are the individual leaders replaced, but the social power structure changes – i.e., the entire ruling class or group of elites, as well, is knocked out of power, and a new group takes their place. Walt adds that 'a revolution creates a new state resting on different social groups, new social and political institutions, different legitimating myths, and novel conceptions of the political community' (Walt, 1992, p. 324). Revolutionary ideologies tend to be optimistic – faithful that they will prevail against the odds, expecting the common people in other countries to support them, and emphasizing the importance of their own people's spirit and conviction as factors in victory. Yet new revolutionary regimes are also insecure, fearful of attempts by both internal opponents and foreign governments to strike them down before they have fully consolidated their power, and thus prone to interpreting the moves of other states in a sinister light or exaggerating foreign threats to rally domestic political support. At the same time, there are several reasons why other states may seek war against a revolutionary state: the revolutionary ideology may be fundamentally threatening to other states' political or economic systems; other states may misinterpret the rhetorical bravado of revolutionary regimes as aggressive intent, such rhetoric usually stemming from insecurity; and outsiders may calculate that the upheaval of revolution has at least temporarily weakened the revolutionary state's war-making capability, giving its enemies a window of opportunity for preventive war. In the longer term, however, the high tensions between revolutionary states and the established powers fade as revolutionary governments become 'socialized' and 'moderate their behavior over time', Walt writes (Walt, 1992, pp. 337–52, 360).

China in the early years of CCP rule largely fitted this pattern. Its revolutionary posture made it prone to conflict with the United States and other status-quo powers. Each side represented a political and economic system which the other side saw as the arch-enemy of its own system. The CCP was keenly aware of the serious threats to its rule posed by domestic opposition, Guomindang-sponsored subversives, and powerful foreign countries such as the USA. Yet Mao often belittled these threats, calling the United States a 'paper tiger' and downplaying the strategic value of nuclear weapons, as a means of encouraging his people and gaining international recognition. It is easy to see how such statements, intended primarily to warn off potential attackers, took on offensive connotations in the minds of Western strategists and politicians who expected the communists to attempt to 'roll back' democracy and capitalism. Unusual mutual hostility and fear prevented an early normalization of relations between Beijing and Washington and contributed to the unwanted Sino-US war in Korea. Only with years of experience did the Chinese and Americans come to see each other as cautious, predictable and pragmatic.

For status-quo-oriented countries in the region, one of the more disturbing means by which a revolutionary China challenged the system was sponsorship of communist insurgencies. Even before the end of the Chinese Civil War, CCP officials had begun to articulate the concept of what became known as 'wars of national liberation'. Although many former colonies in Asia and elsewhere were gaining independence, Beijing took the Marxist viewpoint that these countries were still controlled by the former colonial powers or by the United States through local puppet governments. Furthermore, China, by virtue of its own revolutionary experience and the additional contributions of Mao Zedong Thought to the Marxist Canon, saw itself as a beacon to communist parties and sympathizers in the Third World. 'The path taken by the Chinese peoples in defeating imperialism and lackeys in founding the People's Republic of China is the path that should be taken by the peoples of various colonial and semi-colonial countries in their fight for national independence and people's democracy', proclaimed Mao's deputy Liu Shaoqi in 1949 to an audience of foreign visitors (Choudhury, 1982, p. 13). Chinese support for insurgencies in Southeast Asia began in 1948, but met with little success outside of Vietnam, and was cut back in the early 1950s to await a resurgence later in the decade.

Most Americans considered China a Soviet ally, so US relations with Beijing fell within the context of the US–Soviet bipolar conflict. The CCP had made several overtures toward Washington between 1944 and 1949, and in January 1950 US President Harry Truman announced that the USA was discontinuing aid to the Nationalist government in Taiwan. Yet hostility toward the communist regime was still too strong within the US Congress to allow an early recognition of Mao's government. The Sino-Soviet treaty of February 1950 seemed to confirm the American suspicion that China was a Russian satellite. The Korean War erupted only a few months later, making China and the USA unambiguous enemies.

Mao proclaimed that China was an independent country, but would 'lean to one side', toward Moscow and away from Washington. 'Internationally', he said, 'we belong to the side of the anti-imperialist front headed by the Soviet Union, and so we can turn only to this side for genuine and friendly help, not to the side of the imperialist front' (Mao, 1969, p. 417). While a Sino-Soviet alliance against the United States made sense ideologically, it was also geopolitically expedient. If the Americans were unwilling to enter a serious rapprochement with Beijing, they were even less likely to provide the large-scale economic aid the Chinese wanted. Indeed, the Soviet Union was the only industrialized country to offer China such aid. Furthermore, in the early postwar years, the United States, then at the historical height of its power, was also the most threatening potential adversary of both China and the USSR, which naturally pushed Moscow and Beijing into a united front.

In conjunction with the Sino-Soviet Treaty of Friendship, Alliance and Mutual Assistance, signed after Mao's first visit to Moscow, the Soviets gave the Chinese $300 million in financial credits. These were loans, not grants, and on some the Chinese had to pay interest. The USSR also supported China on certain key diplomatic issues. The Soviets demanded, for example, that Beijing, not the Guomindang, occupy the United Nations seats reserved for 'China'. Soviet representatives had even boycotted the United Nations in protest over this issue (which is why Moscow's UN Security Council representative was not present to veto the resolution condemning North Korea's invasion of South Korea in June 1950). Beijing publicly acknowledged the USSR as the leader of the world communist movement and lavished high praise on Stalin in particular. Mao said on one occasion, for example, 'Stalin is the true friend of the cause of liberation of the Chinese people', and noted 'the Chinese people's whole-hearted love and respect for Stalin'.

China's Intervention in Korea

China's hopes for conquering Taiwan, improving relations with the USA, and rebuilding the Chinese economy suffered a dramatic setback with North Korea's invasion of South Korea in June 1950. Beijing was planning to invade Taiwan later in the year and stood a good chance of success, but Truman's stationing of the US Seventh Fleet in the Taiwan Strait immediately after the outbreak of the Korean War prevented China from finishing its business with the Guomindang. Throughout the Korean War, Chinese leaders complained as bitterly about this 'interference in Chinese domestic affairs' as about the UN intervention on the Korean peninsula.

North Korean forces advanced rapidly in the opening weeks of the war and overran all but the southeastern corner of South Korea, which included the critically important port of Pusan. Then the UN forces regrouped and counter-attacked. General Douglas MacArthur, the Pacific War hero, head of the US occupation forces in Japan, and now commander of the United Nations armies sent to repel the North Korean invasion, strengthened his already Olympian reputation with a successful amphibious landing far behind enemy lines at Inchon. The North Korean defence collapsed soon thereafter. With little effective resistance, UN troops under American command were poised to seize North Korea, which would eliminate a Chinese ally and buffer state and place a united, US-aligned Korea on China's doorstep. Chinese officials began to warn through indirect channels they would not tolerate US forces advancing close to the Yalu River. PRC Premier Zhou Enlai told Indian ambassador K. M. Panikkar on 2 October 1950 that 'the South Koreans did not matter but American intrusion into North Korea would encounter Chinese resistance' (Panikkar, 1955, p. 190). The American high command disregarded the warnings. MacArthur remarked that the Chinese would not dare invade, and if they did UN aircraft would 'slaughter' them. Few officials in Washington disagreed, and the United Nations authorized its forces to push beyond the former North–South demarcation line into North Korean territory.

Intervention in Korea was an agonizing decision for the CCP leadership. Still recovering from the destruction of the Japanese invasion and the Chinese Civil War, China was badly in need of economic reconstruction and development. A new war would further drain manpower and resources. It would also involve combat between US and Chinese troops. If the United States decided to declare war on China, Chinese cities would be exposed to US air and naval bombardment. On the other hand, from the Chinese point of view, American involvement in Korea seemed to be part of a larger US campaign, including the Philippines, Japan, and ultimately China, to subdue and control Asia. MacArthur reinforced CCP fears by saying publicly he wanted to extend the Korean War into China and return Chiang to power on the mainland. More colourfully, Chinese writer Mao Tun was quoted by the official media as saying, 'This mad dog [the USA] seizes Taiwan between its hind legs while with its teeth it violently bites the Korean people. Now one of its forelegs has been poked into our Northeast front. Its bloodswollen eyes cast around for something further to attack. All the world is under its threat. The American imperialist mad dog is half beaten up. Before it dies, it will go on biting and tearing' (quoted in Whiting, 1975a, p. 211). Interestingly, the Chinese view was a mirror image of Washington's perception, which interpreted the North Korean invasion as part of a Soviet plan to communize the region. Thus, the Korean War would be an important reason why both the Americans and the Chinese decided to provide major support to their respective client states in Vietnam.

Evidently, the presence of US troops north of the 38th Parallel, regardless of whether or not they planned to drive on into China, was sufficient impetus for China's intervention. American forces based in northern Korea would force China to maintain a strong defensive line with a high degree of mobilization and readiness, which in the long term would become a serious economic drain. This would also be politically embarrassing to Mao's regime; as Mao told Zhou in October 1950, 'the arrogance of reactionaries at home and abroad [would] grow' if China failed to expel the Americans. These considerations outweighed the dangers of Chinese involvement, which dangers Mao fully understood; he told Stalin, 'We must be prepared [for the possibility] that the United States may, at a minimum, use its air force to bomb many major cities and industrial centers in China. . . . thus leading to the resulting destruction of the economic construction plan we have already begun, arousing dissatisfaction toward us among the national bourgeoisie and other segments of the people' (Christensen, 1992, pp. 147–53). Mao's sensitivity to the domestic pressures on the regime that would result in either case is noteworthy.

Mao's decision to intervene reportedly went against the advice of most of his advisers (Peng, 1981, p. 257). The intervention itself showed signs of caution, indicating Beijing's desire to avert an all-out war with the USA. Rather than moving to attack immediately after UN forces crossed the 38th Parallel, Chinese forces waited until US troops had nearly reached the Yalu River. After their first attack in early November, the Chinese unilaterally withdrew for three weeks, giving the Americans a chance to change their strategy and pull back (unfortunately, they did not). Finally, the Chinese government termed their forces 'volunteers', suggesting Beijing was not officially at war with the United States.

The massive counterattack of some 200,000 Chinese troops sent the UN armies into a long retreat back into South Korean territory. By mid-1951, the front lines settled close to the original demarcation line, and the war devolved into a stalemate that would last two more years. Beijing may have seen extending the war as a means of draining American power through this costly, far-flung operation (Segal, 1985, pp. 94–5). In negotiations for a settlement, the major disagreement was over the issue of repatriation of prisoners of war. Beijing favoured compulsory repatriation – all Chinese and North Korean POWs would be returned to the communist side. The United Nations command wanted each communist prisoner to be allowed to choose between returning home or settling in South Korea or Taiwan. The deadlock in the peace talks was broken after Moscow's post-Stalin leadership stopped supporting the Chinese demand for compulsory repatriation and the new Eisenhower administration threatened to use nuclear weapons against the communist forces. Although conventional wisdom in the West has credited Eisenhower's nuclear threats with ending the war, many China scholars say the evidence for this view is inconclusive (Foot, 1988/89, pp. 101–2). Recently released documents from the Kremlin archives suggest Mao favoured an earlier armistice, but Stalin disapproved because he wanted his two biggest rivals to bleed each other for as long as possible (Ilpyong Kim, 1995, p. 348). Thus, the death of Stalin removed the main obstacle to an agreement. In any case, Beijing finally agreed to voluntary repatriation, clearing the way for an armistice in July 1953. To the PRC's embarrassment, some 70 per cent of the UN forces' Chinese prisoners of war elected not to return to the PRC.

The Korean War saved Taiwan from conquest by the CCP and shattered any hope of an early Sino-US reconciliation. Mao's attempt to expel US troops from the peninsula also failed; while Chinese troops withdrew from North Korea in 1958, American forces remain in South Korea to this day. Nevertheless, China's intervention had preserved a socialist, anti-American regime in North Korea and increased Chinese prestige in the Third World, which saw China fight the world's most powerful country to a draw, albeit at a terrible cost, while the Soviets stood on the sidelines.

Like its alliance with North Korea, Beijing's support for Ho Chi Minh's Vietminh regime in North Vietnam had both ideological and geostrategic justification. Ho's was a national liberation movement that sought to expel Japanese, French, and finally American influence from Vietnam. Chinese trained the Vietminh and gave them US-made weapons captured from the Guomindang, important factors in the Vietminh's successful military campaign against the French colonial forces.

The 'Bandung Spirit'

The Korean War and, soon afterward, the first Taiwan Straits Crisis (1954–5) created a tense atmosphere in the Asia-Pacific that helped Washington find considerable success in recruiting Third World governments for membership in defence pacts designed to 'contain' the Soviet Union and China. Its initial position of hostility toward all but a small number of ideological soulmates, combined with its bitter confrontation with the Americans and its support for insurgencies throughout the region, had earned Beijing many enemies and few friends. Around 1954, the Chinese sought to reverse this trend with a dramatic shift toward an omnidirectional foreign policy. As a conciliatory gesture to the United States, during the Geneva conference of May 1954, which was called to plan Vietnam's future as an independent state, Zhou pressured Vietnamese delegation chief Pham Van Dong to accept a partition of Vietnam, with the southern half under the control of a US-aligned anti-communist regime, and a two-year wait before national elections, giving the southern government time to suppress support for Ho and the communists. China had also smoothed its relations with India in 1954. India agreed that Tibet, the status of which had been hotly disputed, was an integral part of Chinese territory, and Beijing ceased criticizing Nehru as a puppet of the Western imperialists. The two governments published joint communiques announcing that their relationship would be based on 'Five Principles of Peaceful Coexistence'. Apparently authored by Zhou, the Five Principles became, and remain, a mainstay of China's bilateral agreements and other diplomatic pronouncements.

The main showcase for China's new approach was a major conference of African and Asian countries held in Bandung, Indonesia in 1955 – hence the guiding principle for China's diplomacy during this period was known as the 'Bandung Spirit'. The Chinese delegates in Bandung, led by the suave and skilful Zhou, expounded peaceful coexistence, got the Five Principles incorporated into the conference's final manifesto, and enhanced China's image as a prestigious and responsible power. China followed through on its conciliatory rhetoric outside the conference as well. Beijing improved its relations with Britain, signing trade deals and establishing diplomatic relations at the chargé d'affaires level. The PRC reached an agreement with Indonesia on the citizenship of ethnic Chinese. When anti-Chinese rioting flared up in the late 1950s, the PRC government declined to blame Jakarta. In 1956, China signed agreements with Nepal and Cambodia that entitled them to Chinese economic assistance and made conciliatory gestures toward Burma over disputed border territory, which eventually resulted in a border settlement in 1960. The Chinese also invited Thai officials to tour Yunnan Province, which they suspected was a base for insurgency, and proposed a non-aggression treaty with the Philippines, a member of the US-sponsored Southeast Asia Treaty Organization.

The Bandung Spirit sought to unite the Third World nations, to promote Chinese leadership within the Third World, and to assure other developing countries that there was no need to join the American effort to contain China. At the same time, Chinese officials sought to settle the issues with Washington that stood in the way of normalized relations. The two countries held ambassador-level talks for the first time in August 1955, during which the Chinese offered, in effect, to renounce the use of force to recapture Taiwan in exchange for diplomatic recognition by Washington. The Eisenhower administration, however, was unwilling to facilitate a major increase in the PRC's global prestige. While Beijing's suggestions showed considerable flexibility, the American side was uncompromising.

The Taiwan Straits Crises

In addition to Taiwan, the Republic of China (ROC) government also controlled several small islands close to the mainland Chinese coast, the most important of which were Quemoy (Jinmen) and Matsu (Mazu). These offshore islands were a divisive issue between Taipei and Washington. The Americans thought they were a strategic liability: they were within range of PRC artillery, could be captured at will by the mainland, and were difficult to resupply from distant Taiwan. But Chiang believed they would be useful stepping-stones in a campaign to reconquer the mainland, a goal he still clung to. His government told the Americans that abandoning the islands would seriously damage morale on Taiwan, imperilling the ROC's survival. From the PRC's point of view, an attack on the offshore islands was a clever way to exploit a potential weakness in the US–ROC relationship at a time when the two allies were discussing a defence treaty.

After several weeks of warnings in the Chinese media that the offshore islands would soon be recovered, PLA artillery began shelling them in September 1954. In response, US warships steamed toward the Taiwan Strait. Tension continued to escalate through March 1955, when both Eisenhower and his Vice-President Richard Nixon publicly suggested the United States might use nuclear weapons against China in connection with the Straits crisis – threats which provided a strong impetus toward the CCP leadership's decision to undertake its own nuclear weapons programme (Lewis and Xue, 1988; Chang, 1988, p. 121). In April, at Bandung, Zhou said his government hoped to discuss with the United States ways of settling the crisis. Washington accepted Zhou's gesture, agreeing to peace talks, and the shelling quickly wound down.

While the 'Bandung Spirit' ended the first Taiwan Straits crisis, the reverse occurred in 1958, as another crisis over the offshore islands terminated Beijing's conciliatory approach toward the United States. On 23 August Chinese artillery stationed on the coast of Fujian Province began an intensive bombardment of Jinmen and its surrounding waters. Mao told CCP insiders this policy was intended both to 'teach the Americans a lesson' and to probe the US reaction. Of particular interest was whether or not Washington would interpret its defence treaty with Taiwan as obligating the Americans to defend Taiwan's vulnerable offshore islands as well. Mao chose this moment because American troops had landed in Lebanon in mid-July to counter rising Soviet influence in Syria and growing support for Nasser in Iraq. It was a useful pretext: Mao could place the shelling of Jinmen in the larger context of the campaign to oust American imperialist influence in Asia and the Middle East. The gesture of solidarity would please the Arabs, and the Chinese could take advantage of the Eisenhower administration's preoccupation with the operation in Lebanon (Li, Chen and Wilson, 1995/96, pp. 209–10). As in the first Straits crisis, the American response was firm. Once again, Washington sent additional warships, including six aircraft carriers with nuclear-capable planes, to the Taiwan Strait, and they helped escort ROC supply vessels to within three miles of Jinmen. Mao later admitted he had underestimated the US reaction (Whiting, 1975b, pp. 265, 267). The Soviet leadership also saw the shelling as unnecessarily provocative, and suggested they might not back the Chinese if the incident led to a war with the United States. The probe having served its purpose, Mao defused the crisis, sending the conciliatory 'Message to the Compatriots in Taiwan' (in the name of his defence minister Peng Dehuai) on 6 October and cutting back the shelling.

Tensions and hard bargaining between China and the USSR were never absent, but the rivalry was temporarily subordinated to meet the more immediate challenges posed by the capitalist camp. Nevertheless, relations between Beijing and Moscow began to deteriorate seriously only a few years into their alliance. Ostensibly, the principal cause of the Sino-Soviet break was Soviet 'revisionism', the first indication of which came with Khrushchev's 1956 anti-Stalin speech, which was given without prior warning to Beijing and embarrassed the avowedly pro-Stalin CCP. In Beijing's view, the Soviet leadership appeared to be abandoning basic revolutionary principles and retrogressing back toward capitalism and imperialism. While Beijing held that violent conflict with the imperialist states was inevitable, Khrushchev began to promote the concept of 'peaceful coexistence', based on the assumption that capitalist nations might convert to socialism of their own accord as their people saw the light and demanded changes in their socio-political system (the reverse of US Secretary of State John Foster Dulles' notion of 'peaceful evolution').

Throughout the 1950s it was clear that Mao had a different agenda from that of Moscow. Mao was disappointed with Soviet unwillingness to challenge the Americans in an effort to drive US influence out of the region, and in particular the lack of Soviet support in the recovery of Taiwan, which was a vital issue for China but not for Moscow.

The 1958 Great Leap Forward, a radical economic development campaign involving massive collectivization of labour and abandonment of established CCP institutions for new organizations that would give Mao more direct control over the masses, was a repudiation of Chinese reliance on the Soviet Union as well as a challenge to much of the CCP leadership. The Party knew China was heavily dependent on Soviet economic and technical assistance and therefore risked developing into a Russian semi-colony. By the time of the CCP's Eighth Party Congress in May 1958, an intense debate raged among the leadership. The relatively moderate Liu Shaoqi and his supporters argued that despite the risks, continued dependence on the Soviets was necessary for China's development. Mao, whose power had been severely undercut by the Party but who still remained the dominant figure, wanted to break free of this dependence as soon as possible. This was the real goal of the Great Leap, which the Congress approved as Mao's view prevailed (Thornton, 1982, pp. 247–50).

The Soviets had little incentive to build up a China over which they did not have strong influence. In 1957, almost all Soviet credit to China ceased, and the Chinese were required to pay cash for Soviet goods. In 1960, all Soviet technical advisers, some 1,390, left China. Moscow sought good relations with China's unfriendly neighbours. Soon after the large-scale anti-Chinese riots in Indonesia and just before the Sino-Indian border war, Moscow offered generous economic aid packages to Indonesia and India.

The Sino-Indian Border War, 1962

Beijing's desire to maintain good relations with the Third World and, in particular, its favourable exchanges with India in the mid-1950s failed to head off a dispute that culminated in a military clash in 1962. The political atmosphere of Sino-Indian relations was poisoned by India's opposition to the Chinese occupation of Tibet, by suspected Indian complicity in the Tibetan uprising of 1959, by the Nehru government's friendly relationship with Moscow, and by previous Sino-Indian border skirmishing. A new crisis coalesced around the ownership of disputed territory near the Sino-Indian border. The Indian assertions seemed part of a campaign to weaken Beijing's control of Tibet. Furthermore, the Chinese had built a strategically important road through this territory that linked Tibet and Xinjiang Province.

To halt what it described as encroachment by Indian forces, Beijing issued strong warnings, massed forces of its own, and finally attacked on 20 October and again on 16 November 1962. The Chinese won a decisive victory, eliminating Indian military outposts from the disputed area. The Chinese could have advanced further, but instead they unilaterally withdrew. Official Indian losses were about 1,400 killed and 1,700 missing; Chinese casualties were somewhat less.

Exporting Revolution in the 1960s

China's renewed interest in promoting 'armed struggle' abroad paralleled the replacement of the politically moderate defence minister Peng Dehuai by radical leftist Lin Biao in 1958. The goal was to weaken the capitalist bloc by taking away the colonies it exploited to maintain its prosperity. In principle, China would supply arms, money, and training to rebel groups in developing countries whose governments participated in the global capitalist system. In practice, immediate Chinese political interests proved a stronger consideration than the promotion of worldwide socialist revolution, although there was considerable overlap between the two sets of objectives. Rebels in countries that were US allies and/or did not diplomatically recognize Beijing generally got Chinese help, even if they demonstrated little potential for success. On the other hand, the Chinese generally failed to aid insurgencies against governments that were unsavoury from the standpoint of Marxist ideology, but had normal relations with China and were not US allies. Proximity to China also mattered; rebel movements in Southeast Asia got the most attention from the Chinese, those in Africa less, and those in Latin America virtually none. This, too, suggested that narrower Chinese interests took precedence over strictly ideological concerns (Nelson, 1981, pp. 200–1). A study by Peter Van Ness showed that in 1965, when 120 armed revolutionary movements were active throughout the Third World, China supported only the 23 in which the ruling government was a US ally or was unfriendly toward the PRC (Van Ness, 1970).

Decolonization in Africa opened up new opportunities for Marxist revolution and thus attracted Chinese support. Once again, however, Beijing got a poor return on its investment, as military coups overthrew several pro-Chinese regimes in Africa in the mid-1960s.

The disaster that befell the Indonesian Communist Party (PKI) was even more striking. The CCP and Indonesian ruler Sukarno, a revolutionary nationalist who identified with the Maoist anti-Western worldview, developed a friendly relationship in the early 1960s. Beijing supported Indonesia in its 1963–5 'Confrontation' with Malaysia, since the latter was still aligned with Britain. Although not himself a member, Sukarno was a strong ally of the PKI. With his help, the PKI became the largest and most powerful non-ruling communist party in the world. By 1965, the only effective opposition to the PKI was the Indonesian military. China supplied arms to the PKI militia, which attempted to purge its enemies in the military high command. This effort failed, however, and the military responded with an anti-communist and partly anti-Chinese campaign that not only destroyed the PKI, but also led the new government in Jakarta to sever its relations with Beijing and seek conciliation with the West.

After this, China all but shut down its revolution export business. The incentive nearly disappeared in the late 1970s as radical Maoists lost ground to pragmatic moderates seeking improved relations with the developed world to gain access to technology and economic aid and to balance Soviet influence. (Deng Xiaoping even remarked in 1977 that he did not want to see communist parties capture power in the Western European countries because he feared they would try to appease Moscow ['Chronicle', 1978, p. 220].) Beijing nevertheless refused to disavow the concept of 'people's war' and supplied arms to the Khmer Rouge and Burma's communist party through the 1980s (Hinton, 1994, p. 352).

Security Cooperation with North Vietnam

Although they had compromised North Vietnam's interests at the Geneva peace conference, the Chinese provided strong support for Ho Chi Minh's government in the 1960s, reflecting the sense of threat the Chinese perceived from US intervention in Indochina. The Americans had reinterpreted their former Pacific War ally Ho Chi Minh as an enemy and decided to prevent him from bringing southern Vietnam under a 'communist' government, an outcome many in Washington believed would lead to all of Southeast Asia falling under Soviet/Chinese control. For the Chinese, sustaining Ho's fight was therefore an indirect means of draining the United States of blood and treasure. A victorious Vietminh military campaign would increase international respect for China's favoured strategy of open fighting against imperialism, as opposed to the Soviets' new line of 'peaceful coexistence'. Conversely, Ho's defeat might leave an American client state at the Chinese border. After losing patience with the Bandung approach, the Chinese sent 50,000 PLA troops to North Vietnam to man anti-aircraft artillery and to perform logistics duties. A total of 320,000 Chinese soldiers served in North Vietnam in 1965–8, and some 20,000 were killed or injured by American air attacks (*Renmin Ribao*, 1979, p. 4; Shambaugh, 1994a, p. 201). Zhou and the Chinese press also made public statements that China would intervene if US forces invaded North Vietnam. Perhaps intentionally, official Chinese statements used some of the same phrases spoken in warnings to the Americans before Chinese troops entered the Korean War: China and its ally were as close as 'lips and teeth' (based on the buffer state analogy from ancient Chinese military history, '*chuan wang, chi han*': 'when the lips are gone, the teeth get cold'); the Chinese could not be 'expected to look on with folded arms'; and they would not 'sit idly by' in the face of US 'aggression' (*Beijing Review*, 1964a, p. 24, and 1964b, p. 5; Whiting, 1975a, p. 174).

After the 1968 Soviet invasion of Czechoslovakia and promulgation of the Brezhnev Doctrine, which held that the USSR had the right to forcibly prevent political apostasy by Soviet Bloc countries, the CCP leadership feared the Soviets might invade China. Zhou's National Day address of 1 October 1968 mentioned this possibility, as if to prepare the Chinese public. Beijing took a more fearful view of the buildup of Soviet troops near the USSR's border with China. The Chinese sought to make a tough gesture toward the Soviets, evidently in the hope of deterring an invasion. The disputed Zhenbao Island in the Ussuri River became the focal point of increasing Sino-Soviet tensions. After several confrontations between Soviet and Chinese troops, the USSR warned on 25 February 1969 that Soviet soldiers would fire at Chinese patrols found on the island. On 2 March the Chinese moved additional soldiers onto the island and laid an ambush for patrolling Soviet troops, resulting in a battle in which 31 Soviets and 20 Chinese reportedly died. The Soviets sought to retaliate, and another, bloodier, battle broke out on 15 March with Soviet tanks and artillery joining in the fray. While demonstrating Chinese willingness to challenge a superior adversary, the Zhenbao Island incidents also pushed PRC–Soviet relations to an all-time low, even drawing Soviet hints of launching a nuclear attack against China. The incidents also contributed to the political downfall of Lin Biao, who reportedly masterminded the clash (Hinton, 1994, p. 368).

While the Sino-Soviet rift seemed at a superficial level to be a dispute over ideology, the relationship was clearly outgrown by the two countries' view of each other as potential security threats. Conflicts of interest outweighed their common interest in opposing US influence. As an industrialized, nuclear-armed state controlling an empire of satellite regimes, the USSR was a status-quo power, increasingly concerned with managing the international system and avoiding conflicts with the United States. China, on the other hand, was a dissatisfied country – underdeveloped, humiliated, irredentist – trying to move into a better position in the international system.

The Strategic Triangle Period

The 'strategic triangle' refers to the relationship in which China held a flexible position *vis-à-vis* the United States and the Soviet Union, affording Beijing the opportunity to benefit by playing the two superpowers against each other. The relationship began with the Sino-US rapprochement, based on Beijing and Washington's common antipathy toward the Soviet Union. For their part, the Americans recognized that China was not a Soviet satellite state. Moreover, the arguments that the CCP government faced imminent collapse and enjoyed no international standing were no longer tenable. In Beijing's view, ominous recent events suggested the Soviet threat to China was increasing. In contrast, the US military expansion into the region had peaked with the Indochina intervention, from which the Americans were withdrawing in shame. As it had done in the early years of the Cold War, China allied with the less threatening of the two superpowers against the most threatening. Overtures and secret contacts between the US and Chinese governments established a willingness to upgrade their relationship and prepared the way for President Richard Nixon's visit to Beijing in 1972. In the joint Shanghai Communiqué that emerged from this summit, the two countries agreed to work toward deeper, more peaceful, and normalized relations. The Taiwan issue remained a problem, but it was sidestepped through the two sides releasing separate statements. The American statement came close to accepting Beijing's position on Taiwan and committed the American government to 'progressively reduce [US] forces and military installations on Taiwan as the tension in the area diminishes'.

A similar deal was worked out with Japan, which soon followed the US lead in establishing relations with Beijing. Japan agreed to sign a statement criticizing Soviet 'hegemonism', while China agreed to allow Japan to maintain its economic relationship with Taiwan.

This unofficial security relationship perhaps reached its peak in 1979. During that year, China and the USA achieved normalization, the Soviet invasion of Afghanistan further frightened and alienated Beijing, and in a meeting with visiting US dignitaries, Deng Xiaoping, successor to Mao as China's paramount leader, referred to his country's relationship with America as an 'alliance' (*tongmeng*). (A Xinhua report later toned down Deng's comment, replacing '*tongmeng*' with '*lianhe qilai*', or 'become united' [Shambaugh, 1994a, p. 203].) As the USSR and the USA switched roles from that of ally to main threat and vice versa, China's view of the superpowers' perceived regional allies also changed. Previously, the US-aligned states, including Japan, South Korea and Thailand, were essentially considered adversaries. Now Beijing took this view toward the countries friendly with Moscow, including Mongolia, Vietnam, and to some extent North Korea (Hinton, 1994, p. 357–8).

The quasi-alliance with the United States had several important benefits for China. It lowered defence costs by alleviating the US threat, securing US military assistance, and effectually placing China under the US nuclear umbrella. It also increased the PRC's access to the trade, investment and technology of America and its allies. (The United States ended in 1971 an economic embargo against China that had been in effect since 1950.) In particular, Beijing was in a position to exploit Washington's fear of the Soviets for China's own gain; the Chinese attempted to extract additional Western economic assistance and transfer of technology by arguing that a stronger China could tie down greater numbers of Soviet troops (Sheng, 1995a, pp. 113–14). Finally, it increased the PRC's prestige, raising perceived Chinese status to that of a major world player, although Beijing's actual global influence was still low (Shambaugh, 1994a, p. 199).

Many foreign governments had been alarmed by what they saw in China during the Cultural Revolution. While the country was racked internally though the late 1960s by conditions that approximated to a civil war, the PRC's diplomatic activity had almost completely ceased. As China emerged from this chaotic period and showed renewed interest in international contacts, the world moved quickly to reward Beijing and prevent another relapse into isolation. In the early 1970s, some 40 governments, including many US allies, established normal relations with Beijing, and the PRC replaced the ROC as 'China' in the United Nations, taking up as well a permanent seat in the UN Security Council.

The Three Worlds Theory

Developed in early 1970s, principally by Zhou, the Three Worlds Theory was publicly outlined in a 1974 speech by Deng Xiaoping to the UN General Assembly. According to this 'Theory', the First World included the two superpowers; the Second World was comprised of the industrialized allies of the USA and USSR: Japan, Europe, Canada, Australia, and New Zealand; and the Third World took in the remaining countries, the less developed and non-aligned. The two superpowers competed for global hegemony and oversaw the exploitative economic system in which the poorer countries provided raw materials and cheap labour to the richer countries, which reaped disproportionate profits. The Three Worlds Theory's prescription was that the Second and Third Worlds should unite to promote a more peaceful and just international order.

Beijing's rapprochement with the United States had divided the CCP, and the Three Worlds Theory was designed to mollify Party elites who worried that the top leadership was selling out China's revolutionary ideals. The Theory indicated China was still interested in remaking the international system, and that the United States was still seen as an obstacle to this project (Garver, 1993, p. 167). Nevertheless, this was a considerably less ideological view than prevailed during the Cultural Revolution. At that time, Chinese officials and media said international relations were epitomized by the general class struggle between the revolutionary and reactionary peoples. Now, instead of the socialist camp vs. the capitalist camp, the primary struggle was between the superpowers and the rest of the world (Camilleri, 1980, p. 140). Under the auspices of the Three Worlds Theory, cooperation with any government other than the superpowers could be justified as a means of promoting solidarity against hegemonism. This new pragmatism rationalized Beijing's cultivation of relationships even with the fascist regimes in Greece and Spain (Klein, 1989, p. 144).

Conflicts with Vietnam

Despite Washington's (mis)perceptions, cooperation between Beijing and Hanoi during the Vietnam War was an anomaly in a long history of poor relations between the Chinese and Vietnamese. It was the common American threat that had driven them together in a temporary united front. Even during this period Hanoi saw itself played like a pawn in China's larger game, just as Stalin had used the CCP. China had clearly sacrificed Hanoi's interests for its own during the Geneva conference. Later, during the American intervention, China had encouraged the Vietnamese to employ the strategy of 'people's war', implying that Hanoi should avoid seeking heavy weapons and equipment from China's rival the Soviet Union (Hinton, 1994, p. 367).

In early 1974, the PRC opportunistically moved to seize the Xisha (Paracel) Islands, over which Beijing had long claimed ownership, from the crumbling Saigon regime in a brief naval battle. It was better to settle the issue before Hanoi inherited the islands, and there was little chance of the United States intervening to support its abandoned ally.

After Hanoi's forcible reunification, relations between China and Vietnam were severely strained by Vietnam's expulsion of ethnic Chinese, Hanoi's 'Treaty of Peace and Friendship' with the Soviet Union, and a series of border incidents. On 25 December 1978, a *Renmin Ribao* editorial read, 'We serve a stern warning to the Vietnamese authorities: if you take advantage of the Soviet support and reach out for a yard after taking an inch and continue to take actions against China recklessly, you will surely get what you deserve'. That same day, Vietnamese forces invaded Cambodia to overthrow the murderous but pro-Beijing regime of Pol Pot. Although even the Chinese were put off by Pol Pot's cruel excesses, he was their only significant counterweight to Vietnamese influence in Indochina.

PLA forces attacked across the Sino-Vietnamese border on 17 February 1979. Deng said of the campaign, 'Our objective is a limited one – that is to teach [the Vietnamese] that they could not run about as much as they desired' (*SWB*, No. 6054, p. A3/2). Other possible motives for the Chinese incursion were deterring Hanoi from seizing or attacking Chinese territory near the Sino-Vietnamese border; undermining Soviet prestige in the region by showing that China was not afraid to attack the USSR's chief Asian ally; or Deng's desire to demonstrate his control of the PLA to intimidate his domestic political rival Premier Hua Guofeng (Segal, 1985, pp. 215–16; Sheng, 1995b, p. 24). One scholar suggests the attack was to reassure the PLA leadership that national defence would not be completely neglected even though the new programme of reforms (the 'Four Modernizations') placed the modernization of industry, agriculture and science and technology above that of the armed forces (Spence, 1990, p. 659).

In any case, the campaign was largely an embarrassing failure for China: the PLA appeared ineffective during the incursion, and afterwards the Vietnamese continued to occupy Kampuchea and to engage in border skirmishes with the Chinese. Hampered by poor logistics and generalship, the Chinese suffered a surprisingly high number of casualties, estimated at 20,000 or more, most of which occured among Vietnam's border guards rather than its regular army combat units. On the strength of size and numbers, the PLA succeeded in seizing several cities a few miles inside the Vietnamese border. After destroying the economic infrastructure in the areas they controlled, the Chinese withdrew one month after they began their attack.

The 'Open Door' Period

While the strategic triangle period continued, the decade of the 1980s saw a dramatic change in China's orientation toward the world capitalist economy. Mao's death in 1976, followed by a backlash throughout China against Mao's disastrous economic policies and the excesses of Cultural Revolution radicalism, set the stage for a new economic development strategy. Deng, purged during the Cultural Revolution, emerged as the new paramount leader. He virtually renounced Marxism-Leninism as China's economic model, instead giving greater play to market forces, dismantling agricultural collectives, and encouraging foreign trade with and investment in China. The government also began sending students to Western universities; soon there were some 40,000 in the United States alone.

In Deng's view, Mao had overemphasized the risks of economic connections with the outside world. The impressive economic growth of the newly-industrialized countries in Asia, whose success was based largely on their strong links with the international economy, had an important influence on Deng and other pragmatists within the CCP. The experiences of the Japanese, South Korean, Taiwanese, Hong Kong and Singapore economies demonstrated that foreign economic aid and trade could be exploited as well as exploitative. In any case, China would never close the gap with the rich nations without taking advantage of what they had to offer. Deng said in 1980, 'To accelerate China's modernization we must not only make use of other countries' experience. We must also avail ourselves of foreign funding. In past years international conditions worked against us. Later, when the international climate was favourable, we did not take advantage of it. It is now time to use our opportunities' (Deng, 1980, p. L3). To the outside world, Deng proclaimed, 'China has opened its door, and will never close it again'.

The post-Mao CCP also rethought China's basic defence strategy. From the mid-1980s, a consensus of politicians and high military officers concluded that China would probably not fight a full-scale war with a major military power during the near future. The more likely possibility was a limited war on China's periphery. This called for a new PLA posture: fewer troops armed with more technologically advanced equipment.

Beijing reasserted the principle of an 'independent foreign policy' in 1982. The proximate cause was Washington's 1979 Taiwan Relations Act, the backlash by pro-Taiwan Congressmen against the US normalization with Beijing. More generally, the pro-Soviet faction within the CCP complained that Beijing was drawing too close to the United States, in violation of the Chinese principle of non-alignment with a superpower (Barnett, 1985, p. 15). Soviet military pressure on China had considerably abated, giving China the option of shifting to a more equidistant stance between the superpowers (Hinton, 1994, p. 369). Chinese analysts, led by Huan Xiang, argued in 1982 that the balance of power had shifted again, Reagan's defense buildup and more assertive foreign policy having lifted the United States back into a position of rough strategic parity with the Soviets. Many Chinese strategists also felt China's relationship with the USA had grown too close, restricting Beijing's room for manoeuvre (Shambaugh, 1994a, p. 204). At an even deeper level, the independent foreign policy marked a long-term shift from a confrontational to a conciliatory approach toward the foreign powers, based on the declining influence of Maoist ideology and the increasing importance being given to economic development (Garver, 1993, p. 98).

Nonetheless, China expanded its economic, diplomatic and military contacts with the United States through the 1980s. Despite spats over US arms sales to Taiwan and Chinese missile sales to Iran, Sino-US trade and American investment in China steadily increased. The United States government made important concessions: a 1982 communiqué put limits on US arms sales to Taiwan, and in 1983 Washington relaxed licensing requirements for exports of sophisticated technology. America sold the Chinese advanced weaponry and defence systems to strengthen China as a counterweight to the Soviet Union. In 1984 Chinese Premier Zhao Ziyang visited the United States and US President Ronald Reagan visited China. Sino-Soviet tensions also decreased after Gorbachev's Vladivostok speech in July 1986, which signalled Moscow's willingness to address China's major grievances with the USSR. Relations were normalized during a Gorbachev–Deng summit in May 1989, further alleviating Beijing's sense of a strategic threat from the Soviets.

The Impact of Tiananmen

The June 1989 Tiananmen Massacre, in which the CCP leadership dispatched soldiers to brutally suppress mostly peaceful demonstrators in and around Beijing's Tiananmen Square, had important consequences for Chinese foreign relations. Tiananmen effectively terminated the strategic triangle period (Shambaugh, 1994a, p. 205). Within the CCP, the influence of reform-minded moderates such as Zhao Ziyang decreased while that of conservatives such as Yang

Shangkun grew, which led to a more hostile view of the West, particularly the USA, and moves to protect Chinese 'sovereignty' from foreign economic and cultural influence. CCP officials and government media emphasized that foreign enemies of the regime played an important role in the demonstrations, which were allegedly designed to overthrow Party rule and create the kind of chaotic conditions from which China's enemies and domestic 'bad elements' hoped to benefit.

After an initial period of lashing out in self-defence, Beijing sought to repair its damaged diplomatic and economic relationships with the outside world. Within three years, this objective was largely accomplished. In June 1990, Beijing acceded to Washington's request that dissident Fang Lizhi be allowed to emigrate. PRC Premier Li Peng made a foreign tour, meeting US President George Bush among others, as did Yang Shangkun. The PRC established diplomatic relations with South Korea, South Africa, Israel, Saudi Arabia, Indonesia, Singapore and Brunei. Normalized relations with the Southeast Asian states were especially significant because of the region's history of tension between ethnic Chinese and indigenous peoples. Post-Tiananmen sanctions were an important factor leading to Beijing's 1992 diplomatic recognition of Israel, a departure from China's historically pro-Arab foreign policy trackrecord. China's search for new suppliers of advanced defence technologies led Beijing to deepen its relationship with the Israelis, who were too militarily insecure to think about injecting morality into their foreign policy. But despite the progress China made in rehabilitating its international standing, anti-Beijing sentiment among much of the US public, and consequently among many American politicians, would prove persistent.

Tiananmen and the end of the Cold War brought new challenges to Chinese foreign policy-makers, but new opportunities as well. Broadly speaking, in about two centuries the former hegemon of East Asia had nearly come full circle. The lessons and interpretations that Chinese elites have drawn from that momentous recent past are the focus of the next chapter.

3
The View from Beijing

Foreign policy proceeds from basic assumptions about the outside world, assumptions conditioned by a society's unique background and circumstances. Some understanding of Beijing's interpretation of international affairs is vital to comprehending its decisions. Indeed, as R. F. Wye contends, 'In a society where decision-making has certainly tended to be, and probably remains, a much more personal business than it does in the West, the leaders' perceptions matter' (Wye, 1995–96, p. 181). As we shall see, while policy-makers in Beijing face many of the same problems as other statesmen, their worldview is in many respects distinctive.

A methodological question arises here. 'Worldviews' exist in the minds of Chinese elites, but we can access them only indirectly, through the discourse on international affairs produced by PRC politicians, journalists and analysts – and indeed, this is the approach I will take here. A potential criticism is that this discourse might, for various reasons, be irrelevant to what policy-makers are actually thinking. This is a fair observation, but the problem is minimized if we recognize that national security discourse constrains policy-makers in two ways. First, the discourse creates expectations against which the conduct of policy-makers will be judged in the future. If their performance appears out of sync with the conceptual world their own rhetoric has helped create, the authorities will be vulnerable to criticism from their constituencies and political rivals. Second, images and assumptions, even those that were originally formulated as mere propaganda, may become believed if they are repeated enough, and may even persist despite conflicting 'facts'. Therefore, the discourse of CCP officials and state-approved commentators is potentially an enlightening window into the worldview of policy-makers.

This chapter will examine some of the essential elements of Beijing's worldview. We begin with PRC elites' conception of international politics and their view of China as an international actor. Later this chapter elaborates on the regime's belief in the interconnectedness of domestic and international politics, a concept that is crucial to an understanding of the intellectual framework within which Chinese foreign policy-making takes place.

China's View of International Politics

In Beijing's view, all the (other) major states practise 'power politics' (the Chinese term for *realpolitik*, or a policy intended solely to promote relative national power without regard for moral principle). Chinese scholar Wang Jisi says of PRC policy-makers, 'In their eyes, world politics continues to involve a zero-sum game, and in the inevitable hierarchy, the more powerful nations dominate the weak' (Strasser, 1995, p. 30). Manipulating the international balance of power remains the PRC's primary means of managing potential conflict with other strong states or coalitions (Glaser, 1993, p. 253). At the same time, PRC politicians and analysts see important distinctions between the behaviour of capitalist and socialist countries, see the disparity between the rich and poor nations as a major cause of international tension, emphasize the role of the ruling economic class in determining a particular country's foreign policy, and retain a residual suspicion about participation in the world economic order that contrasts with the more liberal view prevalent in the West.

China's Self-Image

As is typical of nations, China has a unique self-image based on its background, culture, endowments and geopolitical circumstances. Perhaps most fundamentally, Chinese think of China as a country that deserves the world's respect. The sheer size of China's population, territory and endowments demands considerable deference. Even in 1980, when China had little global political influence and before it began to reap the fruits of Deng's economic reforms, PRC political commentator Si Mu boasted, 'Though economically and militarily, China is very backward in comparison with the Soviet Union and the United States, . . . Our country is one "pole" by all means' (Si, 1981, pp. 13–14). Si's claim that the PRC was then comparable to the superpowers in importance, even without their economic and military strength, is remarkable. Similarly, commenting on the ineffectiveness of the post-Tiananmen sanctions, Qiao Shi exhulted in 1993, 'China, as a large country with more than one billion people, cannot be isolated. We ourselves are a world and not a small one. There is nothing to be afraid of!' (Qiao, 1994, p. 136).

Pride in the long and accomplished history of Chinese civilization is a factor in China's self-image. As one Ministry of Foreign Affairs official put it, 'With 5,000 years of wisdom, it is unlikely we Chinese will make any major mistakes in our foreign relations' (author interview, 1995).

China also deserves respect for the morality of its behaviour. According to Chinese commentators, China is unique among the major powers in that it pursues a 'principled' foreign policy; China's acts are always noble and never unjust. An important reason for this, say many Chinese, is that China has recently been a victim of abuse at the hands of stronger powers, which gives its leadership sympathy for small countries and victims of injustice.

China's claim of moral superiority is noteworthy in several respects. First, it suggests residual influence from the Sinocentrism of the ancient Middle Kingdom. Secondly, as Samuel S. Kim points out, this understanding of PRC foreign policy contrasts sharply with the Chinese government's approach to its *domestic* political policies, which allows for frequent reinterpretation and even severe self-criticism (Kim, 1994a, p. 19). Finally, Beijing has subjected itself to the charge that the contrast between its words and its deeds is unusually great, even if some allowance is made for the fact that all governments try to make themselves look good in the eyes of domestic and world public opinion.

The Chinese stand out in the frequency and intensity of their claims of moral rectitude. Often they prefer to deny their violations of a general principle, such as 'no country should base its forces in another country' or 'China never attacks other countries', rather than attempt to rationalize why the principle does not apply to a particular policy decision. In the 1960s, for example, when there were 50,000 Chinese troops stationed in North Vietnam to deter an American invasion and another 15,000 in Laos in 1964–72 to balance Thai troops supporting the Royal Lao, Beijing not only refused to publicly ackowledge these foreign-based forces, but continued to insist that 'China does not have a single soldier stationed outside its own borders' (quoted in Whiting, 1975a, p. 236). The PRC's image of itself as a moral actor of admirable accomplishments contributes to a sense of Chinese exceptionalism and even messianism. This emerges in straight-faced statements by CCP officials that 'All countries in the world may see that China has a different attitude and that China stands up for justice' (Qian, 1994, p. 114). While many Americans like to think of their country as the 'last, best hope of mankind', the Chinese might make a similar, if more reserved, claim. Foreign Minister Qian Qichen has argued, for example, that since the collapse of European communism, China's

> international prestige has not declined, but increased. . . . we have not boasted [of] our achievements. . . . Now, [developing countries] all say: 'China is our only hope, the only country that can speak for us, and the only power that can represent our interests'. . . . For the people of the world, China's very existence indicates that the claims that Marxism does not work and that socialism has collapsed are wrong. . . . Wherever we [CCP officials] go [in the developing world], they put up eye-catching slogans such as 'China is the hope of Africa'. (Qian, 1994, p. 110)

'China Stands for Peace'

China's use of force, PRC politicians and scholars insist, has only occurred in self-defence or for other just purposes. This approach reputedly harks back to traditional Chinese beliefs that war is wasteful, that martial strength must never be used for selfish gain or to abuse the weak, and that 'an unrighteous army is destined to fail of itself'. As PRC President Jiang Zemin recently told a Malaysian audience, 'China has consistently stood for the settlement of international disputes through peaceful negotiations and opposed the threat or use of force in international relations' (Jiang, 1995, p. 3). Some counterexamples immediately come to mind, but they can be explained away. Beijing's threats to use force to recapture Taiwan do not count, since Taiwan is an 'internal' rather than an 'international' issue. In the 1962 border war with India, the Indians were in the wrong to begin with and attacked first. The Chinese, by contrast, showed great restraint by voluntarily withdrawing after defeating the Indians. Similarly, the 1979 campaign against Vietnam had the righteous objective of aiding Chinese ally Cambodia.

The PRC proclaims its foreign policy is based on implementation of the Five Principles of Peaceful Coexistence, which since the 1950s have been a mainstay in Chinese bilateral agreements and, Chinese scholars point out with pride, have also influenced several United Nations documents. The Five Principles are 'mutual respect for sovereignty and territorial integrity, mutual non-aggression, non-interference in each other's internal affairs, equality and mutual benefit, and peaceful co-existence'. The central place of the Five Principles in Chinese diplomatic rhetoric remains unchallenged. Jiang added that even after 40 years and vast global changes 'these five principles are becoming even more vital and important', and that 'Facts have proven that as long as the Five Principles of Peaceful Coexistence . . . are strictly observed, nations can overcome their differences' (Jiang, 1995, p. 3). Qian Qichen told the United Nations General Assembly that the Five Principles were virtually the key to world peace: 'All nations, notwithstanding their differences in social systems, ideologies, values or religious faiths, can live in amity and carry out mutually beneficial cooperation as long as they abide by these principles. Failure to do so will lead to frictions, confrontation or even military conflicts' (Qian, 1995b, p. 5).

While the 'principles' are discernible, the original statement of the Five Principles that is now so often quoted verbatim like a CCP mantra is remarkably poorly worded. There seems to be a lot of overlap in 'mutual respect for territorial integrity' and 'mutual non-aggression', which are listed as separate principles. 'Equality and mutual benefit' is a rather unclear expression of the idea that international economic relationships should not be exploitative. And 'peaceful co-existence' is listed as the fifth of the 'Principles of Peaceful Co-Existence'. The gist of the Five Principles has often been rephrased more cogently than in the original statement (Jin, 1991, p. 10; Geng, 1992, p. 9; Liu, 1994, p. 18). That PRC officials and scholars today continue to quote the original statement verbatim and mantra-like, even when better versions are available, is perhaps a commentary on the rigidity of the CCP political system.

Although Chinese officials and PRC-based scholars have maintained in public statements and published writings that Chinese foreign policy is consistently moral, they undoubtedly recognize that Chinese foreign policy also has a Machiavellian streak. Some Chinese analysts privately concede, for example, that although China presently stands by the principle that no country should station its military forces in a foreign land, this might change in the future as China's capabilities grow (author's interviews in Beijing, October 1995). It seems fair to say, nevertheless, that Chinese elites tend to see their own foreign policy behaviour as more principled and less cynical than that of the other major powers.

International Politics in the Post-Cold War Era

The end of the Cold War left the Chinese, like many others, less certain about who their potential adversaries are. Chinese analysts accept the view common in the West that the structure of international politics is devolving from a bipolar (two 'poles', or major powers, the USA and the USSR/Russia) to a multipolar (several major powers) structure. The collapse of the Soviet Union left the United States as the sole superpower and reduced China's importance as the third point of the 'strategic triangle'. Nevertheless, Chinese analysts generally believe multipolarity is a positive development, allowing China and the other Asian states greater control over their own destiny, in contrast to the rigidity of Cold War bipolarity.

Most Chinese observers of international affairs believe that the post-Cold War era has greatly decreased the chances of *major* war (a war between major powers), but that the possibility of minor wars (between a major and a minor power, or two minor powers) has persisted or even increased. Some PRC analysts tend to be optimistic about the new developments, and others more pessimistic. Thus, while some see the Asia-Pacific as unprecedentedly 'relaxed' and 'stable' (Shen, 1992, p. 13; Geng, 1992, p. 2), others emphasize the endurance of old sources of conflict and the emergence of a few new ones, including minor regional wars and civil wars (Qian, 1995a, p. 2).

The end of the Cold War also left China the undisputed leader of the world communist movement. Although it rings hollow these days, the CCP continues to maintain that it is committed to socialism, that the Marxist view of history's inevitable march toward universal communism is still correct, and that the collapse of the communist regimes in the Soviet Union and Eastern Europe resulted from poor leadership and therefore has no relevance to China (Yuan, 1994, pp. 111–12).

Beijing believes the West desires an economically fruitful, capitalist, politically compliant China, but fears a powerful, socialist

China under CCP rule. Thus, the West wants to '" Westernize" and "divide" our country' (this is a common sentiment among CCP leaders; in this case the speaker was Jiang Zemin, as quoted in 'China Completes Missile Tests Off Taiwan', *The Washington Times*, 26 August 1995, p. A7). 'Westernizing' refers to political liberalization, including institution of a multi-party system and the ouster of the CCP. China's economic growth poses something of a dilemma for the West: Western business people want the Chinese market to become affluent enough to consume Western goods and services, but Western strategists worry that economic development gives China greater military capability. A 'divided' China would solve the dilemma, allowing the various parts of China to develop independently, as spokes of a foreign-centred hub, unable to unite politically in opposition to Western interests. Thus, the United States and its economic allies practise 'peaceful evolution', protect Taiwan's independence, support separatism in Tibet and economic autonomy in the east coast provinces, and made 11th-hour attempts to institutionalize democracy in Hong Kong before its return to PRC rule.

Fortunately for China, the West's strength is sapped by economic underperformance, increases in crime and other forms of social pathology, and disputes among the Western countries (including Japan) themselves (Jin, 1995, pp. 9–10). The West's power is in decline even as the power of China and most of the rest of East Asia rises.

Key Issues for the Leadership

Political and economic issues of immediate concern to the PRC leadership in the post-Cold War era have included the following:

1. Maintaining the CCP's sole authority to govern China. The Party's legitimacy has been greatly diminished by the Cultural Revolution, Deng's reorientation of the economic system from socialism toward capitalism, and the Tiananmen Massacre of 1989.
2. Managing the PRC's economic development. Party leaders see an urgent need to raise living standards quickly enough to meet the population's expectations, contain social discontent, and catch up with the developed countries. Reforming the economy

too quickly, however, may be counterproductive (e.g., generating high inflation that might contribute to a recession, or leaving millions more workers unemployed through the shutdown of unprofitable state-owned industries), while appeasing foreign governments to maximize economic opportunities risks compromising China's sovereignty and opens the country to further cultural and ideological 'pollution'.

3. Defending Chinese interests against various forms of pressure and obstruction by certain foreign countries, particularly the United States.

4. Holding the Chinese empire (including Taiwan) together amidst separatist challenges.

These concerns inescapably involve Chinese foreign relations; even those that seem primarily domestic in nature are viewed in Beijing as strongly connected to the outside world.

Internal–External Linkages

From the beginnings of the PRC, its leaders have worried deeply about the symbiotic nature of internal discontent and external attack – *nei luan, wai huan.* The CCP distinguishes less than most other governments between internal and external threats. Indeed, a popular concept in Chinese analyses of the PRC's national security is 'comprehensive national strength', a term that includes not only military defence but also such internal conditions as economic prosperity, political stability, and cultural and ideological purity (Shichor, 1995, pp. 4–5). Similarly, Chinese elites see a close connection between domestic political problems and foreign influence. There are two important reasons for this.

First, the Chinese political system equates regime security with national security. Continued leadership by the CCP is vital to the maintainence of China's progress, prosperity and stability. Members of many a ruling party throughout the world would like to be taken seriously when they tell their populace that removing them from power will ruin the country. The CCP has managed better than most parties to give this claim some credibility. The Party is associated with the end of the Century of Humiliation, the expulsion of exploitative foreigners, the (not yet complete) restoration of China's rightful territory, the international recognition of China as an important country, and the recent advances in the social and economic life of the mainland Chinese people. By the same token, taking leadership out of the Party's hands would risk throwing away these gains and returning China to its wretched former state of disorder, weakness and vulnerability. The distinction between national and regime security is nearly erased. As Party officials say, 'If there were no CCP, there would be no new China' (in this case, the official is Peng Zhen, during an address to the National People's Congress standing committee in January 1987; quoted in Wang, 1992, p. 67). The overthrow of CCP rule threatens national disaster comparable to what a war might inflict; therefore, domestic opponents of the Party are as dangerous as potential foreign military foes. Second, because of China's historical experience of imperialist intrusion and because China has only recently re-established strong ties with the West after a long period of relative isolation, Chinese leaders are highly sensitive to the negative influences of the outside world.

Thus, the connection between China's internal problems and its foreign relations is arguably greater than is the case for most of the other major powers. Most of China's serious internal problems have significant foreign policy implications. One such set of problems arises from the difficulty of holding the Chinese empire together. Since Tibet, Xinjiang and Inner Mongolia are largely captive nations, these 'internal' problems are in a sense foreign policy issues as well. In any case, these problems are closely related to Chinese foreign relations. To maximize business opportunities and tourism revenue from abroad, Beijing must minimize ethnic discontent in minority regions. Furthermore, the PRC accuses foreign governments, especially Washington, of encouraging separatism. From the Party's viewpoint, other internal problems, as well, such as regionalism and pressure for political liberalization, are intensified – sometimes intentionally – by Chinese contact with foreigners.

Cracks in the Empire

China's 55 minority groups constitute only 8 per cent of the PRC's population, but they are concentrated in parts of China that are rich in resources, are sparsely inhabited (making minority groups a relatively high percentage of the local residents), and encompass a large proportion of PRC territory. Mao promised the Chinese minorities special privileges to gain their cooperation during the Chinese Civil War. Today several areas in China heavily populated by minority groups are designated 'autonomous regions', but Beijing retains authority over most important administrative matters. Ethnic identification has risen considerably in China during the 1980s and 1990s, with many people previously listed as Han, or ethnic Chinese, on official records asking to be reclassified as members of various minority groups (Gladney, 1995, p. 5).

Chinese analysts share the Western conventional wisdom that the end of the Cold war has seen an increase in ethnic nationalism as a force in international politics, the principal results of which have been conflict and instability.

In particular, Chinese analysts believe separatism within the PRC's empire was exacerbated by the breakup of the Soviet Union (Chen, 1993, pp. 238–9), which freed many national and ethnic groups on the Russian periphery to form their own states – another reason for the CCP to loathe Gorbachev. The nationalisms Gorbachev unleashed contribute to disorder that could send waves of refugees across the Chinese border. Even if this does not occur, the old problem of holding the empire together persists, made more difficult in some respects by modern communications, modern political ideas and the spread of Islam.

Tibet

Depending upon whether or not one accepts the legitimacy of Beijing's sovereignty over Tibet, the region is at minimum an internal issue with major foreign policy implications, and at maximum a foreign policy issue in its own right. The Tibet issue thus deserves extended elaboration here.

Controlling Tibet is important to the PRC's national security for several reasons. First, Tibet provides a buffer region between China and India, and adds strategic depth in case of a Russian invasion (Tibet comprises 13 per cent of the PRC's territory). By the same token, if China did not occupy it, Tibetan territory might serve as a site for another foreign power's military bases. Second, Tibet is a source of natural resources, for which Chinese demand is especially great as it pushes for developed nation status. Tibet's Mandarin name, Xizang, means 'western treasure-house'. Finally, Chinese control of Tibet is vital to maintaining the Chinese empire; if Tibet was granted independence, other groups of 'separatists' would increase their own demands for autonomy from Beijing.

Tibet was independent through most of its history, but fell under Manchu control during the last two centuries of the Qing Dynasty. With the dynasty's collapse, Tibetans successfully expelled the Manchu garrisons and declared independence in 1913. They found little international support for their position, and although China remained preoccupied by internal turmoil, subsequent Chinese governments consistently asserted that Tibet was part of China.

The official line from Beijing is that Tibet was historically a backward, feudal society 'darker and more cruel than the serf societies of the European Middle Ages' (*Beijing Review*, 1992b, p. 15; 1992a, p. 4). The lamas, the ecclesiastical authorities of Tibetan Buddhism, were repressive, parasitic and widely hated, living a sumptuous lifestyle while the great majority of Tibetans lived in poverty, ignorance and semi-slavery. Tibet was also subject to the molestation of foreign imperialists, such as the British expedition to Tibet in 1904 commanded by Francis Younghusband. The Chinese descibe Younghusband's invasion as an orgy of destruction and atrocities, while most Western histories say that the British force was interested only in establishing a commercial treaty with Tibet, and that after doing so the British soldiers withdrew, leaving the Tibetan civilian population and their religion undisturbed.

The People's Liberation Army (PLA) invaded Tibet in 1950 to enforce its claim to ownership of Tibet, to 'liberate' the Tibetans from feudalism, and to 'wip[e] out British and American influence there' (1950 Xinhua news bulletin, quoted in Whiting, 1975a, p. 13). This latter objective might have been mere propaganda – postwar Western influence in Tibet was minimal – but it may also have reflected real Chinese fears of one of the traditional buffer regions on their underpopulated western flank being controlled by foreign powers.

The operation was mounted only a few months after the foundation of the People's Republic and involved many logistical challenges, indicating the high priority Beijing placed on establishing control over Tibet. The small Tibetan army resisted but was quickly overwhelmed. The Tibetan government pleaded in vain for intervention from the United Nations, saying they did not need to be 'liberated' from anyone but the Chinese. Tibet's chief religious figure, the Dalai Lama, fled the capital, and Tibetan representatives, with few cards left to play, signed an agreement with Beijing in May

1951. The central government would control Tibet's military forces and foreign affairs. In return, Beijing promised to allow Tibet a high degree of autonomy and continuation of its culture and religion. Chinese hopes for a smooth assimilation of Tibet into the new Maoist civilization were not realized. Attempts by CCP authorities to agitate the rural population into rebellion against the landlords and lamas met with little success. The feelings of many Tibetans were summarized by one defiant old man who reportedly told a Chinese official during a public gathering,

I have this to say to you Chinese: ever since you entered our land, we have been barely able to tolerate your behaviour. Now you try to force some new-fangled 'democratic reforms' on us, that all of us think are ridiculous and nothing but a mule-load of conceit. What do you mean you will give us land, when all the land you can see around has been ours since the beginning of time? . . . If anyone is oppressing us, it is you. (Norbu, no date, pp. 102–3)

The Chinese then resorted to more heavy-handed methods: forcible confiscation of property for redistribution, attacks on ordained Buddhists, and infringement of religious practices. Enraged, many Tibetans began guerrilla attacks against Chinese troops and installations. The Chinese brought in reinforcements, including aircraft, and retaliated ruthlessly against Tibetan villages and temples. A host of atrocities ensued: murder, torture, rape, destruction of cultural sites and relics, and abduction of locals for forced labour or 're-education' elsewhere in China (Michael, 1988, pp. 278–9).

Tibetan resistance grew to a crescendo in 1959. In March, Chinese military authorities appeared ready to arrest the Dalai Lama, who was back in Lhasa. Thousands of his subjects assembled around his palace to block the Chinese from capturing him. When the Chinese responded a few days later by shelling the palace, the Dalai Lama fled to India. Chinese troops killed thousands of rebels and activists in the capital of Lhasa and crushed guerrilla units in the countryside. The CCP authorities also tried to crush Tibetan Buddhism, which they saw as a rival political system. The Chinese closed temples, destroyed sacred books and artwork, harassed and tortured monks, forbade photographs of the Dalai Lama, and revamped the Buddhist-oriented education system.

Conflict continued between the PLA occupiers and Tibetan opposition groups, both armed and unarmed, throughout the

1960s and 1970s. The Cultural Revolution brought a new wave of persecution, as Tibetan Buddhism made an easy target for self-styled Red Guards looking for vestiges of feudalism to destroy.

The Dalai Lama, with corroboration from human rights monitoring groups and many other observers, complained that his people have 'not only been shot, but also beaten to death, crucified, burned alive, drowned, vivisected, starved, strangled, hanged, scalded, buried alive, disembowelled, and beheaded' (Gyatso, 1983, p. 222). There have been numerous reports of dissidents, including monks and nuns, arrested en masse, tortured and often killed during detention; excessive force used by PLA troops against demonstrators; especially shocking atrocities, encompassing a variety of cruel tortures, during the infamous Cultural Revolution; forcible abortions performed on Tibetan women found pregnant with a second child, even though overpopulation is not a problem in the region; and even young Tibetan children arrested, beaten and tortured with electric shocks (*Tibetan Bulletin*, 1990, p. 14). 'Torture is routine, sometimes resulting in death', says Lodi G. Gyari, the Dalai Lama's envoy to the United States. 'In many cases, Tibetans remain imprisoned under inhumane conditions for years without being formally charged with an offence' (Gyari, 1992, p. 25). Tibetan prisoners have the additional hardship of serving their time under mostly Chinese administrators, who habitually treat Tibetans as ethnic inferiors.

As in China proper, the Chinese authorities in Tibet organized 'struggle sessions', public hearings in which local landowners, clergymen and others the regime considered 'counter-revolutionary' were denounced, humiliated and beaten, with the audience encouraged to participate. Egged on by Chinese officials, mobs murdered and cruelly abused untold numbers of people, often on the flimsiest of pretexts. The Tibetan government-in-exile has estimated that the Chinese occupation has killed 1.2 million Tibetans, nearly 20 per cent of the Tibetan population.

Beijing is also frequently charged with attempting cultural genocide in Tibet. According to outside estimates, some 6,000 temples and monasteries have been destroyed by the Communist Chinese during their occupation of Tibet (Cranston, 1992, p. 2). In the education system administered by the Chinese government, Tibetan culture and language are belittled, while Chinese culture and history are extolled.

The Chinese administration in Tibet has overseen unrestrained pollution, large-scale extraction of timber and other natural resources for shipment back to China proper, and the offering of parts of the land as dump sites for the hazardous wastes of foreign countries. Of course, uncontrolled exploitation and degradation of the land are also occurring in China proper; the question is China's right to carry out such activities in what is arguably 'occupied' territory. Tibetan exile Dorje Tsephel raises what may be a legitimate complaint: 'The Chinese claim they've come to help the Tibetans, but all they do is rob us and take all our natural wealth to China. When they arrive, they come with empty bags, but they go away with two or three truckloads of possessions. A posting to Tibet is a guarantee that they will make their fortune' (Craig, 1992, p. 241). This view was corroborated by Hu Yaobang, then considered the most likely successor to Deng, when he visited Tibet on a fact-finding mission in 1980. Hu reportedly concluded of the Chinese occupation, 'This is plain colonialism' (*Emancipation Monthly* (Hong Kong), no. 115, December 1987; in Donnet, 1994, p. 97).

All of this has contributed to separatist pressures that force the Chinese to maintain in Tibet up to 200,000 PLA soldiers whose primary mission is to suppress internal revolt rather than to guard against foreign invasion (Malik, 1995a, p. 320). During the post-Mao moderation of the 1980s, Chinese officials allowed the Tibetans greater religious and cultural freedom. (Some critics say these changes were less indicative of religious tolerance than of Beijing's desire to generate revenue from tourism and to mollify foreign complaints about human rights abuses.) Nevertheless, separatist sentiment remained strong, even among younger generations of Tibetans. In 1988 and 1989 there was a series of violent clashes between demonstrators and Chinese troops. The Chinese claimed the disturbances were instigated by a small number of trouble-makers hoping to profit by creating social disorder. Other witnesses, however, said the demonstrations were broad-based and met with brutal, excessive force by the Chinese.

The Chinese authorities declared martial law in Tibet in March 1989, shortly before the Tiananmen Square crackdown. Foreigners were required to leave, curtailing outside media coverage of Chinese atrocities and abetting the Chinese government's disinformation campaign. Hundreds of Tibetans were imprisoned, with accompanying reports of beatings and torture of prisoners. Later that year, to Beijing's chagrin, the Dalai Lama won the Nobel Peace Prize, his fame built on his efforts to publicize human rights abuses in his homeland and to generate international support for Tibetan independence.

For its part, Beijing denies systematic human rights abuses in Tibet and argues that in material terms, the average Tibetan is far better off as a result of PRC administration. Some Tibetans have clearly benefited from the opportunities brought by Chinese rule, and the CCP continually produces pro-Beijing Tibetan spokespeople, such as regime-approved 'Living Buddha' Donggar Losang Chilai, who asserts that 'the living standard of Tibetans has greatly improved' under Beijing's administration (*Beijing Review*, 1992a, p. 5).

The fear of foreign influence in Tibet intended to divide and weaken China remains strong among the CCP leadership. These fears are not completely unfounded. The US Central Intelligence Agency (CIA) trained Tibetan exiles in guerrilla warfare tactics at a remote camp in Colorado during the 1960s. Many Westerners in both private and public positions campaign for Tibetan self-rule. CCP officialdom maintains that the Dalai Lama and other Tibetan separatists are 'under the direct guidance of foreign hostile forces' (Ren, 1995, p. 107) and that foreign agitation explains why Tibet remains so unruly despite the benefits it enjoys under PRC rule. This claim is undermined, however, by accounts such as that given by a foreign visitor to Tibet who witnessed the uprising of 1988: 'I saw with my own eyes how the whole Tibetan sector, as many as 10,000 people, rose up against the Chinese. It was as though years of pent-up frustration suddenly came to the surface'. The strength of this frustration was apparent in the 'hopelessness' of the demonstration; 'There were the tin-hatted Chinese soldiers, thousands of them, with tear gas and machine guns, and all the Tibetans could do was throw stones' (Craig, 1992, p. 272).

In the long term, more subtle policies are likely to succeed where naked force has failed to repress Tibetan separatism. Beijing has moved to gain control of the next generation of Tibetan Buddhist leadership. After the Dalai Lama named a young boy to the position of Panchen Lama, Tibetan Buddhism's second-highest ecclesiastical office, in May 1995, Chinese officials put the boy under house arrest at a hidden location. In June 1996, under pressure from the government, a group of senior Tibetan lamas chose another boy, the son of CCP members, as an alternative Panchen Lama. By tradition, he will select the next Dalai Lama.

To neutralize Tibetan political power, Beijing has gerrymandered provincial borders to keep Tibetans geographically divided; more than half of the 6 million Tibetans live in Chinese provinces other than Tibet. Perhaps the greatest threat to Tibetan civilization is Beijing's policy of resettling ethnic Han Chinese in Tibet. The government has provided attractive financial incentives to lure Han settlers to Tibet, including two to four times the usual salary, additional hardship pay for the high altitude, free furniture and guaranteed housing, extra vacation time, and increased pensions. The result has dramatically altered the region's demography. Besides dominating economic and cultural life, Han residing in Tibet now outnumber the native Tibetans by over a million (*Tibetan Bulletin*, 1992, p. 8). As Tibetans become a minority in their own land, their case for independent homeland is seriously weakened.

Tibet epitomizes the linkage between internal and external threats to the CCP's political project. In addition to the traditional problem of maintaining control of a far-flung yet strategically and politically vital corner of the empire, the Party seems convinced that local opposition to Chinese rule is upheld by the support of foreigners whose ultimate goals are to overthrow the CCP and subjugate the PRC. Tibetan separatism is also an indirect threat to the careers of the PRC's top leaders; having backed themselves into a corner by continually proclaiming Tibet an integral part of the 'motherland', they could not give it away without suffering disastrous domestic political damage.

Pan-Islamicism and Pan-Mongolianism

Many Chinese analysts worry about pan-Islamicism, seeing the possibility that it might unite predominantly Muslim countries in the Middle East and Central Asia into a political bloc that might represent 'a new pole' in the international system (Glaser, 1993, p. 255; Malik, 1995a, p. 344). Islam tugs at another weak link in the Chinese empire: the province of Xinjiang ('New Territory'), which is about half Muslim. Many Xinjiang Muslims resent such aspects of Chinese rule as forced birth control, restrictions on building mosques, unsustainable exploitation of the region's natural resources, and nuclear testing (the PLA's primary nuclear test site is located at Lop Nur [Lop Lake] in Xinjiang). In the past, China has allowed Xinjiang Muslims considerable cultural leeway in order to promote good relations between Beijing and the Arab states. Thousands of

Xinjiang residents made the pilgrimage to Mecca in the 1980s, and Beijing allowed the Muslim World League to fund Islamic education in Xinjiang. These were significant concessions for a regime that sees religion, and Islam in particular, as a competitor for the loyalty of the Chinese populace. The CCP has viewed Xinjiang's ties with Muslim outsiders more narrowly, however, since a Muslim uprising broke out in Xinjiang in 1990 that ultimately drew some 200,000 PLA soldiers and cost the lives of as many as 1,000 demonstrators (Wang, 1994, p. 42). In February of that year, Premier Li Peng warned that 'We must heighten our vigilance' against 'reactionary and splittist forces. . . . donning religious outer garments' (Li, 1990, p. B2/1). As with Tibet, CCP officials have taken the position that 'foreign hostile forces' are supporting non-Han Xinjiang Chinese in an often violent campaign to gain independent statehood (Ren, 1995, p. 107). Support from neighbours in Central Asia was evident in the thirty bombings carried out by activists for an 'independent Turkestan' reported in 1994. A Uighur riot against Chinese rule in February 1997 that resulted in ten (the official Chinese figure) to several hundred (outside estimates) deaths and was rapidly followed by 100 executions was also blamed on 'foreign hostile forces' (*Straits Times*, 1997a, p. 2).

Along with the suppression of insurrectionists, Beijing sees economic development as a key part of its strategy for combating the lure of pan-Islamicism. Although Khazakhstan's economic growth has been slowed by post-USSR disorder, Khazakhstan controls an infrastructure that is superior to that of neighbouring Xinjiang. PRC strategists therefore believe it is imperative that Xinjiang makes rapid economic strides in the next few years as a hedge against Xinjiang Chinese envying the living standards of their fellow ethnics in Khazakhstan. 'Common sense tells us that generally poor families yell out for separation', writes Ma Zongshi. 'Poverty is the root cause of unrest [and] national separation elsewhere in the Third World. Since China is now eradicating age-old poverty, unity in diversity, not family property division, will prevail in the process' (Ma, 1994, p. 75).

Despite border disputes and unhappiness about PRC nuclear tests in Xinjiang, Beijing, Moscow and the Central Asian states have formed, in Harlan W. Jencks's term, a modern-day 'holy alliance' to defend the political status quo against religious separatism in the region. Indeed, Uzbekistan's president recently publicly praised 'the role which China plays in this particular region in preventing separatist feelings and establishing peace and stability' (Jencks, 1994, p. 79). Similarly, Beijing and Tajikistan's government agreed in September 1996 to jointly 'oppose all forms of national separatism; oppose attempts to stir up contradictions between nations, nationalities and religions; and disapprove of separatist activities by any organisations or forces within a country directed against the other country' (Karniol, 1996, p. 22).

The Chinese see Mongolia, like Tibet, as an important buffer region, and would like to see all the Mongols absorbed into the Chinese nation and the territory now administered by Mongolia incorporated into the PRC. Chinese propagandists have even claimed that the legendary Mongol conquerer Ghenghis Khan was actually Chinese, apparently in an effort to weaken Mongolian nationalism (Malik, 1995c, p. 291).

Many Mongols, on the other hand, hope to see all their people, including those in the Chinese province of Inner Mongolia (known to the Chinese as 'Nei Monggol'), united under the auspices of a single, indepedent Mongolian state. Indeed, the most prominent theme in Mongolia's recent history is its struggle to protect itself from Chinese domination. Mongolia took advantage of the Qing Dynasty's collapse in 1911 to declare itself an independent state, only to see the Chinese send troops into Ulan Bator while the Russians were preoccupied with their own revolution in 1919. The victorious Bolshevik government eventually expelled the Chinese in 1921. The Mongolian People's Republic regained independence, but only under a socialist regime that was highly dependent on the Soviet Union for defence against China. Beijing did not recognize Mongolian statehood until after the Second World War.

The PRC's fears have been realized as Mongolia has become an important base for pan-Mongolian and anti-Chinese agitation in Inner Mongolia, further straining tensions there between long-established Mongols and more recent Chinese settlers (as in Tibet, the relatively sparse population of Inner Mongolia makes it feasible for Beijing to establish a Han majority through resettlement programmes). Mongolian nationalists in China are supported by the General Coordination Committee of Inner Mongolian Rejuvenation Movements, a nationalist organization that operates legally (as of early 1993) in Mongolia. The Dalai Lama visited Mongolia in 1991 and was warmly welcomed, to Beijing's open chagrin. Furthermore, Mongolia in 1990 embarked on a programme of political and economic reform that is converting it to a democratic-capitalist system. If these reforms prove successful, Mongolia will become even more attractive, and pan-Mongolian agitation more persuasive, to Chinese Mongols. At minimum, Beijing hopes to keep Mongolia from aligning with another great power. The Sino-Mongolian Treaty of Friendship and Cooperation signed in 1994 was partly intended to preclude reassertion of Russian influence in Mongolia, providing that 'neither party shall join any military or political alliances targeted against the other or sign with any third country any treaties that infringe on the other side's sovereignty and security', or allow a 'third country' to 'hurt the other side's sovereignty and security' (Jencks, 1994, p. 77).

Regionalism

Fragmentation of the country through regional rebellions against central authority is a fear as old as China itself. The opening line of Lo Kuanchung's classic 14th century historical novel *Romance of the Three Kingdoms* reads, 'Long united, the kingdom must divide; long divided, it must unite. It has always been thus'. The Communist leadership has recognized this problem from the PRC's inception, which is why they quickly took steps to attempt to bolster national unity, including introducing a national currency (the *renminbi*, or 'people's currency'), making Mandarin Chinese the national dialect, standardizing education curricula, and disbanding or restructuring regional armies. Allen S. Whiting sees the historical difficulty of holding together the Chinese empire as the principal reason for a 'far greater degree of anxiety in Chinese estimates of linkage between internal vulnerability and external threat than would be found elsewhere' (Whiting, 1975a, p. 203). Cultural and ethnic divisions, such as those which distinguish the Tibetans, Uighurs and Mongolians from the Han, are one type of challenge to central control; another is the tendency of the provinces, even those that are predominantly Han, to resist the dictates of Beijing.

   This type of regionalism has greatly increased in recent years, a side-effect of Deng's promotion of economic and political decentralization. Seeing both their political and economic fortunes increase under these reforms, provincial governments, an increasingly influential interest group, have lobbied Beijing for rapid rather than restrained economic growth. They have also opposed the conservative campaigns to combat 'spiritual pollution', peaceful evolution and 'bourgeois liberalization', which inevitably translate into restrictions on foreign trade and investment (Harding, 1994, p. 34). The provinces now routinely evade and even defy instructions from Beijing, looking out instead for their own interests and practising what Lucien Pye terms 'the great Chinese art form of feigned compliance' (Harding, 1994, p. 34; Pye quoted in Kaye, 1995a, p. 18). Provincial leaders massively underpay the taxes they owe the central government, and Beijing is constrained from pushing the provinces too hard lest it further alienate them. Provinces engage in protectionism and even trade wars against each other, again in violation of Beijing's orders.

There is a wide range of predictions regarding China's future composition. A breakup is certainly not inevitable, as the forces pulling China apart are perhaps balanced by powerful countervailing conditions. The provinces are highly interdependent economically. Beijing remains in control of the PLA and other important overarching institutions. Chinese nationalism also has a cohesive effect, although many PRC elites doubt that national identity is enough to hold the country together (Segal, 1994a, p. 10), and Chinese communities outside of the mainland are comfortable identifying themselves as 'Chinese' but not PRC citizens. Fear of the disorder that might result from a collapse of central authority may be the strongest force holding the country together.

While establishment elites publicly deny that this scenario is possible, the political breakup of China is a chilling prospect, reminiscent of the disorder and shame of the warlord period and the anarchy of the Cultural Revolution. Dread among Chinese elites of an erosion of central authority is manifest in their renewed interest in the nineteenth-century scholar-general Zeng Guofan. In 1995, Zeng's biography was a national bestseller and his calligraphy was selling for hundreds of thousands of dollars (Kaye, 1995b, p. 24). Zeng's storied career was devoted to propping up the declining Qing Dynasty. His most famous accomplishment was defeating the Taiping Rebellion (1850–1864). Led by Hong Xiuquan, who was heavily influenced by foreign missionaries, the Taiping ('heavenly peace') movement was at once Christian and anti-Beijing. Hong built up an army that posed a serious threat to the regime, capturing several major cities in Southeast China and holding its own against Beijing's troops. A ruthless but shrewd commander, Zeng turned the tide against the Taiping by uniting the private armies of local landowners. In the PRC's early years Zeng was vilified as a counter-revolutionary in the service of a feudal government run by foreign invaders. The rehabilitated Zeng, however, is widely admired as a man who tried to preserve order against looming chaos. The revision suggests many newly prosperous Chinese deeply fear disorder and believe maintaining stability is worth putting up with even an imperfect central government.

While the causes of regionalism are largely internal, foreigners play a significant role. Deng's reforms gave greater freedom to the provinces to pursue their own foreign economic policies. Each of the provinces now has its own unique pattern of links with the international economy. Consequently, each also has its own political agenda, with the potential for disagreement with some of Beijing's directives. Foreign investment and trade turn the interests of particular provinces outward, creating potential disincentives for obedience to Beijing's commands. Gerald Segal notes, for example, 'One of the reasons why Britain is able to take such a tough line on Hong Kong is that Beijing has lost important aspects of control of Guangdong Province, adjacent to Hong Kong, which relies heavily on investment from the British colony and wants to get on with business, not raise tensions' (Segal, 1994b, p. 11). Fujian Province, which has strong economic links with Taiwan, would face a similar conflict of interest should Beijing call for a military assault across the Taiwan Strait.

Overseas Chinese, who provide some 80 per cent of the foreign direct investment in China, also bring their more cosmopolitan, pluralistic outlook to the PRC, which undermines the notion that a single political authority must circumscribe all mainland Chinese (Segal, 1995, pp. 68–9).

PRC elites note that some Western scholars have seized upon regionalism as another means by which foreigners can use their economic influence to divide and weaken China. Segal, for example, wrote a major study that concluded that as a result of Deng's economic decentralization much of China was only nominally under Beijing's rule. 'The centre . . . did not foresee the longer-range implications of its experiments. It never thought it would lose, and be unable to regain, control', Segal wrote (Segal, 1994a, p. 11). The assertion by this Western scholar that China was politically breaking up clearly pricked a raw nerve. The PRC establishment called Segal's study 'irresponsible, baseless and malicious' (Goh, 1994, p. 9) and Segal found himself temporarily unable to obtain a Chinese visa.

Liberalization and 'Peaceful Evolution'

A variety of recent developments have damaged the CCP's legitimacy, including the Cultural Revolution, Deng's shift to 'Market socialism', and the 1989 Tiananmen Massacre. At the same time, the PRC's economic, cultural, and educational intercourse with the outside world make it increasingly permeable by foreign political ideas. It is understandable, therefore, that domestic pressure for political liberalization is one of the Party's greatest fears (although some members of the Party fear it more than others). 'Bourgeois liberalization', as it is known in CCP terminology, principally means abandoning the one-party political system. As mentioned earlier, this prospect threatens disaster for the careers of CCP politicians and raises doubts about the sustainability of China's general development. The CCP, therefore, has consistently maintained a consensus on intolerance of any challenges to the Party's authority to rule China, a tenet institutionalized as one of the 'Four Cardinal Principles' Deng laid down to mark the boundaries of acceptable political debate. (The Four Cardinal Principles are socialism, dictatorship of the proletariat, leadership of China in the hands of the CCP, and Marxist-Leninist-Maoist thought as the foundation political philosophy.) In many respects, Chinese officialdom's fear of liberal subversion parallels the fear of communist subversion manifest among many Americans during the Cold War.

To combat domestic pressure for political liberalization, the Party leadership has taken several steps in the 1990s. These measures include purging moderate CCP officials who have shown sympathy for political liberalization; devoting more attention and resources to suppressing dissidents; and securing greater Party control over the military by intensifying soldiers' political education, increasing the PLA's budget, and removing politically unreliable commanders (some PLA units reportedly responded reluctantly to the orders to crack down on the demonstrators in and around Tiananmen Square).

As an illiberal-socialist state in a world dominated by liberal-capitalist powers, China sees strong links between outsiders and 'bourgeois liberalism' at home, and not without good reason. In early 1953, US Secretary of State John Foster Dulles began enunciating what became known as the strategy of 'peaceful evolution': the US government was committed to the overthrow of communist governments, including China's, but war was not the only way to achieve this goal. An indirect, long-term, peaceful campaign of cultivating demands for liberalization from within countries such as China could be equally effective. With outside support to help the process along, democratic elements within China would eventually force the CCP out of power and replace it with a more liberal regime (which, the Americans assumed, would also be a more cooperative, responsible and peaceful international actor).

Mao reportedly took Dulles's peaceful evolution speeches very seriously, especially as the Khrushchev government in the Soviet Union seemed to grow less revolutionary and more accommodating toward the USA in the late 1950s. He saw linkages between US attempts at subversion, Soviet 'revisionism', and his own enemies within the CCP politburo, such as Peng Dehuai (Qiang, 1995/96, pp. 228–31).

The renewed antipathy of many foreign governments and non-government organizations toward the CCP in the wake of the Tiananmen Massacre heightened many Party members' fears of foreign subversion. CCP official Wang Renzhi provides a representative statement of the post-Tiananmen view of peaceful evolution:

> Western capitalism . . . has stepped up political, economic, ideological, and cultural infiltration into socialist countries, and built up anti-socialist forces operating within socialist countries to pursue a policy of 'peaceful evolution'. Under these circumstances, bourgeois liberalization is bound to appear and expand into a force in China. Such a force inevitably seeks support from international reactionary forces. The international anti-Communist forces are certain to lend support. (Wang Renzhi, 1990, p. 2)

Anti-CCP nations such as the United States are believed to train and fund Chinese provocateurs, invite Chinese students to attend their universities in the hope of liberalizing them, and spread liberal ideas among the Chinese populace through systematic means such as Voice of America radio broadcasts or informal means such as conversations by visiting foreigners with the local people. PRC officials and the Chinese press assigned 'hostile foreign forces' a prominent role, for example, in the Tiananmen demonstrations of 1989. Western countries offer blandishments such as financial aid and preferential trade status to governments that shift to more liberal economic practices, while withholding economic assistance from socialist states or even laying siege against them with sanctions and embargoes.

Beyond the shrill propaganda of a Party looking over its shoulder at potential rivals, many Chinese are apprehensive about the possible impact of political liberalization. Even among intellectuals, a group that has often clashed with the CCP leadership, this evaluation of multiparty democracy offered by Ma Zongshi is not uncommon:

Frankly, experiments with Western parliamentary democracy have not been a success story in Asia, let alone in China. We had it even in the warlord era in the twenties, nothing but a mockery of democracy. . . . Pluralism? Good Heavens, there were thousands of rival Red Guard factions in the country in the ten chaotic years of the so-called Cultural Revolution (1966–76) when party committees were kicked aside in the name of making 'revolution'. It was anarchy, pure and simple. . . . Whether one likes it or not, the CCP . . . remains the only organized political force capable of holding the vast country together. (Ma, 1994, pp. 76–7)

America's peaceful evolution campaign epitomizes the connection between external and internal threats to the CCP. Some Party officials see it as a deliberate attempt to weaken China (by promoting political instability and the social evils that allegedly accompany democracy), while others recognize that many American politicians believe democracy would be good for China. In general, Chinese elites consider foreign support for political liberalization an unwelcome intrusion into China's internal affairs.

Internal Problems Driving Chinese Foreign Policy?

As we have seen, PRC policy-makers believe many of China's serious internal problems are closely connected with its foreign relations. Up to now we have examined areas in which, from Beijing's point of view, outsiders trouble China. To complete the discussion of internal–external linkages, we should consider the converse possibility that domestic developments move China to trouble outsiders. This question assumes that internal problems, even those over which foreigners have little apparent influence, may shape China's foreign policy. It is commonly asserted that national leaders who are unable to overcome domestic difficulties sometimes pursue an aggressively extroverted foreign policy to distract their people from the problems at home. Samuel S. Kim seems to have this idea in mind when he argues that 'Today the main danger to the peace and stability of the Asia-Pacific region stems more from China's domestic weaknesses than from its external assertiveness. . . . a weak, reactive, insecure, and fragmenting China is more unpredictable and dangerous than a strong, confident, and cohesive China' (Kim, 1995, p. 487).

From this perspective, China's growing energy shortfall is particularly worrying. China became a net energy importer in 1990 and will become a net oil importer by the end of the decade. With its reserves shrinking (presently known reserves would be exhausted in 20 years if economic growth averaged 8 per cent annually) and demand growing, China faces heavy dependence on foreign suppliers of this vital resource unless it discovers new deposits on Chinese territory. The two areas with the greatest potential are the Tarim Basin in Xinjiang Province and the South China Sea. The Tarim Basin will be exceptionally difficult and expensive to exploit because of the harsh, sandstorm-swept surface terrain, the depth of the deposits, and the complexity of the subterranean rock formations. Surveys in the South China Sea have thus far proved disappointing; despite very high Chinese estimates of the amount of oil in the area, most of the wells drilled there have yielded neither oil nor natural gas, and most of the deposits found have been small (Salameh, 1995–96, pp. 133–4, 138–41). One way or another, China's energy shortfall will become an important foreign policy consideration. The prospect of increased dependence on foreign suppliers will alarm the more xenophobically inclined elites who believe China has already made itself too vulnerable to the control of outsiders in its rush for development. One possible outcome is a greater attempt to secure Chinese control over new energy supplies outside China proper. Proponents of a stronger Chinese military capability have already taken this approach in connection with the disputed Spratly Islands (Garver, 1992, pp. 1018–19).

Despite China's rapid economic growth and increased living standards in the 1980s and 1990s, there is significant potential for the kind of large-scale domestic discontent that might push the leadership to search for a foreign affairs issue to capture the public's attention and rejuvenate their support for the regime. While the average Chinese is richer than ever before, serious economic and social challenges loom in China's near future – some created or intensified by rapid growth itself. High inflation has accompanied rapid growth; the inflation rate was 20 per cent in 1994, and has hovered at around 15 per cent since then. At the same time, state-funded welfare programmes have shrunk dramatically, leaving many working-class urban Chinese struggling to make ends meet. Tens of millions of former peasants have flooded China's eastern cities in search of better-paying jobs, creating new slums and ample opportunities for exploitation by sweat-shop bosses. The government is reluctant to privatize many of China's largely unprofitable state-owned industries for fear of the social consequences of laying off huge numbers of workers. State-owned firms employ about 70 per cent of the country's industrial workers, and one-third of them might lose their jobs if the entire sector was privatized (*The Economist*, 1995, pp. 25–6). In the meantime, however, these firms are a drag on economic growth. Even with its harsh one-child policy, China's population, now 1.25 billion, will probably continue to grow for another 20 years, peaking at perhaps 1.5 billion. This strains resources of all kinds, but particularly land. With its ratio of population to arable land already relatively low in global terms, China has been losing additional farmland at the rate of about 500,000 hectares annually to urban development (Smil, 1996, p. 35). Yet by the year 2015, China's population will need about 50 per cent more grain than the country was able to harvest in 1994 (Starr, 1996, p. 17).

Collectively, these and other developments mean most Chinese will probably be unable to attain the standard of living of their neighbours in Asia's Newly-Industrializing Countries for the fore-seeable future. Yet the economic boom of the 1990s created high expectations generally and severe discontent among those Chinese, particularly peasants, who have benefited less than their better-placed countrymen (Swaine, 1995, pp. 44, 45). Many Party officials and other elites see the government's most important task as keeping economic development a step ahead of widespread public dissatisfaction.

Indeed, dissatisfaction is already serious enough that its manifestations are being called 'public order crises'. In 1993, for example, China reportedly suffered 78 uprisings involving 1,000 or more people, and 2,400 internal security police and soldiers were killed or injured. Greg Austin argues that rising public disorder has increased the leadership's sense of vulnerability and 'contributed to a call at senior levels of the PLA for a new foreign policy specifically designed to oppose US "intervention" in China' (Austin, 1995, pp. 9, 14).

Foreigners, it seems, are never far from domestic instability in China, either as instigators or would-be profiteers. Along with distinctive views of the international political system and of China's role within it, the linkage between internal and external threats is an essential plank in the intellectual framework of PRC foreign policy-making. This intellectual framework has a more tangible counter-part in the collection of organizations that conduct China's foreign relations, which is the subject of the next chapter.

4

The Structure and Process of Foreign Policy-Making

The Chinese government has two parallel governmental structures: one set of organs and institutions run by the Chinese Communist Party, and the other run by the state. Following the Soviet model, the top party organizations are the Politburo (Political Bureau) Standing Committee, and below it are the Politburo itself and the Central Committee. The most powerful state organizations are the National People's Congress (NPC) and the State Council. The NPC is China's highest legislative body, equivalent to the British Parliament or US Congress, while the State Council is chief executive body. Like the Party's Central Committee, the State Council, which oversees the various government ministries, is too large to be an effective decision-making body; its leadership is therefore distilled in a smaller State Council cabinet, headed by the Premier of the PRC.

Although the two structures are parallel, they are not co-equal. The PRC's history, ideology and even its constitution make it clear that the party is the source of all political power and authority in China, including the legitimacy of state organizations. To facilitate the Party's supervision and control over the state, Party organizations are interlocked with their state counterparts. Leaders at the highest levels may be members of both Party and state bodies. Further down the chain of command, Party organizations employ specialists charged with overseeing particular operations of the state bureaucracy. Indeed, it has always been difficult to tell where the Party ends and where the state begins in China.

The intermeshing of Party and state institutions is evident in the process of foreign policy-making. The most powerful general decision making body in China is the Politburo Standing Committee. Although a Party organ, this group ordinarily includes the State President (who is also tasked with ratifying treaties and other

63

agreements with foreign governments) as well as the Chairmen of the CCP, Central Military Commission, Chinese People's Consultative Conference, and Standing Committee of the National People's Congress. The CCP Secretariat is officially charged with overseeing the implementation of the Politburo's policy decisions, but the most important liaison between the decision-making and executive organs may be the Foreign Affairs 'Leading Small Groups' of the CCP Central Committee, which consists of some members of the Politburo Standing Committee, plus a senior military officer and top officials from the state bureaucracies involved in foreign affairs. These bureaucracies include the Ministry of Foreign Affairs (MFA), which conducts political, legal and humanitarian relations with other countries; the Ministry of Foreign Trade and Economic Cooperation (MOFTEC, economic relations); the Commission for External Cultural Liaison (cultural and mass media activities); the State Science Commission (scientific and technical exchanges); the Ministry of Defence (military relations), which encompasses the People's Liberation Army (PLA); the Commission for Overseas Chinese Affairs; and the Xinhua ('New China') News Agency. Of these, the MFA and the PLA are the most significant, and will be discussed further below. Countless smaller organizations also have direct contacts with foreigners, and thus have the potential to formulate and carry out their own foreign policy on a small scale. Over half of all PRC ministries, including those that supervise such portfolios as public health, forestry and aeronautics, have their own foreign affairs departments, which act as liaisons between Chinese officials and their counterparts overseas (Sutter, 1996, pp. 20–1).

The PRC's foreign policy-making progress has undergone important changes in recent years. First, the growth of Beijing's international contacts in the last two decades has both increased the number of Chinese organizations with input into foreign policy-making and enhanced policy-makers' knowledge of the outside world. Second, Deng's reforms have changed foreign policy-making from what was virtually a one-man dictatorship to a process with greater scope for haggling among bureaucracies and groups representing special interests, although major decisions are still made by a handful of top leaders. Deng's restructuring efforts have also resulted in greater influence for state institutions and less for party institutions, shifting power from ideologues to technocrats. The State Council, which oversees the MFA, MOFTEC and the Ministry of Defence, is empowered to make minor foreign policy decisions on its own, while referring weighty questions to the CCP Secretariat. Even in these cases, the Secretariat largely relies on the State Council's advice. Thus, in recent years, China's foreign-policy making process has become more professional and institutionalized, with the party retaining the final say over the major tenents of China's foreign relations, but with less involvement in the routine operation of PRC diplomacy.

Within policy-making organizations, decisions are generally reached through discussion and consensus. Regardless of official titles, the authority of members of an organization is unequal, stemming from a variety of subtle factors that accord certain members greater prestige. During discussion of an issue, each group member in effect casts a vote by expressing an opinion. When a highly ranked member of the group expresses an opinion, however, junior members tend to acquiesce. At the highest levels, there is greater pressure for the group to come to a unanimous decision, which all the group members will then publicly support (Lu, 1997, p.16). In a political system with strong inertial forces stemming from the sheer size and complexity of the government bureaucracy and from the need to build a consensus among the relevant officials, foreign policy-making is further prone to falling back on the status quo because the implications of particular foreign-policy issues for current domestic power struggles are often unclear (Zhao, 1996, p. 86).

While various tasks of government appear thoroughly articulated and rationally distributed throughout the bureaucracy, foreign policy-making itself is not highly systematic or formalized. As is typical of Chinese policy-making in general, a small group of top civilian and military leaders has made the important decisions, generally with a broad view of national security in mind. Since the PRC leadership considers foreign affairs an especially sensitive sphere of government, the foreign policy process has been particularly subject to secrecy and concentration at the top level of Party leadership. Below this pinnacle of power, however, is a vast bureaucratic structure, separated and inter-related in complex ways, and subject to the usual dynamics of bureaucratic struggle between self-interested organizations.

Like most other organizations, the groups and institutions involved in the making of Chinese foreign policy pursue their own bureaucratic interests though the established channels and procedures. Generally stated, these interests include: (1) maintaining the organization's survival; (2) preserving what the organization considers to be its appropriate missions; (3) securing greater funding; and (4) increasing the organization's autonomy (seminal works on the politics of organizational input into foreign policy-making include Halperin, 1974 and Allison, 1971). While ideological divisions within the Chinese government are less acute than in the past, and thus less likely to generate disputes over foreign policy options, bureaucratic politics in the making of Chinese foreign policy remains significant for other reasons. Deng Xiaoping intentionally took steps to decentralize the PRC's political system. Jiang Zemin, Deng's successor as top PRC leader, is unable to personally dominate the policy process the way his predecessors did; indeed, it is unlikely that any individual will ever again command unquestioned control over the party, government and military simultaneously. Furthermore, China's foreign relations have become 'pluralized' because the PRC's linkages with the outside world have become so numerous that they are no longer manageable by a small group of high-ranking officials, let alone a single paramount leader (Hamrin, 1994, p. 89). Consequently, the various bureaucracies with input into Chinese foreign policy-making have found opportunities to increase their influence, some of which will inevitably be directed toward the pursuit of relatively narrow organizational agenda (Lu, 1997, pp. 35, 163). In Quansheng Zhao's formulation, the foreign policy-making process has 'shifted from vertical authoritarianism' characterized by a dominant leader, a single chain of command, and a unified set of policies, to 'horizontal authoritarianism', typified by multiple power centres representing a variety of interests, resulting in a less coherent set of policies (Zhao, 1996, p. 81).

There is a geographic as well as a bureaucratic aspect of this decentralization. During the 1990s, certain provincial and municipal governments became both more autonomous foreign policy actors and more powerful lobbyists with Beijing. Shanghai, Guangdong, Fujian, Shandong, Tianjin, Jiangsu, Zhejiang, Liaoning and the Special Economic Zones (such as Shenzhen and Xiamen) are notable in this regard because of their success in attracting foreign investment and/or trade, which provides a supply of foreign currency (Zhao, 1996, p. 104). Analysts note the 'striking new power of local governments to shape decisions by the central government' (Montinola, Qian and Weingast, 1995, p. 69). This raises the prospect of Chinese cities and provinces not only influencing Beijing's foreign policy-making, but also carrying out their own diplomacy. As a case in point, in July 1990, when a US government angry over the Tiananmen incident of 1989 was generally shunning high-level Chinese officials, a delegation of Chinese mayors (including Zhu Rongji, then mayor of Shanghai) travelled to Washington seeking to 'improve bilateral relations' and managed to meet with the Speaker of the US Congress's House of Representatives, the National Security Adviser, and the Deputy Secretary of State (Zhao, 1996, pp. 105–6).

Variations within the Elite

The PRC leadership is probably more unified in its basic assumptions today than at any time in its history (Harding, 1994, p. 26). Nevertheless, significant distinctions in outlook exist among individuals and between key groups within the PRC's policy-making elite. For our purposes, the differences in viewpoints among groups are more permanent and therefore matter more than those among individuals. Perhaps the most important of these distinctions is the tendency of the 'conservatives' to see the world differently from the 'moderates'. The conservatives tend to be older bureaucrats with general political training and practical administrative experience but little formal or technical education. They prefer an authoritarian political system, gradual or minimal economic reform and slow growth, fearing that the benefits of rapid prosperity are not worth the disorder that would accompany a dismantling of the old system of state planning and control of the economy. As for international outlook, the conservatives are suspicious of foreign economic influence, highly sensitive to the dangers of subversion and 'spiritual pollution' through contact with outsiders, and pessimistic about the long-term possibility of the other major powers living in peace with China. These concerns are not given due consideration, conservatives believe, if China merely strives for rapid development at all costs and grabs everything foreigners offer.

The moderates are mostly associated with the younger, better-educated technocrats, many of whom have studied or at least travelled abroad. They support (and, indeed, have benefited from) Deng's commitment to rapid economic reform. Like the conservatives, however, most moderates oppose anything more than minor political liberalization, convinced that the instability and dislocation caused by the economic restructuring demand continued authoritarian rule to keep them under control. The moderates are less averse than the conservatives to the risks of rapid reform, including inflation, high unemployment, loss of social welfare benefits, and unsavoury ideas brought into China from the outside world. In the long run, moderates believe, prosperity is the best means of dealing with China's problems, including those created by economic reform. The moderates welcome greater foreign trade, investment and economic cooperation, believing the benefits outweigh the dangers. They also tend to be more optimistic about the capacity of economic interdependence to restrain 'power politics' by China's adversaries.

In one form or another, the struggle between the conservatives and the moderates has produced important shifts in the centre of gravity of Chinese foreign policy throughout the PRC's history, and this dynamic will likely continue in the post-Deng era. As one group gains ascendancy, it brings into power its particular worldview, which in turn implies a particular orientation in China's foreign affairs. One worldview or another may dominate a given organization; differing outlooks on foreign affairs may thus provide an additional basis for conflict among organizations competing for foreign policy influence. This phenomenon is clear in the relationship between perhaps the two most important foreign policy bureaucracies in China, the MFA and the PLA, which will now be examined in some detail.

The Ministry of Foreign Affairs

The MFA is the most influential of the PRC's bureaucracies in the day-to-day conduct of foreign policy. With over 3,000 employees in the early 1990s, the MFA is nearly twice the size of China's next-largest central bureaucracy (Guojia Jigou Bianzhi Weiyuanhui, 1991, p. 215). In keeping with the general intermingling of the Party and state bureaucratic structures, the MFA is officially under the supervision of the State Council, but in practice it reports to the Foreign Affairs Leading Small Group of the Politburo Standing Committee (Lu, 1997, p. 20)

The MFA has separate departments for Asian Affairs, Russian and Eastern European Affairs, North American and Oceanian Affairs, West Asian and North African Affairs, Western European Affairs, African Affairs, and Latin American Affairs. Below the department level are divisions: the United States Affairs Division, for example, within the North American and Oceanian Affairs

Department (Sutter, 1996, p. 21). Some employees are trained at an MFA-affiliated institute, the Foreign Affairs College in Beijing.

In addition to overseeing the activities of Chinese diplomatic missions abroad, the Ministry makes policy recommendations, analyzes foreign affairs, and amasses news on overseas developments. MFA staff receive regular cables from PRC diplomats and also monitor foreign news reports from the major wire services and America's Cable News Network 24 hours a day. The single most important source of foreign affairs information for MFA staff is *Cankao Ziliao* (*Reference Material*), a compilation of translated articles from the foreign press produced daily by the Xinhua News Agency. Distribution of the ordinary version of *Cankao Ziliao* is restricted, and a top-secret version containing articles that discuss Chinese activities that Beijing claims do not exist (missile sales, espionage, etc.) is available only to top officials.

The MFA plays an important role in interpreting how principles decreed by the top leadership, which are broad or even ambiguous, are to be translated into more specific policy goals. Through its internal publications and analyses based on information forwarded by Chinese diplomats abroad, the MFA also has a critical impact on the top leadership's perceptions of international affairs. MFA reports process the raw input from sources such as *Cankao Ziliao* into assessments and arguments that are taken seriously by the PRC leadership because of the MFA's reputation as one of the more professional of China's principal bureaucracies (Lu, 1997, p. 117).

As it is charged with managing Chinese diplomacy, the MFA has an organizational interest in promoting and preserving good relations with other countries. Consequently, MFA officials tend to favour policy options that would minimize contention between Beijing and other governments, even if this means making short-term concessions with a view toward enjoying the long-term benefits of a stable relationship. This has often left the MFA vulnerable to criticism from other bureaucracies that it plays the role of advocate for the interests of foreigners instead of sticking up for Chinese interests (Lu, 1997, p. 164).

The PLA as a Policy-Making Body

Western scholars often base their analysis of the People's Liberation Army upon the observation that it is essentially a 'political' army, designed to defend the interests of the Chinese Communist Party rather than the interests of China. The PLA certainly has unique characteristics, but these should not be overblown. Comparatively heavy involvement of the armed forces in domestic politics is not unusual in developing or socialist countries (Shambaugh, 1996a, p. 268). The CCP has maintained a Chinese tradition of civilian control over the armed forces, an idea China shares with the West (Dreyer, 1996b, p. 2). Furthermore, like their Western counterparts, many PLA officers have developed a strong sense of professionalism. Finally, the PLA and some of its components have their own sets of organizational self-interests, which they pursue in much the same way as is visible in bureaucratic power struggles everywhere.

At the pinnacle of the military hierarchy are the three most senior members of the Central Military Commission (CMC). The chairman is the paramount civilian leader, with two PLA officers as co-chairmen. The advice of other senior Party members, such as the other members of the Politburo Standing Committee, is usually taken seriously. The same is true for the next most influential members of the PLA leadership: the remaining CMC members, including the heads of the PLA General Logistics (GLD), General Political (GPD) and General Staff (GSD) Departments. Others with an important voice are the directors of three other PLA institutions: the Academy of Military Science (AMS), the National Defence University (NDU), and the Commission on Science, Technology and Industry for National Defence (COSTIND). In the next tier of influence are the chiefs of the PLA Air Force, the PLA Navy, and the Second Artillery, and the commanders of the seven military regions. Retired generals of high prestige may offer their opinions on certain issues, and if several of them unite in strenuous opposition to a certain policy, it will likely be dropped. It should not be surprising considering the size of the Chinese military bureaucracy that lower-level bureaucrats are not closely supervised on most matters, which gives considerable scope for organizational self-interests in the implementation of general foreign policy directives from the top (Swaine, 1996, pp. 377–9, 390).

The PLA itself is not a monolithic organization in either structure or viewpoint. Each of its principal components, including the GPD, GSD, GLD, COSTIND, AMS, and NDU has its own separate budget and activities. Like the Chinese economy (Chapter 5), these components have historically had a lot of vertical but little horizontal integration (Shambaugh, 1996a, p. 283). These intra-PLA institutions have tended to develop distinct identities and interests, as is typical of all organizations. The GSD, for example, pursues an agenda favourable to the PLA ground forces, supporting a continental strategy (in contrast to the PLA Navy's maritime strategy) and increased funding for the army to allow it to enhance its units guarding China's borders with Russia, Central Asia and India (Swaine, 1996, p. 381). Some analysts argue convincingly that it is a 'fiction' to believe there is '*one* Chinese defence budget, *one* defence strategy, *one* defence system and plan, and *one* military–civilian relationship' (Lewis, Hua, and Xue, 1991, p. 90).

Besides institutional biases, there are other factors that divide the PLA against itself. The PLA is subject to the same 'generation gap' that is in evidence among the CCP civilian leadership. Many reports suggest older PLA officers see themselves as defenders of traditional virtues such as austerity, self-sacrifice for the good of the group, and patriotism, while younger officers are more individualistic, apolitical, and concerned with amassing material wealth (*Xinhua* report, 15 May 1993; *Renmin Ribao,* 26 July 1993; cited in Wang, 1994, p. 102). Younger officers thus tend to be more supportive of economic reform and less supportive of political indoctrination programmes than their older comrades-in-arms.

Regionalism is another potentially divisive factor. Before the foundation of the People's Republic, China had a well-established history of separate regional armies. Based on long historical wisdom and practice, the PLA commonly rotates provincial commanders to prevent them from building up their own 'independent kingdoms'. The chances of the PLA fracturing along regional lines in anything short of extreme circumstances are probably minimal (Segal, 1994a, pp. 24, 28), but regional consciousness and rivalry have not disappeared from among the generals. A recent example has been the concern among some PLA leaders that a 'Shandong clique' is becoming disproportionately powerful. Natives of Shandong Province fill about a quarter of the top 175 PLA leadership positions, and three of the nine seats on the CMC, while Shandong contains only about 7 per cent of the PRC's population. According to one report, Jiang Zemin has been working to offset the influence of Shandong natives by elevating PLA officers from Jiang's own Jiangsu Province (Yen, 1996, pp. 38–40).

The tension between politics and professionalism also creates conflicts within the PLA. This can be understood as another aspect of the old issue of 'red vs. expert': which matters more, political rectitude or technical competence? (Or, to coin a famous phrase by Mao Zedong's third wife Jiang Qing, is it true that 'a socialist train running late is better than a capitalist train running on time'?) To professionally-minded PLA officers, political education takes time and resources away from strictly military training and preparation, and the contributions of talented potential officers should not be squandered because they lack sufficient enthusiasm for the politics of the day. The advice of the political commissars assigned to PLA units is not always appreciated, and is sometimes ignored, by combat commanders (*Jiefangjun Bao*, 3 July 1993; *World Journal* (New York), 6 August 1993; cited in Wang, 1994, pp. 102–3).

If the PLA has not shown much of an inclination to use its military force to influence the outcomes of domestic political debates, it *has* proven a vigorous lobby group. The specific objectives for which the PLA lobbies include getting a greater share of the annual central budget; maintaining or enlarging its own revenue-generating activities; improving living standards for PLA personnel; acquiring improved, modern military equipment and weapons systems; and, for many PLA officers, making the Chinese armed forces more professional.

In addition to these organizational interests, the PLA has exhibited a particular outlook on foreign relations. In general, the PLA appears especially sensitive to what may be construed as challenges to Chinese sovereignty or indirect threats to national security, and less willing than other groups within the Chinese government to make concessions in these areas for the sake of maintaining favourable diplomatic or trade relations. Thus, in recent years PLA officers have been among those who interpret US policies as an effort to 'contain', suppress and divide China, and who call for stronger protective measures against the USA's peaceful evolution campaign. The PLA clearly favours a relatively hard-line PRC position on Taiwan's efforts to raise its global diplomatic status. Finally, the PLA has been reluctant to accept Chinese participation in regional multilateral security organizations or to accommodate foreign complaints that the PRC's force structure and defence expediture is insufficiently transparent.

The influence of the PLA leadership over foreign policy in general is not as great as its influence over the more narrow field of defence policy. In the former case, the generals have a significant say through both formal and internal channels, but state and Party organizations make the final and important decisions. In the making of defence policy, however, senior PLA leaders, especially the second and third highest-ranked members of the CMC, probably have decisive power on almost all major decisions (Swaine, 1996, pp. 373, 377). In political proposals that bear directly on national defence, as well, the civilian leadership often submits to the PLA's wishes. Deng, for example, reportedly attempted to abolish the military region system and put the PLA's group armies under more direct control by the CMC, a move that would have strengthened the ruling civilian faction's command of the armed forces. Deng had to drop this idea, however, in the face of strong opposition by PLA generals (Wang, 1994, pp. 16–17). The PLA also reportedly resisted Deng's efforts to make Hu Yaobang head of the CMC and probably contributed to the CCP leadership's decision to purge Hu in 1987 (Dreyer, 1996a, pp. 15–16). That this version of events was widely believed in China was confirmed when a high PLA official took the extraordinary step of publicly denying that the PLA was responsible for Hu's ouster (*Ming Pao* [Hong Kong], 25 July 1987, p. 1; cited in Wang, 1992, p. 195).

Most outside analysts believe that high PLA officials were among those elites pushing the Chinese government to take tough positions in the 1990s over issues such as Taiwan, the Spratly Islands, and Chinese relations with the United States and Russia, even at the risk of worsening Beijing's relations with some of the other major powers. How strong a factor this lobbying by PLA 'hardliners' has been in recent Chinese foreign policy is unclear. The not-always-reliable Hong Kong press reported that angry PLA officers sent about 100 letters of protest per day to Jiang's office before ROC President Lee Denghui visited the United States, and 800 letters per day immediately after Lee's visit (*South China Morning Post*, 1995). Many leading analysts of Chinese security issues believe these reports are exaggerated (Dreyer, 1996b, pp. 3–4; Swaine, 1996, p. 366), but the general orientation of the PLA's input into the foreign policy-making process seems clear.

More tangibly, increases in PLA defence budgets in the early 1990s were probably at least partly a result of PLA lobbying. Many outside analysts have plausibly speculated that these funding increases in the 1990s may be understood as the price the generals demanded for coming to the Party's rescue during the Tiananmen demonstrations of 1989.

The PLA Navy's lobbying campaign in the late 1980s and early 1990s provides an illustrative case study. According to John Garver's oft-cited analysis, the PLA Navy (PLAN) had the same agenda as most other organizations. The Navy first had to find a mission for itself that would necessitate increases in its funding, capabilities and importance. Controlling the Spratlys served this purpose, as this would make the PLAN a key strategic player and require great increases in its ability to sustain naval operations far from the Chinese coast. To defeat rival claimants for limited funds as well as opposition from the Foreign Ministry, the Navy could not win the argument on the strength of its own self-interests, but instead had to argue that what it wanted was best for the nation. Some of this lobbying was public. In 1988 and 1989, several articles in the PLA's authoritative journal *Jiefangjun Bao* argued that it was essential for China to protect its potential maritime resources. In a typical passage, one of these articles argued, 'In order to make sure that the descendants of the Chinese· nation can survive, develop, prosper and flourish in the world of the future, we should vigorously develop and use the oceans. To protect and defend the rights and interests of the reefs and islands within Chinese waters is a sacred mission. . . . [E]very reef and island is connected to a large area of territorial water and an exclusive economic zone that is priceless' (Cai Wenyi, 'Reefs, Islands, Oceans, and the Future of a Nation', *Jiefangjun Bao*, 11 March 1988; cited in Garver, 1992, pp. 1018–25). Naval officers maintained the argument in the early 1990s. PLA Navy Commander-in-Chief Zhang Lianzhong warned in 1992, 'As the world is suffering from rapid population growth and resource exhaustion, all countries are turning their eyes to the ocean . . . triggering a world-wide competition for ocean resources' (Huang, 1992, pp. 16–17). Zhang's Deputy Commander Zhang Xusan similarly maintained that since 'the country's available land resources can hardly shoulder the heavy population burden . . . It is high time for China to readjust its maritime strategy and make more efforts to recover the oil and gas resources of the South China Sea'. Of course, Zhang added, 'The navy is ready to offer assistance' in this endeavour (Gao Anming, 'Navy to Participate in Economic Reform Drive', *China Daily* [Beijing], 6 April 1992; cited in Jun, 1994, p. 182). The PLAN's lobbying efforts have apparently paid off, making naval modernization a high priority in China's recent defence budgets.

Bureaucratic Infighting: The PLA vs the MFA

Distinct sets of organizational interests inevitably bring groups vying for influence over foreign policy into conflict. The some-times-contentious relationship between the PLA and the Ministry of Foreign Affairs (MFA) illustrates this dynamic. In recent years, the PLA leadership appears to have increased its scrutiny and criticism of MFA actions, believing these are weakening PRC sovereignty. As we saw above, national sovereignty is an area in which the PLA takes particular interest, while the MFA is often willing to accommodate foreign governments to smooth over potential disputes. On issues such as ownership of the Spratly Islands, the future status of Taiwan, the reincorporation of Hong Kong, PRC military transparency, Chinese participation in multilateral security organizations, PRC nuclear testing, and certain trade disputes, the MFA has generally favoured a more conciliatory position than the PLA. Not surprisingly, the PLA brass tends to believe the MFA has been too compromising in its relations with some foreign governments, especially Washington, failing to stand up to pressure and even humiliation by the Americans on a variety of issues. Some recent disagreements between the PLA and the MFA have reportedly been so intractable and prolonged that they had to be resolved by the paramount leader (Swaine, 1996, p. 375).

An example of PLA–MFA infighting centred on the Law on Territorial Waters and Contiguous Areas promulgated by the National People's Congress in February 1992. The Law explicitly included the Diaoyutai/Senkaku Islands, which are claimed by both China and Japan, in its list of Chinese-owned territories. The Foreign Ministry had objected, arguing that this would damage Sino-Japanese relations and jeopardize Japanese economic aid to China. Senior PLA officials, however, wanted the Diaoyutai in, and their view prevailed (Wang, 1994, pp. 53–4).

On some occasions, the bureaucratic battle is not resolved internally before it reaches the stage of policy implementation. The result is irrational foreign policy-making: self-contradictory signals or behaviour arising from two actors with differing agenda pursuing their own, conflicting policies. Perhaps the best recent example of this phenomenon is the conflict between the PLA and the MFA over Chinese arms sales. Chinese arms sales have been one of the greatest sources of tension in recent Sino-US relations. Washington has sometimes received assurances from the MFA that China will restrict sensitive arms sales involving sophisticated weaponry, particularly nuclear technology and missiles, to politically unstable areas such as the Middle East, only to find that the sales go ahead anyway. Often the MFA makes these promises in good faith. The problem is that the MFA cannot control Chinese arms sales; most of these come under the purview of the PLA, which is more willing than the MFA to tolerate a deterioration of relations with the United States to maintain a good source of revenue.

Oversight and control of the PLA-owned corporations that conduct China's arms export business is made more difficult by the close involvement of these firms with some of the privileged children of high-ranking CCP officials. When the MFA complains about an arms sale, these corporations are likely to respond that 'We are determined to devote ourselves to raising funds for promoting the four modernizations of China. . . . It is wrong to sacrifice the number one mission for the sake of foreign affairs' (this statement comes from a senior COSTIND official interviewed in Lewis, Hua and Xue, 1991, p. 95). Deng had the power to bring PLA arms sales into compliance with the Foreign Ministry's wishes, and Jiang does as well, but they chose not to do so. Aware that economic reforms have forced the military to raise more of its own funds, Deng often sided with the PLA. In one illustrative case, Deng was called on to settle a dispute between a PLA corporation and the Foreign Ministry over the sale of advanced missiles to Saudi Arabia. Deng asked the firm's representative how much money they made. The answer was \$2 billion. '*Bu shao* [That's quite a lot]', said Deng, thereby settling the matter (Lewis, Hua and Xue, 1991, p. 96).

Having discussed the ideational and organizational structure of China's foreign relations, we now move on to some specific issue areas, beginning with the PRC's relationship with the global economy.

5

China and the World Economy

Throughout its history, the PRC has pursued widely varying strategies in pursuit of the same goal: development rapid enough to enable China to catch up economically with the major powers. Beijing's dramatic changes of course in its foreign economic policy point up the importance of two variables, one internal and one external. The internal variable is the difference in outlook among individuals and factions within the CCP leadership – between Mao and Deng, for example. While all Chinese leaders recognize that the world economy has great potential to both help and harm China, the more radical, typified by Mao, have emphasized the dangers of strong Chinese economic links with other countries, while the more pragmatic such as Deng have emphasized the opportunities of interdependence.

The external variable that helps account for China's changes in orientation toward the world economy is the PRC's changing relationship with the great powers, which can sometimes significantly constrain Beijing's options. China entered into an economic relationship with the Soviets when the USSR was willing to offer trade and aid but the other superpower was not; tried near-autarky when both superpowers were hostile toward Beijing; and welcomed economic assistance from the Americans when they were ready to provide it.

The postwar world economy has been, and still is, a basically capitalist system dominated by the United States and its allies. China has pursued all three of the possible approaches to the world economy: establishing an alternative system (the 1950s); isolating itself from the system (the 1960s to mid-1970s); and participating in the system (the late 1970s onward).

To understand the assumptions underlying these differing Chinese approaches to the world economy, it is useful to invoke the three grand theories of global trade, as each encompasses a distinctive view of the international political economy (for a useful summary of the three main theories of international political economy, see Gilpin, 1987, pp. 25–41).

The first of these three theories, Liberalism, emphasizes the capacity of unfettered international trade to promote economic growth among participating states. Liberal theory encompasses the principle of comparative advantage, which holds that any and all participating countries may benefit from international trade. Every state, regardless of its circumstances, can produce certain goods or services relatively efficiently. By supplying to the world market goods and services in which it maintains a comparative advantage and importing what others can produce more efficiently, trading states find a profitable niche while ensuring their citizens enjoy favourable price and quality in a wide range of products. Liberalism stresses the power of market forces to erode and penetrate political boundaries. This is viewed in a positive light, as these forces often reduce political tensions by creating economic ties of common interest among peoples divided by political restrictions and barriers that are, from the standpoint of economic efficiency, irrational. Free trade also has positive consequences for international security. Trading states discover that trade is a more profitable way to build national wealth, and even national security, than conquest. Therefore, states that are enmeshed in the international economy have strong incentives to avoid military conflict: a state would only hurt itself by making war on its trade and investment partners, and the free flow of capital, goods and services among the nations is predicated upon a stable and peaceful international environment.

The second major theory of international political economy is Neo-Mercantilism, which is essentially Neo-Realism applied to economics. According to this view, national governments harness economic activities, both domestic and international, as a means of pursuing state interests such as nation-building and national security. National leaders realize economic ties make their state vulnerable to foreign coercion and penetration, and they strive to guard against any erosion of state sovereignty through foreign trade or participation in international economic organizations. Governments attempt to protect their domestic economy from the possible damaging effects of the international marketplace. In contrast to Liberal theory, which sees trade as a positive-sum game, Neo-Mercantilism holds that governments pay close attention to who benefits more from trade, and are unwilling to see their economic cooperation result in disproportionate gains by a potential adversary. Consequently, economic relations between states are competitive and conflictual – taken to its extreme, Neo-Mercantilism is war by economic means.

Finally, the Neo-Marxist view holds that trade between developed and underdeveloped nations is inherently unequal. The underdeveloped nations, which can supply only raw materials and cheap labour, gain less from economic exchanges than countries with large amounts of capital, which reap the majority of profits in a capitalist system. International trade not only widens the gap between the rich and poor countries, it also increases the developing world's dependence on the capitalist states, which strengthen their dominant position by basing exploitative multinational corporations overseas and by co-opting authoritarian Third World governments. There are two possible ways the developing world can break out of this deleterious arrangement. The more radical prescription is for the underdeveloped nations to band together and form a more just economic system of their own as an alternative to the capitalist system. The less radical solution is for the poor countries to force the developed nations to recognize the injustice of the capitalist system and provide massive assistance and concessions that will enable the developing world to close the economic gulf that separates it from the rich states.

As we will see, elements of all three of these theories recur throughout the history of the PRC's foreign economic policy.

A Socialist Partnership with the USSR

China was remarkably dependent on the Soviet Union from 1950 to 1959, in contravention of past tendencies to maintain closer ties with Asia than the West and to avoid a close relationship with any major power. Not surprisingly, Beijing was never comfortable with its heavy reliance on the Soviets; dependence was a means of achieving independence. Zhang Huadong, PRC Minister of Trade, said in 1955, 'The purpose of importing more industrial equipment from the Soviet Union is to lay the foundation of China's industrial independence, so that in the future China can make all of the producer goods it needs and will not have to rely on imports from the outside' (quoted in Ross, 1994, p. 438). Beijing would have desired and perhaps even preferred economic relations with the richer, more technologically advanced US camp as well, but this option was unavailable. In early 1949, the US government began banning exports of products considered 'strategic' to CCP-controlled areas of China. When the communists proclaimed their new government in October 1949, Washington put China under the same export restrictions as the Soviet satellite states in eastern Europe. This embargo was broadened twice again before the Korean War, whereupon Chinese assets in the United States were frozen and virtually all US trade with China was outlawed until 1972.

Foreign businesses in China were closely identified with imperialist intrusion, and therefore had to be evicted. Instead of simply nationalizing Western firms, which would have required Beijing to pay fair compensation under international law, the Chinese sought to harass foreign businesses – through strikes, high corporate taxes, the kidnapping of foreign businessmen, etc. – into choosing to withdraw their operations from PRC territory. These tactics were effective; within a year of the communist takeover, most of the substantial foreign business community had left. Kicking foreign businesses off Chinese soil did not necessarily mean Beijing was not interested in continued trade with foreign countries, but few in the West comprehended this nuance.

The Soviets, on the other hand, were willing to provide loans and technical and engineering assistance. If economic links with the capitalist nations were not forthcoming, Beijing hoped the socialist countries themselves could band together and form a self-sufficient and eventually superior international economic system. Chinese trade in the 1950s was redirected from North America and Japan, which were China's main trading partners prior to the founding of the PRC, to the USSR and Eastern Europe. PRC foreign trade was controlled by a small number of state-owned corporations, in mimicry of the Soviet model.

China's immediate objective, which was to embark upon a crash programme of heavy industrial development, would be impossible to achieve without relying heavily on the Soviets and Eastern Europeans, as the Chinese lacked the machinery needed to engage in heavy industry. (The requirements of its economic development strategy were a major impetus for Beijing's alliance with Moscow in 1950 [Garver, 1993, p. 183].) Over a quarter of China's gross national product was being invested in heavy industrial development by the late 1950s. For their part, the Soviets helped the Chinese build and equip over 200 factories, sent 10,000 technicians to China, and gave the Chinese some 10,000 sets of blueprints (very useful in the process of reverse-engineering) for various types of equipment. The scale of Soviet aid made this the communist counterpart to American assistance to Western Europe under the Marshall Plan (Garver, 1993, pp. 183–4).

China's dependence on the Soviets had its downside, of course. The Soviets required repayment with interest for most of their aid, and China paid them between $200 and $360 million per year, finally clearing its debt to Moscow in 1965 (Cheng, 1964, pp. 213–14). Beijing constantly complained that the USSR's assistance to China was inadequate. The Soviets gave more aid, for example, to East Germany, Poland, and even India than to China. Worst of all was the vulnerability to a cutoff of assistance, which occurred in 1960. After the Great Leap Forward, the Soviets had begun to fear that China was squandering their aid, and Moscow was also unhappy with Beijing's unwillingness to enter into closer military cooperation, which the Soviets had proposed in 1958. For Mao and other high CCP officials, this experience reaffirmed the lesson that foreign countries will inevitably attempt to use their economic influence to politically coerce China.

Even before the Sino-Soviet rift, as the new regime in Beijing became more confident, it sought to alleviate its dependence on the Soviets by expanding its trade with other countries in Asia, Africa, and even the West (minus the United States) after the embargo against China was loosened. Beijing also began a foreign aid programme that included even some countries in Eastern Europe, an early indication of China's aspirations as a rival to the Soviet Union for leadership of the socialist movement (Ross, 1994, pp. 439–40).

The Soviet model command-style economy the Chinese largely copied in the 1950s was highly effective in the mobilization of resources, and combined with Soviet assistance, it helped China develop a solid industrial base relatively rapidly. The weakness of this system, however, was that it bred inefficiency in the operation and management of this infrastructure. By the 1970s China's rate of return per unit of capital invested was low even for a Third World country, and still falling. This system was also poorly suited to international trade, which requires familiarity with market forces. The Soviet-style economy would become a major hindrance to economic growth when China adopted a strategy of export promotion in 1978 (Garver, 1993, pp. 186, 195).

Withdrawal from the International Economy

Mao noted in 1961 that Khrushchev's strategy of 'peaceful coexistence' with the West was tantamount to 'changing two de facto world markets into two economic systems inside a unified world market' – in other words, the Soviets had abandoned the effort to create an alternative socialist world economic system and had effectually joined the capitalist world economy. Without the USSR, the socialist alternative was not viable (Cumings, 1996, p. 31). That same year, 'Self-reliance' (*zili gengsheng*) became an important Party principle. Mao's developmental strategy during this period was to build up Chinese economic power by harnessing internal resources, particularly the effort and dedication of the Chinese people – revolutionary enthusiasm was supposed to compensate for the absence of foreign technology and capital. Mao also decentralized economic control to encourage regional self-reliance. Consequently, China had minimal economic relations with the outside world for over a decade. Foreign trade played only a small part in Mao's strategy, while foreign investment in and foreign aid to China had no place at all. Although Chinese officials never said they favoured a complete absence of foreign trade, China came close to this, especially during the Cultural Revolution. China's legal foreign trade during the 1960s consisted almost solely of the deals negotiated at the semi-annual 'trade fairs' in the old treaty port of Guangzhou (Canton). While limited, China's foreign economic relations were pragmatic, and often diverged from Beijing's rhetoric. Shifting the emphasis from heavy industry to agriculture and consumer goods, Mao's economic planners exported agricultural products and light industrial goods, then used the earnings to import Western technology and machinery. Japan became China's top trading partner by 1965 despite several outstanding political disputes between Beijing and Tokyo, and trade flourished with Hong Kong, a bastion of the capitalism and colonialism the CCP excoriated (Ross, 1994, pp. 440–1).

Was autarky a choice or a necessity for Beijing? The Soviets had withdrawn their assistance and the United States still maintained an economic embargo against China. But Beijing was not left completely bereft of opportunities. West Germany, Britain, France and Japan had broken ranks with Washington and relaxed their trade embargo in the mid-1950s. A decade later, Chinese imports from Japan and Western Europe were growing, and the Soviets too were trying to renew trade relations with China. China's diplomatic progress, evident in its return to the United Nations, the restoration of trade with America, and the normalization of relations with Japan, West Germany and Canada, encouraged many Party leaders to adopt a more internationalist outlook, including a more positive view of foreign trade as a means of facilitating national development (Ross, 1996, p. 444). The Cultural Revolution, however, saw this outlook abruptly discountenanced and Beijing turn away the opportunities of international trade in favour of self-sufficiency; accordingly, imports fell again (Garver, 1993, p. 187). Perhaps this is what Deng, who was purged during the Cultural Revolution, meant when he said in 1980, 'In past years international conditions worked against us. Later, when the international climate was favourable, we did not take advantage of it' (Deng, 1980, p. L3).

Throughout this period the CCP was riven by a debate not unlike that which took place among Chinese elites during the Qing Dynasty: should apparently superior Western techniques be imported at the risk of corrupting China? The more pragmatic Party officials argued that China should adopt the most effective forms of production and organization, regardless of their political connotations. Maoist radicals, on the other hand, argued that political purity was more important than technical expertise and efficiency. Even if Western practices seemed to be more productive, they came at the cost of exploiting workers and other kinds of social injustice. Even if such practices raised productivity in the short term, they would weaken rather than strengthen China in the long term.

Perhaps no incident better illustrated Beijing's attitude during this period than its reaction to the massive earthquake of 28 July 1976 that destroyed the city of Tangshan in Hebei Province. With an official death toll of 242,000 (the actual figure was probably much higher), this was one of the worst natural disasters in Chinese history. Yet China refused offers of aid from the United Nations and individual foreign governments, relying instead on the PLA and medical teams from other provinces for disaster relief.

Chinese foreign aid had begun soon after the establishment of the communist regime with arms shipments to the Vietminh, then fighting the French colonial administration, and to North Korea during its attempt to conquer South Korea. During the 1960s and 1970s, Beijing expanded its military assistance to include various anti-American non-communist groups, and also supported civilian projects. Revolutionary rhetoric aside, the placement of this aid seemed to be guided primarily by Chinese *realpolitik*. It bought political influence and UN votes favouring China in the Third World, opened markets for Chinese exports, and promoted China as a worthy rival to the USSR as leader of the socialist movement (Ross, 1994, pp. 441–2). Beijing's aid combined with the Hoxha government's relative independence from the Soviet Union formed the basis of a close Chinese relationship with Albania. The Chinese spent perhaps US$2.6 billion on the Tanzam railway, built in 1970–5, which was designed to give Zambia access to the sea via Tanzania instead of relying on pre-established routes through the powerful and despised state of South Africa (Garver, 1993, p. 245n). Chinese foreign economic assistance remained substantial until the Cultural Revolution, when it nearly disappeared. Thereafter, however, it reached its highest levels in the mid-1970s. North Vietnam, North Korea and Albania got the largest shares, but Beijing also gave an average of US$100 million per year to non-communist countries (with Pakistan leading the list) between 1956 and 1977. China's overseas aid dropped off precipitously after 1978, as the leadership decided to channel more resources into China's own economic development (Garver, 1993, pp. 221–2).

The autarky period was clearly damaging to China's economic growth. Much investment in the interior was wasted; attempts to make the regions self-sufficient in grain production led to huge inefficiencies; and China fell further behind the developed countries technologically. While the need to counter the strategic threat posed by the Soviet Union is the most important explanation for the 1972 rapprochement with the United States, the realization of autarky's deficiencies also helped create support among China's political elite for cooperation with the American camp (Naughton, 1994, pp. 49–50).

In 1976–8, with domestic politics unhinged by the death of Mao, China reactivated the conservative, Soviet-influenced economic planner Chen Yun and temporarily reverted back to the economic development strategy of the 1950s: giving priority to the building of heavy industry, especially steel, and practising import substitution through the export of Chinese raw materials to raise foreign exchange to buy advanced foreign machinery and equipment. This last gasp of the central planners was ineffective, largely because Chinese oil sales failed to generate sufficient revenue to import the goods China desperately needed (Cumings, 1989, pp. 207–9).

The 'Open Door': Joining the International Capitalist Economy

In the mid-1970s, Deng, Zhou Enlai and others started questioning China's policy of isolation, saying the effect was to perpetuate Chinese weakness by cutting off access to advanced science and technology, the same mistake the last emperors of the pre-modern era had made. These pragmatic officials were also heavily influenced by the experience of the East Asian Newly-Industrializing Countries (NICs), which had used foreign trade and investment to achieve rapid economic growth. If international trade was a desirable means for building China's national power, many CCP leaders also began to see it as a possible way to head off growing domestic discontent with the Party. China's efforts to accumulate capital for industrialization condemned most of the population to an austere lifestyle: meagre diets, inadequate housing, overtaxed transportation systems, and few consumer goods. By the 1970s the Chinese public began to grow weary of these hardships. The Party's legitimacy was further damaged by the ideological excesses of the Cultural Revolution. A rapid improvement in living standards was needed to preclude serious challenges to the CCP's exclusive right to govern China.

The radical Maoist faction of the CCP, led after Mao's death in 1976 by his widow Jiang Qing, opposed anything more than minimal trade links with the capitalist nations. The radicals accepted strategic cooperation with the United States as necessary to check the Soviet threat, but they warned that letting in foreign economic influence would destroy the socialist revolutionary spirit and leave China vulnerable to manipulation by hostile governments. The arrest of Jiang Qing and her three top allies, known collectively as the 'Gang of Four', in October 1976 cleared the way for a consensus among the Party leadership for what became known as China's 'open door' policy, a consensus formalized during the historic Third Plenum of the Eleventh Central Committee in December 1978. During this meeting the view prevailed that 'large-scale turbulent class struggles of a mass character have come to an end' – i.e., the Maoist revolution was over. The authority of Mao's annointed successor Hua Guofeng went into decline, Mao's own role in PRC history began to be downgraded, and pragmatists Hu Yaobang and Zhao Ziyang soon ascended to the top rung of leadership along with Deng. 'We must abandon once and for all the idea of self-sufficiency', said Zhao, the PRC's new premier. 'All ideas and actions based on keeping our door closed to the outside world and sticking to conventions are wrong. . . . [W]e should boldly enter the world market' (quoted in Cumings, 1996, p. 32).

Internally, China's new economic strategy involved reduced emphasis on heavy industry; less investment and more consumption; concentrating economic development in the coastal provinces rather than the interior; partial demobilization and reduced funding for the PLA; and most importantly, a shift in economic policy away from central planning toward giving market forces a greater role in determining prices, wages and production. Externally, China would expand its foreign trade, beginning with a programme to produce light industrial goods for export, and welcome foreign investment.

The 'open door' foreign economic policy reflected a fundamental change in China's developmental strategy. There are two basic approaches: 'extensive' development and 'intensive' development. With extensive development, production is increased by adding more inputs – more of the available capital and workforce are diverted into building the desired product, more factories are built, workers work longer hours, etc. – and this accumulation comes at the expense of other sectors (e.g. consumer goods). Intensive development, on the other hand, aims to boost productivity through increased efficiency – working 'smarter' instead of working harder. The number of factories, machines, and workers might remain the same, but they produce more through improvements in organization, management, motivation, or technology. The PRC employed the strategy of extensive development, also called capital accumulation, from its inception until 1979, first through Soviet assistance and then through an austere programme of low consumption during the self-reliant period (Garver, 1993, pp. 195–7). After 1979, Beijing moved closer to a strategy of intensive development, which required supplies of advanced foreign technology and management expertise.

China's economic and political relations proved mutually reinforcing. The desire to get greater access to US economic assistance and technology provided impetus for Beijing to work for improved relations with Washington. These efforts paid off; the United States granted Most Favoured Nation trading status to China in July 1979 and gradually loosened COCOM (Coordinating Committee for Multilateral Export Controls) restrictions, shifting the PRC to the category of 'friendly, non-allied' country in May 1983. Conversely, Beijing used trade as a means of improving political relations with countries such as South Korea and Taiwan – a practice Chinese officials termed 'economic diplomacy' (Harding, 1987, p. 242).

China opened – or perhaps 're-opened' is the better word – to the Soviet Union as well as the West. Economic cooperation with the Soviets had several advantages for China: it offered some of the land-locked interior provinces, which were clamouring for their own share of the international marketplace, an alternative source of foreign trade and investment; Soviet products were generally cheaper than their Western counterparts, and the Soviets usually accepted barter trade, sparing China's precious stocks of foreign currency; and Soviet assistance was needed to renovate or upgrade China's industrial plant, so much of which the Soviets themselves had furnished in the 1950s (Garver, 1993, p. 208).

Although there has been no serious challenge since the inauguration of the 'open door' policy to the assumption that China's development requires participation in the world economy, there has been contention since the 1980s within the Party over the speed and scope of reforms. The more conservative elites accept that some foreign investment and limited market reforms are necessary to speed up economic development and the improvement of Chinese living standards, but they intend to keep market forces and foreign activities under the state's control. Other Party officials, whose views are in some respects consistent with the assumptions of Liberal economic theory, welcome market forces and foreign competition, believing these will push the Chinese economy to be more productive and increase China's access to Western expertise and technology. New moves toward economic liberalization have typically been followed by new regulations designed by conservative officials to reign in market forces (Ross, 1994, pp. 446–8).

Thus, in terms of the three major theories of international trade laid out at the beginning of this chapter, China's basically Neo-Mercantilist orientation toward the international economy has persisted into the open door period. The leadership has generally viewed interdependence as a 'one-way street': foreign countries are invited to import Chinese goods and to supply China with funding and advanced technology, but China expects to retain the full measure of its sovereignty, maintaining strong controls over the Chinese economy and filtering out those foreign influences, ideas and products that do not fit into the authorities' plan for Chinese development. Nevertheless, the open door period has seen a robust element of liberalism enter into the thinking of the Chinese elite. Many have begun to see interdependence as mutually beneficial and non-threatening. Chinese analysts studied and debated the merits of 19th century economic thinker David Ricardo's liberal views on trade during the 1980s. Some observers argue the result was a perceptible shift in Chinese elite attitudes toward acceptance of global economic interdependence (Harris, 1996, p. 10).

Some Chinese analysts effuse about their country's potential to serve as 'a new engine for growth in Asia', suggesting acceptance of the liberal notion of trade as a positive-sum game (Ma, 1994, p. 78). Officially, Beijing supports free trade: 'In the interest of common development, we call for the abolition of protectionism and discrimination in international economic relations and trade', Foreign Minister Qian Qichen recently proclaimed before the United Nations (Qian, 1995b, p. 7). Liberal economists would certainly applaud the Chinese government's commitments to 'resolutely open our doors to the outside world. . . . make full use of the sources and markets both at home and abroad, further develop an open economy, and use the relative advantages enjoyed by China's economy . . . to enable our economy and the international economy to dovetail with and supplement each other', as enshrined in the PRC's Ninth Five-Year Plan adopted by the National People's Congress in March 1996. Of course, the Plan also contains qualifications to this sweeping statement: market forces must remain under 'state macro-control' and 'At no time [will] spiritual civilization be sacrificed as a price in exchange for momentary economic development' (Xinhua, 1996, pp. 29, 30, 57). Although worldwide reaction to Tiananmen produced calls among Chinese conservatives to limit Western influence, a consensus still remained that China could not return to a strategy of development through self-reliance (Robinson, 1994b, p. 190). Yet there are also vestiges of Neo-Marxism, manifested in fears about the corrupting influences of doing business with foreign capitalists and in the abiding belief that 'the Chinese economy must remain an independent and relatively complete system' (the statement was made in 1990 by CCP official Yuan Mu, quoted in Ross, 1994, p. 444).

In sum, my assessment is that Neo-Mercantilist assumptions appear to bear the strongest influence on China's orientation toward the world market today, although the Liberal view also holds considerable sway. My view is contestable; other observers would contend that I have overemphasized the influence of Neo-Mercantilism. Nicholas R. Lardy, for example, argues that 'on balance, [China's] economy is more open than that of other East Asian economies at comparable stages of economic development and in certain respects is even more open than they are now' (Lardy, 1994, p. 127). Besides Neo-Mercantilism and Liberalism, a residue of Neo-Marxist impulses persist among some conservatives. The result is an ongoing tension between openness and liberalization on the one hand, and defensiveness and continued central control on the other hand. This tension is visible in China's policies toward foreign trade and investment and in its engagement with international economic organizations and institutions during the open door era.

Foreign Trade

In the main, Beijing has pursued a trade strategy of import substitution. This means a country imports only the goods necessary to its economic development that it cannot itself produce, and once it attains a domestic production capability, it stops importing those goods. This implies engagement with the international market is limited and temporary, intended only to rectify specific deficiencies. This approach even carried over to China's exports, which have consciously been used primarily as a means of generating foreign exchange for the purchase of advanced foreign technology – an 'import-led' export strategy, as opposed to the familiar concept of 'export-led' growth made famous by the rapidly-developing Asian NICs (Harding, 1987, p. 171). Once strictly followed, the import substitution approach has become less pronounced with the economic decentralization of the 1980s, but it remains a guideline for many Chinese economic strategists. .

China's imports fall mainly into one of two categories: raw materials (food, energy, lumber, wool and synthetic fibres, fertilizer, chemicals, steel, etc.) from the developing countries, and advanced technology (machinery, software, etc.) from the developed countries. Chinese exports, in keeping with China's comparative advantage, are mostly relatively cheap labour-intensive manufactured goods, which are particularly attractive in lower-income countries. In terms of World System Theory, China generally 'buys in the core and sells in the periphery', and is thus classed as a semi-peripheral state. The pattern is reproduced within China itself, where the richer, more industrialized coastal provinces (which belong in the category of the semi-periphery) export heavily to the interior provinces (the periphery). This points up an asset that distinguishes China from the other NICs: a large and potentially lucrative domestic market (Cumings, 1996, p. 33).

Consistent with the principle that higher-tech products earn higher profits on the capitalist world market, China tends to run trade surpluses with developing countries and trade deficits with developed countries (the USA, which absorbs 20 per cent of Chinese exports and has a substantial trade deficit with China, is an exception).

China's foreign trade has of course grown exponentially since the opening to the world market. Exports comprised about 2 per cent of China's GDP in 1980; in 1996, they accounted for 10 per cent (Harris, 1996, p. 7). China's list of trade partners expanded throughout the 1980s to include most countries of the world – 180 by 1990 (Ross, 1994, p. 445) – including some with which Beijing still had political disputes.

Even with the post-Mao economic liberalization, the state intervenes heavily in China's foreign trade. Most of it is still controlled by government agencies and state-owned banks and trading firms, which work to keep foreign business from undermining the state's economic objectives. The main result of decentralization has merely been to move decision-making powers to a lower level of bureaucrats. On a larger scale, the Chinese government tries to avoid unhealthy imbalances with any particular trade partner. If a single country becomes a dominant supplier, Beijing will seek to diversify; if a country such as Japan develops a large trade surplus with China, Beijing will likely exercise political pressure toward redress.

Foreign Investment in China

The PRC kept out foreign investment until 1979, when the previously heavy restrictions were relaxed, allowing eventually for full foreign ownership of firms operating in China. Beijing hoped thereby to raise hard currency from exports produced by foreign-funded projects and to gain access to foreign technology. Initial enthusiasm among Western investors in the late 1970s cooled in the early 1980s as they realized that China remained, in many ways, a difficult place for them to do business, with its excessive regulations, arbitrariness and ambiguity in the enforcement of these regulations, inconsistency in the quality of local services and production, corruption, and the widespread, if unspoken, assumption that foreigners are wealthy and therefore should pay extra for everything. In the 1980s and early 1990s, the Chinese government reformed and clarified the laws governing foreign investment and generally sought to reduce the uncertainties that had bedevilled foreign businesses operating in China. After the dust from Tiananmen settled, robust foreign investment continued, reaching US$81 billion in 1994 alone (Klintworth, 1995, p. 496). Before reincorporation into the PRC, Hong Kong was the leading foreign investor in China, followed by Taiwan, the USA, Japan and Singapore.

Despite significant liberalization in the investment regulations, Chinese authorities ensure that the foreign investment they allow is consistent with Beijing's guidelines, and mid-level Chinese bureaucrats still hold the power to approve or disapprove most major projects (Ross, 1994, p. 450). 'We should tell foreign businessmen which projects we welcome and which we do not', says Premier Li Peng (Xinhua, 1990, p. 31). Another reminder of the limits of Chinese liberalization in this area is Beijing's persistent desire to limit the amount of annual profit foreign investors can keep (in recent years, China has set the figure at 12–15 per cent).

To attract foreign direct investment, the PRC government opened 'Special Economic Zones' (SEZs) on the Chinese coast. Modelled after the export processing zones in South Korea and Taiwan, these areas offered relatively low tax and tariff rates, plus an infrastructure and trained labour force already in place. The PRC intentionally situated SEZs in Shenzhen, Zhuhai and Xiamen close to the relatively wealthy (and ethnically Chinese) capitalist dynamos of, respectively, Hong Kong, Macao and Taiwan. Beijing hoped the SEZs would generate foreign exchange, promote Chinese exports, and give the Chinese access to foreign technology and managerial skills. Regional politics, as well, spurred the establishment of the SEZs. Guangdong Province lobbied particularly strongly for the plan, seeing it as a means of independence from Beijing and access to foreign markets. Within a few years, many other Chinese cities, including some in the interior, also sought and gained approval to offer foreign investors special incentives. After the breakup of the Soviet Union, the Chinese moved quickly to establish three SEZs in

Xinjiang Province, all connected by rail to the Central Asian republics, as well as three additional zones in the provinces of Jilin, Heilongjiang and Inner Mongolia aimed at economic cooperation with Mongolia and the Russian southeast. Movement across these borders by both Chinese and Russian/former Soviet traders, many of them small-time entrepreneurs, is now heavy. Thus far, they find that economic conditions are generally better on the Chinese side of these borders, which the Chinese press freely reports (Dittmer, 1994, pp. 106–7). Observers note that 'Beijing and Chinese cities in the Northeast are full of burly Russians with gray duffel-type bags buying up light industrial goods and flying back to Russia with the overweight baggage to sell the contents at considerable profit' (Lampton, 1995, pp. 85–6).

This experiment with foreign investment and export-led growth involved minimal risk to the CCP regime for two reasons. First, of the vast industrial infrastructure the CCP regime had built, almost none of it was located on the southern coast. This comparative neglect of the southeast was largely because these provinces were the most likely site of a Guomindang invasion, but also because many Beijing officials disliked the commercial tradition of the southeastern Chinese. Thus, very little of the real core of the Chinese economy would be exposed to the potential negative results of economic experimentation. Second, it was correctly anticipated most of the overseas investors would be ethnic Chinese, which mitigated concerns about foreigners gaining influence over the PRC's economy (Garver, 1993, pp. 200, 204; Naughton, 1994, p. 58).

GATT, the WTO, and APEC

Even after Beijing attained the 'China' seat in the United Nations in 1971, it was initially uninterested in joining the General Agreement on Tariffs and Trade (GATT), which Beijing viewed as a 'rich man's club' (Feeney, 1994, p. 242). The Chinese did not formally apply for GATT membership until 1986, well into the open door era. The process proved contentious. One problem was Taiwan. To preclude PRC opposition, Taiwan applied for membership as a 'customs territory' rather than a state. This was the same basis upon which Hong Kong had joined GATT, with Beijing's acquiescence, in 1986. Beijing did not object to Taiwan's membership in GATT, but argued that Taiwan should not be allowed to join before the PRC did; rather, the PRC should join GATT first and then sponsor Taiwan's application, just as Britain had sponsored Hong Kong's GATT membership.

Another problem was the status under which the PRC would join GATT. The Chinese wanted China to be categorized as a developing country, which under GATT rules may maintain relatively formidable barriers against foreign imports to protect infant domestic industries. If, on the other hand, China was categorized as a developed but non-market economy, other GATT members would be allowed to maintain barriers against Chinese goods.

Serious negotiations and hard bargaining, principally with American negotiators, over China's GATT membership began in 1993. Beijing wanted to join GATT before it was succeeded by the World Trade Organization (WTO) on 1 January 1995; this would allow China to enter the WTO as a founding member. The Americans, however, challenged China's application over the issues of Chinese non-tariff trade barriers, especially those restricting foreign service industries and agricultural products; the inconsistency of regulations at the various entry points of imports into China; lack of transparency of Chinese regulations and quotas; and the Chinese government's apparently slack enforcement of foreign intellectual property rights. The US position was that China must make convincing headway in curtailing such practices before being fully accepted as a responsible member of the international trade regime. In their defence, the Chinese pointed out that individual countries have typically negotiated their own deals, based on their particular circumstances, for entry into GATT; China should be allowed to do the same, especially if it is recognized (in accordance with the Chinese position) as a developing country. The Americans were also criticized for holding Chinese authorities to an unfairly high standard of enforcing GATT/WTO rules, especially when the USA itself was unable to control the influx of illegal immigrants or trafficking in narcotics within its own borders.

The Americans effectually won the debate, as the talks failed to resolve these issues before the inauguration of the WTO, and China thus missed out on the chance to join the organization as a founding member. A high Chinese official said bitterly that 'some countries, disregarding the plain facts, had erected barriers to block China's re-entry and to stop it from becoming a foundation member' (quoted in Klintworth, 1995, pp. 507–8). In retaliation, Beijing suspended a 1992 agreement to lift import barriers against a long list of US products. Washington responded by raising tariffs on selected Chinese goods to punish China's allegedly inadequate protection of American copyrights.

WTO membership offers China many potential advantages. First, entry into the organization would enhance China's prestige in the developed world as a stable, responsible power and an attractive host for foreign investment. Second, trade opportunities would increase, as China could expect to gain automatic Most Favoured Nation (MFN) trading status with its fellow WTO members, which account for some 90 per cent of China's foreign trade. This would greatly reduce the threat of protectionism against Chinese exports, a major concern now that China is an efficient producer of many cheap manufactured goods of reasonable quality. Third, if China was a WTO member, it would be more difficult for the United States to use economic sanctions to punish China for human rights abuses. (Washington has, however, left this possibility open by announcing that US domestic law, including the Jackson–Vanik Amendment that links MFN to human rights progress, takes precedence over the international agreements the USA enters into.) Fourth, the WTO, like other international regimes, provides its members services that have economic value: rules and expectations, market information, and a procedure for resolving disputes. Membership would enable China to share in these benefits.

On the negative side, WTO membership would require of the Chinese numerous and deep economic reforms, including making certain areas of its economic policy more transparent, restructuring its exchange rate for the Chinese *renminbi* (which gives Chinese exports a competitive advantage), and phasing out a host of other practices, such as erecting barriers against imported goods and services, subsidizing domestic producers, restricting the movement of foreign currency within China, and dumping (i.e., selling goods at a price below the cost of production in an effort to capture the market) Chinese products overseas. Even if Beijing is willing to abide by WTO guidelines, the decentralization of power Deng initiated makes it more difficult for the regime to guarantee the observance and enforcement of these rules throughout China (Segal, 1994a, p. 56).

The Pacific Economic Cooperation Council (PECC), the precursor to Asia-Pacific Economic Cooperation (APEC), was founded in 1980. After some vigorous haggling over Taiwan's title, both China and Taiwan joined the PECC in 1986, despite Beijing's earlier criticism of the organization as a Japanese attempt to increase Tokyo's economic and political influence. APEC was founded in 1989 with the stated objective of promoting trade liberalization in the region, which export-intensive China favours. The organization's 1994 Bogor declaration commits its developed member nations to work toward free trade by the year 2010, with developing states to follow suit by 2020. China became a member in 1991, its accession delayed by the fallout from Tiananmen, along with Taiwan and Hong Kong.

As would be the case with the WTO, China enhances its prestige by participating in APEC, demonstrating a commitment to international cooperation in support of regional stability and open trading. APEC membership is also good for the ruling regime, allowing Jiang Zemin to publicly stand alongside the US president and the Japanese prime minister. APEC has sometimes served as a useful facilitator of dialogue between Beijing and other governments. The meeting between Jiang and Clinton at the APEC summit in Seattle in November 1993 was the first such contact between the two governments since Tiananmen. APEC also brings together high-level PRC and Taiwanese delegates, as China has accepted (limited) Taiwanese participation. The Republic of China has sent its economics minister to join the heads of state from other member countries at APEC summit meetings. PRC and ROC officials have met together in both Taiwan and China under the auspices of APEC programmes. Finally, APEC affords China the opportunity to rally support from fellow Asian governments against the United States on issues that tend to find Americans on one side and Asian leaders on the other. As Gary Klintworth puts it, 'China is effectively multilateralizing the bilateral United States–China relationship within APEC' (Klintworth, 1995, p. 508).

Some observers favour using APEC as the basis for building a multilateral security framework that would encompass the major Asia-Pacific powers, including China. Thus, there are constant suggestions that APEC broaden its agenda to include talks on political matters (human rights, democratization, the Spratly Islands dispute, the status of Taiwan, etc.). Beijing, which strongly opposes APEC's discussion of issues unrelated to economic and technical cooperation, has successfully blocked an expansion of APEC's agenda; most of the APEC countries are reluctant to antagonize the Chinese, seeing Beijing's cooperation as essential to APEC's viability.

International Economic Institutions

After years of criticizing the International Monetary Fund, the International Finance Corporation, the International Development Association and the International Bank for Reconstruction and Development (more commonly known as the World Bank) as tools of capitalist exploitation, the PRC joined these organizations (known collectively as the World Bank Group [WBG]) in 1980. Samuel S. Kim succinctly describes the attitudinal change associated with the open door period: 'Beijing began to ask more and more what international organizations could do for China, and less and less what China itself could do to reform or transform the existing world order' (Kim, 1994b, p. 431). Dominated by liberal economic theory, the WBG has been anxious to fund China's economic development; dominated by a Neo-Mercantilist approach, China has been anxious to accept this funding. In economic terms, the Chinese have benefited hugely from their pragmatic reorientation toward the WBG and their willingness to make occasional 'symbolic kowtows', especially after Tiananmen. China got funding for the construction of its economic infrastructure, technical assistance, administrative advice, and, indirectly, expanded opportunities for foreign trade and investment. IMF loans and guidance helped China through several potential economic crises in the 1980s. The post-Tiananmen suspension of assistance lasted less than a year-and-a-half, demonstrating the WBG's willingness to get back to business as usual. China currently receives more World Bank funding loans than any other country, although this funding provides only a fraction of what the Chinese need to meet their developmental targets. China gets concessionary rates on its loans from the World Bank, which also provides technical support (Feeney, 1994, pp. 229, 238).

Consequences of Interdependence

China's international economic engagement has been a key factor in its remarkably rapid economic development since the foundation of the PRC. Very few states have matched China's record of sustained industrial growth – about 10 per cent annually through the 1980s, and as high as 13 per cent in the 1990s. Indeed, China is becoming a source of investment capital rather than just a destination, with PRC nationals funding projects in the developed world, such as factories in America and mines in Australia.

While developing countries with heavy trade and investment links often worry about the possible effects of international economic shocks upon their domestic economies, this has not been a serious problem for China, partly because of the size and scope of its economy. The inconvertibility of the Chinese currency provides a layer of insulation between world and Chinese domestic prices. Indeed, connections with the international economy have actually helped China ride out potential domestic economic difficulties relatively smoothly (Naughton, 1994, pp. 55–6).

China's engagement with the world economy gives China enhanced influence that in some cases may carry over into political issues. Interdependence, after all, entails *mutual* vulnerability that may potentially work in China's favour. The foreign governments and firms that have found China an attractive business partner now face paying a stiff price for displeasing Beijing. Thus, complaints from the American business community forced US President Bill Clinton to announce in May 1994 that China's progress on human rights issues would no longer be a criterion for MFN trading status with the United States. Similarly, governments that violate Beijing's unwritten rules of engagement with Taiwan (by selling to Taipei certain types of weapons systems or hosting high-level Republic of China officials, for instance) risk losing lucrative trade opportunities through PRC retaliation.

A growing number of Chinese analysts believe that 'in the post-Cold War era, the main threat is not necessarily from a particular country or military invasion', but 'from multi-level economic and scientific challenges' – that is, staying ahead of regions such as Eastern Europe, and catching up with the West, Japan, and even the Asian NICs (Chen, 1993, p. 240; Glaser,1993, p. 253). From this standpoint, a return to autarky would be disastrous. The only avenue that gives China a chance of improving its relative technological capability is diffusion of technology to China from the leaders in research and development (principally the United States and Japan), which Chinese engagement with the world economy makes possible.

Of course, openness toward the world economy has disadvantages as well, not all of which were fully understood or anticipated by the Chinese leadership. Many scholars emphasize the power of the international system to shape the domestic structure and politics of its member states. This viewpoint suggests the extent to which enmeshment in the world economy has changed China should not be overlooked (Kim, 1994c, p. 31). One aspect of this phenomenon is the impact that Chinese participation in international economic institutions such as the WBG has made on Chinese domestic policy-making. For example, pro-reform leaders such as Zhao Ziyang have used the views and advice of these institutions to strengthen their position in debates with their domestic opponents (Jacobson and Oksenberg, 1990, p. 141).

The unruly forces of the international market have also changed China, probably unalterably, and are likely to bring about further, rapid change in the near future. Chen Yun, the patriarch of China's central planners, argued that market forces can be contained like a bird in a cage; 'rarely', says Bruce Cumings, 'has an analogy so confirmed an utter misunderstanding of the world market's inexorable logic. . . . In this sense the Colonel Sanders dummy, standing in front of the Kentucky Fried Chicken outlet at Tiananmen Square, knows more than all the leaders who have stood atop the Gate of Heavenly Peace, scratching around for another way to wall in their people' (Cumings, 1996, p. 36).

Ties with the world economy can trigger suboptimal behaviour by various regions of the PRC. With central control over the national economy reduced, local economies have sometimes imported far more than they exported, creating in the aggregate a sizeable Chinese trade deficit. Regions have also competed with each other for foreign business, each attempting to offer the foreigners the lowest tax rates and overhead costs, when China as a whole would benefit more if a national cartel negotiated such deals on behalf of all the regions. An illustration of where provincial avarice can lead occurred in 1985, when officials on Hainan Island used US$570 million of their foreign currency allowance from the central government to purchase thousands of cars, motorcycles, television sets and other consumer goods from overseas, then marked up the prices and sold them inside China (Garver, 1993, pp. 206–7).

Interaction with the world economy contributes to what the CCP regime terms 'spiritual pollution': a host of social vices have emerged or increased as market-oriented reforms left Chinese society less tightly controlled and generated new wealth. As it becomes more capitalist, China is beginning to suffer many of the same forms of social pathology that plague the capitalist West. (This social phenomenon has ominous political implications for the Party, as it undermines a key argument for CCP legitimacy: that the Party's exclusive control of PRC politics has maintained public order.) CCP official Ren Jianxin offers a typical lamentation of the changing times:

> [T]he major crime rate keeps rising. . . . Bandits are still running wild, the number of theft cases is still high, and there are more and more serious fraud cases. Gang activities are rife, and some of these clearly bear the hallmark of underground societies. Public security is deteriorating in a number of rural areas, and hooliganism and feudal clan forces prevail. All sorts of local tyrants have emerged, and some even openly defy the local authorities. Unpleasant social phenomena are becoming more and more open: prostitution is still spreading, pornographic activities are appearing in new forms and in some places have practically become a semiopen line of business. (Ren, 1995, p. 108)

Li Peng and other conservatives clearly see a correlation between reform and social decay: 'We must never attract foreign investment by sacrificing our spiritual civilization. . . . We must not go down that path. In the course of speeding up the reforms and opening-up, we must thoroughly purge all [social vices]' (Li, 1994, p. 128). As Li's statement implies, the conservatives would prefer slower growth in the PRC's wealth and economic capacity to halt the decline in public order and morality.

Besides spawning crime and eroding morals, opening to the outside world has also brought a new awareness of foreign lifestyles, culture and attitudes to millions of Chinese. Some of these ideas, such as liberal political philosophy, are potentially threatening to the communist regime, which explains periodic government campaigns throughout the 1980s and 1990s against 'bourgeois liberalism' (i.e., questioning the CCP's monopoly of political power). While PRC trade with Taiwan, now at US$20 billion annually, has served Beijing's interests by severely eroding Taipei's previous policy of 'no contact, no negotiation, no compromise', the CCP regime faces the danger that pressures for democratization will accompany the economic influence emanating from newly-annexed Hong Kong into the rest of southeastern China (Cumings, 1996, p. 37).

As part of the opening of China's door to the outside world, thousands of Chinese students have gone abroad to study, with

American universities the most popular choice. Many of these students have decided not to return home. This is not always for political reasons; these students often fear they will be assigned to a job in which they will be unable to use their newly-acquired skills. Beijing has tried several measures to reduce this problem: indoctrinating students before their departure and requiring them to report regularly to the closest Chinese consulate while abroad; making it difficult for spouses and children to join students overseas; and sending older rather than younger students, on the assumption that older students would be more likely to return (Garver, 1993, p. 205). In any event, Chinese officials must weigh the costs of this 'brain drain' against the gains of sending their future elites overseas for training.

How does China's engagement with the world economy affect regional security? China's development poses what Stuart Harris terms an 'economic security dilemma' (Harris, 1995, p. 37) for the other powers: on the one hand, the world wants strong Chinese economic growth to preclude the dangers of internal instability and to deepen China's participation in the international economy, potentially making China both a more responsible international actor and a lucrative trading partner for its neighbours; on the other hand, a strong economy would provide China with the basis for immense political power, which Beijing might employ to force its own self-serving agenda upon its neighbours.

The potential pacifying effects of economic interdependence may be divided into two types. The first is voluntary: a government chooses to cooperate in the maintenance of the international order, and to avoid antagonizing its trade partners, out of a desire to keep the economic benefits flowing in. The second is coercive: governments use economic ties as a weapon to force a trade partner to change its behaviour. In China's case, interdependence has produced better results through voluntary inducement than through coercion.

Some analysts argue that economic interdependence has had a socializing effect on Beijing, as 'China has shown itself capable of learning that constructive cooperation in international economic institutions . . . is in its own interests' (Harris, 1996, p. 12). China's modernization drive also gives the Chinese a strong interest in the preservation of regional stability, which may help account for Beijing's contribution to resolving Cambodia's civil war and to keeping the 1994 Korean crisis from escalating (Klintworth, 1995, p. 488). It must be understood, however, that while economic interdependence is a factor in PRC policy calculations, it is inadequate by itself to preclude all instances of Chinese behaviour that other states find uncooperative and overly assertive. Substantial Chinese economic interdependence with the Association of South East Asian Nations (ASEAN) states and a strong Chinese interest in the continued prosperity of Hong Kong did not prevent Beijing's direct challenge to an ASEAN state in the South China Sea (the Mischief Reef incident of 1995: see Chapter 8, pp. 188–9) or a belligerent reaction to Hong Kong Governor Chris Patten's democratic reforms (Segal, 1996, pp. 108, 115–23). Maintaining the movement of goods and capital between China and the region was obviously not the overriding consideration when the PRC chose to fire missiles near the Taiwanese coast during the Republic of China (ROC) presidential election campaign in 1996.

Attempts by foreign governments to change Chinese policies by cutting off or restricting economic contacts have been even less successful. The American policies of containment and embargo during the 1950s slowed Chinese economic growth, but failed to produce the kind of Chinese behaviour Washington wanted. Indeed, Chinese became even more anti-American. Soviet punishment of the Chinese through the withdrawal of their economic aid in 1960 had a similar result. The US attempted in 1981–2 to use China's desire for US economic assistance to force Beijing to accept an upgraded US–Taiwan relationship, but this effort also failed. Post-Tiananmen economic sanctions did not push the CCP regime any closer to political liberalization (Garver, 1993, p. 241).

There are three main obstacles to successful foreign economic coercion against China. First, because of its size and well-rounded resource endowments, China's has been a relatively self-sufficient economy. A near-autarkic PRC would not be able to develop rapidly or catch up with the leading economic powers, but it could certainly survive. Some Chinese elites believe China is becoming too heavily engaged with the world economy anyway, and are disappointed with the rate at which China has acquired advanced foreign technology. In their case, the threat of foreign economic retaliation for undesirable Chinese behaviour has minimal deterrent effect (Austin, 1995, p. 16).

Second, the countries that cut their economic ties to China find they hurt themselves as well as the Chinese. The Chinese leadership realizes this; Deng quipped after Tiananmen that China is 'too big a piece of meat' for foreign businessmen to stay away for long (quoted in Sullivan, 1992, p. 21), and he proved correct. Even in the democratic states, the concern of ordinary people with moral questions has only a limited impact on the foreign policies pursued by their leaders. This was starkly illustrated by Li Peng's visit to several European countries in the spring of 1994. While he was confronted with embarrassing public protests over human rights issues, he managed to bring home business deals with European firms worth over $3 billion (Bachman, 1995, p. 45).

Third, many policy-makers in foreign capitals fear taking steps that might 'isolate' China and drive it back into the dark ages of the 1960s and 1970s. Many drew the lesson from those years that if Beijing lacks a stake in the international order, it is more likely to be an irresponsible, trouble-making power. This fear re-emerges with any contemplation of a policy of economic coercion against Beijing.

Beijing has not fared any better in its own attempts at economic coercion. For example, Kishi Nobusuke, Japanese prime minister from 1957 to 1960, incurred Beijing's displeasure by campaigning for closer relations between Japan and Taiwan (Kishi even visited ROC President Chiang Kai-shek). China pulled various economic levers to attempt to weaken Kishi and his Liberal Democratic Party (LDP) relative to the Japan Socialist Party (JSP), including cancelling contracts with Japanese firms, dropping its plan to hold a trade fair in Japan, calling upon Southeast Asian countries to boycott Japanese products, and harassing Japanese fishing boats. Beijing's efforts, however, were counterproductive. Kishi and the LDP won the 1958 elections, anti-China sentiment in Japan increased, and support for the JSP and pro-China pressure groups fell (Garver, 1993, p. 243).

The Future of Chinese Economic Policy

It remains for China to take the next decisive step toward interdependence. Outside analysts commonly distinguish between the relatively wealthy coastal provinces and the poorer interior provinces, but to understand China's links with the world and regional economies, this coastal region must itself be conceptually divided in two. Unlike the southeastern provinces of Guangdong and Fujian, the northeastern coast is part of what Barry Naughton (1994) terms the 'Communist Core' – China's industrial heartland, a region with a relatively high degree of central planning and subsidization, and perhaps the only section of China over which Beijing is able to exercise direct supervision.

While reformers such as Zhao Ziyang have favoured integrating this industrial core into a Northeast Asian economy, with strong links and a broad range of common economic groundrules between China, Japan and Korea, conservative Party officials have fought to limit foreign economic penetration, fearing this would jeopardize China's largely inefficient state-run industries and increase pressure for political liberalization. Another problem is the political sensitivity of Japanese and South Korean investment, which the northeastern provinces of Shandong, Hebei, Tianjin and Liaoning are geographically suited to attract. Japanese economic penetration revives memories of Japanese domination of northeastern China during the Pacific War. South Korean investment is a sore point with Chinese ally North Korea.

For all these reasons, the northeast has been slower than the southeast to create the market-oriented environment that appeals to foreign investors. While Guangdong and Fujian are moving rapidly towards deep interdependence with other Asia-Pacific nations, this process faces strong structural and political obstacles in the northern coastal provinces (Naughton, 1994, pp. 57–68).

Most scholars of PRC economic policy concur that while many Chinese elites are apprehensive about further economic liberalization and deepening interdependence, these trends will probably continue (Ross, 1994, pp. 451–2; Harris, 1996, p. 12; Naughton, 1994, p. 67), both because of the difficulty of controlling market forces once they gain momentum and because continued openness toward the world economy is necessary for the Chinese to achieve their developmental goals. If and when China does take steps to further reduce the structural barriers to deeper economic integration with the outside world, a likely outcome is a Northeast Asian regional economy in which more Japanese, South Korean and Taiwanese manufacturers relocate their operations to China. Northern China would specialize in the production of raw materials, energy and heavy machinery, with southern China concentrating on producing light consumer goods (Naughton, 1994, pp. 67–8).

A final question relevant here is how important a factor domestic economic development is in PRC foreign policy-making. Many scholars believe the economic imperative is now the driving force of PRC foreign policy. Barry Naughton, for example, argues that by the 1980s Chinese elites believed their external environment had become much less threatening than during the regime's early years. This allowed economic development to surpass military security as China's primary concern (Naughton, 1994, pp. 48–50). Others, such as John Garver, argue that while domestic economic development is one of Beijing's chief goals, it must be balanced against other objectives. Naughton is probably correct to conclude that after 1979 economic development rose in importance relative to deterring an invasion of China. But as Garver points out, 'PRC diplomacy is replete with instances in which Beijing sacrificed economic objectives to other interests', even in the open door era (Garver, 1993, pp. 240–1). Examples include the regime's harsh crackdown against peaceful demonstrators in and around Tiananmen in full view of the Western press in 1989; and Beijing's decision to recover Hong Kong rather than extend Britain's lease even though the territory's vast economic value (even for the PRC) has been largely premised on British administration.

Ultimately, however, the two objectives of internal economic development and external security are interrelated. With the passage of the Mao era, the role of ideological purity and fervour in nation-building has been downgraded. More recently, the collapse of the Soviet Union graphically illustrated to Chinese observers that 'national security depends more upon . . . a solid economy rather than simply upon military might' (Yan, 1993, p. 6). Consequently, Chinese elites are more inclined than ever to view economic development as a means of strengthening national security. This applies at least as much to the matter of *regime* security in an age when the CCP's legitimacy is based on little more than its ability to raise the Chinese people's living standards.

6
Defending the PRC

The sheer size of China, which shares borders with twelve different countries, imparts both strategic advantages and disadvantages. Physical conquest and occupation of China is practically impossible given the vastness of its territory and population, most of which lives in the countryside. China is relatively well-endowed with useful minerals and is as self-sufficient in this area as the former super-powers. Unlike its neighbour Japan, China is also self-sufficient in food production, but just barely, and the population continues to grow more quickly than agricultural output. On the downside, China's vast territory and uneven levels of infrastructure development make it difficult to move large numbers of troops quickly to every potential trouble spot. This may increase the chances of attempted territorial encroachment by neighbouring states (e.g., the Sino-Indian war of 1962). Furthermore, since China is an empire, the danger of internal insurrection competes with external threats for the attention of Chinese security forces. Most of China's industrial infrastructure is centralized in a handful of key areas, including Beijing, Shanghai and Tangshan, while energy production is concentrated in Manchuria, Zhejiang and Loyang. A nuclear strike therefore has the potential to wipe out most of the country's growing economic wealth. All told, nevertheless, a complete military 'defeat' of China by either conventional or unconventional means would seem out of the question as long as the country remained politically coherent. In any case, the chances of this proposition being tested are minimal in the relatively benign political environment of the post-Cold War era.

This is the strategic landscape within which China's armed forces, collectively known as the People's Liberation Army (PLA), operates. As its name implies, the PLA was formed on the premise that it would enforce the socialist revolution (in 1946, when the PLA was founded, China was still mostly under Guomindang control and thus not yet 'liberated' by communism) and serve and protect the

Chinese masses thereafter. Indeed, among most rural Chinese, Mao's Red Army, the forerunner of the PLA, had distinguished itself favourably during the Chinese Civil War from the comparatively rapacious and undisciplined troops of the Guomindang. In line with its desired image as an army that serves the people, the PLA has been active in disaster relief and civilian construction throughout the PRC's history. (About a third of China's railways, for example, were built by PLA personnel.) The PRC constitution affirms that the armed forces 'belong to the people', and specifies that the military is duty-bound to 'participate in national reconstruction, and work hard to serve the people'. In practice, as the Tiananmen Massacre so vividly illustrated, the PLA is also charged with protecting the Party *from* the masses. In the more tactful phrasing of Chinese officialdom, part of the PLA's mission is 'to protect the existing Chinese socialist system' (Central Military Commission Vice-Chairman Zhang Zhen, quoted in Wang, 1994, p. 41). The PLA officer corps is demonstrably unenthusiastic about suppressing domestic dissent, which explains why the government created the People's Armed Police, a strictly internal security force whose numbers have swelled from 500,000 to 1.2 million since Tiananmen.

Earlier we examined the *advisory* role the PLA plays in China's foreign relations. The PLA also fulfils an *executive* function of using force or threatening to use force against foreigners in defence of PRC interests. Belying China's self-image as a peaceful country that eschews the use of force except as a last resort, the PRC has fought more wars and suffered more casualties in battle since 1949 than any other major country over the same period (Segal, 1985, p. 1). Despite the PLA's initial orientation toward fighting an all-out defensive war against an invasion of the Chinese homeland, all the PRC's wars have been limited wars, and all have been fought on either foreign or disputed territory. The PRC sent troops into combat beyond the PRC's recognized borders in each of its first three decades, including the Korean War intervention, the border war with India, the seizure of the Paracel Islands from South Vietnam, and a second campaign against Vietnam overland. Indeed, David Shambaugh argues that even during the Mao era, despite the official emphasis on the principle of 'luring the enemy in deep', the PLA's de facto doctrine was a 'frontier defence policy' of meeting enemy forces at the border with resolve and heavy firepower (Shambaugh, 1994b, p. 53).

Beijing clearly considers both the use of military force and the threat of using military force as instruments of foreign policy. PLA firepower has served a variety of purposes: to regain 'lost' Chinese territory (the campaign to conquer Tibet in 1950–1; the Paracel Islands grab); to destroy foreign-based anti-PRC guerrillas (crossing into Burma to attack residual Guomindang soldiers); to test the resolve of its superpower adversary (The Taiwan Straits crises); to demonstrate its own resolve (the 1969 border clashes with the USSR); to rescue an ally and buffer state from conquest (the Korean War intervention); to punish a neighbouring state pursuing anti-China policies (the incursion into Vietnam in 1979); and to extend deterrence to an ally under threat of invasion (the stationing of Chinese air-defence troops in North Vietnam during its war with the USA). China has also employed the PLA in strategic movements without hostilities, such as the occupation of some islands in the Spratly group in the 1980s and a mobilization of Chinese troops along the Sino-Indian border to force India to divert some of its forces away from the war with Chinese ally Pakistan in 1965.

The PLA–Party Relationship

Western scholars often base their analysis of the PLA upon the observation that it is essentially a 'political' army, designed to defend the interests of the Chinese Communist Party rather than the interests of China. The PLA certainly has unique characteristics, but these should not be overstated. Comparatively heavy involvement of the armed forces in domestic politics is not unusual in developing or socialist countries (Shambaugh, 1996a, p. 268). The CCP has maintained a Chinese tradition of civilian control over the armed forces, an idea China shares with the West (Dreyer, 1996b, p. 2; more on this below). Furthermore, like their Western counterparts, many PLA officers have developed a strong sense of professionalism. Finally, as we have already seen, the PLA and some of its components have their own sets of organizational self-interests, which they pursue in the much the same way as is visible in bureaucratic power struggles everywhere.

Unlike the Japanese *samurai* and feudal European knights, military men in China traditionally had comparatively low social status. War was not glorified. Rather, it was considered a breakdown of the proper order, a failure of government. When needed, armies were to be composed mainly of the uneducated and unskilled (why send useful men out to be wasted on the battlefield?), then quickly demobilized after the campaign was finished. Mao, who often spoke of warfare in romantic and heroic terms, is something of an exception to the general current of Chinese tradition. There was little interest among the Chinese elite in military professionalism. What did develop was a strong tradition of civilian control over the military. In this respect Mao showed continuity with his pre-modern counterparts, insisting that 'Our principle is that the Party commands the gun; the gun shall never be allowed to command the Party' (quoted in Segal, 1985, p. 46). Deng concurred, saying that 'At all times, the armed forces must unconditionally be subordinated to the leadership of the Party' (British Broadcasting Corporation, 1994, p. G/13).

Realizing this goal has required constant attention and manoeuvring by the Party from the PLA's inception until today. Wang Shushin argues that Western scholars exaggerate the Party's control over the PLA. Mao controlled the PLA only through his immense personal prestige and skilful playing of different factions within the army against each other. Similarly, Deng has been forced to provide the PLA with rewards and incentives to gain its backing on particular issues. The Party's control over the PLA should therefore be understood as 'relative and not absolute', says Wang (Wang, 1994, p. 37).

The paramount civilian leader is also typically the head of the armed forces (such has been the case with Mao, Deng, and Jiang Zemin). This integration at the top is complemented by compartmentalization at the bottom: lower-level military organizations and units tend to be functionally self-contained and linked to the vertical chain of command that leads back to Beijing rather than to their counterparts in other regions of China, which works against them getting involved in politics (Joffe, 1996, p. 302). The PLA command system is highly centralized, with orders originating in the Central Military Commission (CMC) and passing through the General Staff Department (GSD) down through the military region headquarters and finally to individual units. The movement of troops from one military region to another is forbidden without CMC permission. The Party also maintains indoctrination and supervision of the troops through a structure of Party committees, departments and commissars that extends through the ranks of the PLA.

As Ellis Joffe notes, the PLA is 'a Party-army with professional characteristics'. Although established and run by the CCP, the PLA 'has acquired basic features of professionalism which have brought it into an enduring, albeit fluctuating, conflict with the Party'. Nonetheless, it is this same professionalism that has steered PLA officers away from intervening in domestic political struggles (Joffe, 1996, p. 300).

As a result of its own apoliticism stemming from military professionalism, combined with Party efforts to 'control the gun', the PLA has not demonstrated much interest in politics. The army has generally entered domestic politics with guns drawn only when it was ordered, dragged or sucked in. The PLA is, in Shulong Chu's characterization, a 'passive political force' (Chu, 1994, p. 185). When the civilian leadership is divided, such as during parts of the Cultural Revolution, immediately after the death of Mao or during the 1989 Tiananmen crisis, the PLA may settle the contest by backing one side or another. Significantly, in the latter two cases, the PLA supported the strongest faction, and the one that offered the best prospect of maintaining political stability (Segal, 1994a, p. 24). In the case of Tiananmen, PLA participation was less than enthusiastic; according to one estimate, over 2,000 PLA soldiers accused of refusing to obey orders or sympathizing with the demonstrators were punished, and perhaps one or two hundred were executed *(Central Daily News* [Taipei; Overseas Edition], 24 November 1992 and 6 November 1989; cited in Wang, 1994, pp. 11–12).

It seems fair to say that the PLA has never forcibly intervened in China's domestic politics merely to promote its own organizational interests (Joffe, 1996, p. 308). Antipathy within the PLA towards involvement in domestic politics may well be on the increase, as younger officers, tomorrow's PLA high command, tend to have a stronger commitment to professionalism, including the ideal of an apolitical military (Chu, 1994, p. 185).

After Deng worked throughout the 1980s to reduce PLA influence in the civilian government, he and Jiang have brought the military back in as a means of maintaining the Party's monopoly of political power and consolidating support for economic reforms and for Jiang's ascension to the position of paramount leader. At Tiananmen, of course, Deng resorted to PLA firepower to suppress a challenge to CCP authority. Afterwards he reportedly warned that

'If any democracy movement comes back again, the army will do the same job as it did in Tiananmen Square in June 1989' (*Renmin Ribao* report, 6 May 1992; Wang, 1994, p. 42). As part of his campaign to reverse the post-Tiananmen effort by CCP conservatives to roll back his economic reforms, Deng reportedly secured the support of PLA elder statesmen Yang Shangkun, his half-brother Yang Baibing and Liu Huaqing, then warned his domestic opponents in 1992, 'If the Politburo of the Party is unable to engage in economic and personnel reforms, I will ask all commanders of the seven great military regions to force it to do so'. This threat helped Deng successfully reassert his agenda at the 14th Party Congress later that year. At the same Congress, reassignments significantly increased the proportion of PLA officers in key government bodies. Of 189 members of the Central Committee, for example, 44 were servicemen (Wang, 1994, pp. 5, 55).

Paradoxically, Deng's other major domestic political objective, instituting Jiang as his successor, contributed to the purge of the Yangs only a few months after they had backed Deng in his struggle with the anti-reform faction. The ambitious Yangs were suspected of packing the PLA leadership with their protégés, prompting complaints that the PLA was becoming 'the Yang family army' (*Christian Science Monitor*, 14 May 1990; in Wang, p. 25). Deng feared that a Yang-dominated PLA could challenge Jiang's position as the new paramount leader. Both Yang brothers exited the CMC, and subsequently many of their appointees elsewhere in the PLA were also purged. Zhang Zhen and Liu Hauqing rose to fill the Commission's second and third most senior positions (Jiang Zemin is CMC chairman). The aged Zhang and Liu were thought not to have higher political aspirations, and thus would be more likely to accept Jiang's leadership (Dreyer, 1996a, pp. 23–4).

While Long March veterans Mao and Deng commanded great respect and prestige from the PLA, most outside analysts believe Jiang does not. Indeed, Jiang appears to be devoting considerable energy to winning the PLA's support for his paramount leadership. In 1994 and 1995, for example, Jiang promoted 27 lieutenant generals to the rank of full general in sumptuous, conspicuous ceremonies held in the Great Hall of the People (Shambaugh, 1996a, p. 271).

While Deng and Jiang have invited increased representation from the PLA as a means of promoting their agenda, the Party has simultaneously attempted to bolster its control over the military through increased indoctrination and disciplinary activities within the PLA and a re-emphasis of the slogan 'absolute loyalty to the Party'. The Party leadership's concern is evidently based on disturbing recent events such as the failure of the armed forces of the Eastern European countries to defend their beleaguered communist regimes as well as the reluctance of many PLA units to suppress the Tiananmen demonstrators in 1989 (Shambaugh, 1996a, pp. 274–5). That efforts to subordinate the PLA to Party authority should accompanying a larger role by PLA officers in China's political process is consistent with the government's determination to maintain civilian control over the military.

PRC Military Capabilities in the Late 1990s

The PLA is a numerically large force (some 2.93 million active duty troops, plus 1.2 million reserves) that has developed 'pockets of excellence' in certain areas, including the production of ballistic missiles, anti-ship weapons, and some aspects of submarine operations. Overall, however, the PLA operates with equipment that is mostly obsolete. The Chinese themselves often describe their military as having 'short arms and slow legs'. The PLA's relative weaknesses include long-range surveillance and reconnaissance, precision guided munitions, C3I (the collective term for the related capabilities of command, control, communications, and intelligence), and electronic warfare (Shambaugh, 1996a, p. 266; Bitzinger and Gill, 1996, p. 26). The *sine qua non* of a major military power is its ability to project force beyond its borders. Most analysts believe the PLA to be 10 to 20 years away from such a capability. While the leadership is committed to modernizing the force, structural barriers and limited finances allow only for gradual upgrading of the PLA's hardware and doctrine. In the meantime, the militaries of the other major powers and even the smaller Asia-Pacific states continue to make qualitative advances.

The strength and efficiency of the PLA ground forces have greatly improved in recent years as a result of downsizing and the incorporation of new doctrines such as combined arms operations. The ground forces are also acquiring more modern weapons systems, including improved Russian tanks, advanced ground-based radar systems and attack helicopters, as funds are available. The PLA recognizes, however, that both its new defence strategy and its capability to project military power beyond China's borders depend largely upon enhancing the PRC's air and naval forces.

Typical of China's armed forces as a whole, the PLA Air Force (PLAAF) is large but under-equipped. The inventory includes nearly 5,000 combat aircraft, including 48 advanced Su-27 fighter-bombers recently purchased from Russia. Most of the PLAAF, however, is composed of Chinese versions of Russian warplanes designed in the 1950s and 1960s. Chinese pilots lack proficiency in night, all-weather and over-water flying (Godwin, 1996, p. 479) – some of the very capabilities necessary for power projection, which requires a constant air force presence to protect advancing ships and troops. The PRC plans to produce an advanced, indigenously designed fighter, designated the J-10, which is supposed to have capabilities comparable to early variants of the US F-16 (generally recognized as the world's best fighter aircraft). But China's past efforts to create its own fighters have had only limited success (Godwin, 1996, p. 480), and even if no major new problems arise, the J-10 will probably not be ready for deployment before 2003, by which time it may already be a full generation behind the international state-of-the-art in aircraft technology. A highly respected 1995 RAND study on the PLAAF pointed to deficient pilot training, weaknesses in logistics and maintenance, a lack of the necessary infrastructure for producing hi-tech air combat systems, and inadequate funds to carry out the comprehensive modernization programme the PLAAF needs. The study concludes, 'The PLAAF does not constitute a credible offensive threat against the United States or its Asian allies today, and this situation will not change dramatically over the coming decade. If anything, the PLAAF's overall capabilities relative to most of its potential rivals will diminish over the next ten years' (Allen, Krumel and Pollack, 1995, p. xiii). Among its many weaknesses, however, the PLAAF enjoys at least one bureaucratic advantage: both the ground forces and the navy realize they need a powerful air force to fulfil their own organizational aspirations, and thus support devoting significant funds to PLAAF modernization (Swaine, 1996, p. 381).

The PLA Navy (PLAN) operates some 55 surface combatants, but less than 10 of these are fitted with up-to-date weapons systems (Shambaugh, 1996b, p. 27). Once capable of little more than coastal defence, the PLAN is now considered a 'green-water navy' that can periodically operate moderate distances off the Chinese coast, but is perhaps a decade or more away from becoming a 'blue-water navy' that can operate at great distances for long periods of time. Its main limitations in this respect have been insufficient capabilities for re-supplying and protecting ships at sea. The replenishment problem will be improved by the recent commission of two supply ships equipped with helicopters. But PLAN vessels generally carry inade-quate defences against aircraft, submarines, and surface-to-surface missiles, and land-based Chinese aircraft cannot provide air cover far from the Chinese coast. Yet building a blue-water navy is clearly the PLAN's objective. In a downsizing effort similar to that taking place among the ground forces, the PLA Navy has in the last decade decomissioned half its vessels and modernized much of the other half (Godwin, 1996, pp. 477–8). More modern frigates and destroy-ers are being constructed. Liu Huaqing has said, 'I'll die with everlasting regret if China does not build an aircraft carrier', and the PRC leadership reportedly plans to acquire two carriers by 2005 (Chanda, 1996, p. 20). A carrier is the key to projecting naval force; it allows the fleet to carry its own air cover wherever it goes, plus providing the offensive capability of placing a naval air base off the shores of any potential adversary or hot-spot.

Commissioning a carrier, however, presents immense challenges to the PLA. First, there is the financial expense of either building or purchasing the vessels (two or three are necessary to provide a continuous capability, as a carrier requires regular and lengthy periods of maintenance). Devoting such a large share of limited funds to this single project is a difficult proposition when the entire PLA is in great need of modernization. Second, operating a carrier is immensely complicated, requiring skills and experience no one in the PLA has – from landing aircraft on a deck rocking in rough seas, to managing the efficient storage and movement of aircraft between the hanger deck and flight deck, to incorporating a carrier into the existing logistics infrastructure and combat doctrine. Finally, a potential target as large, costly and militarily important as a carrier requires a big investment in its protection, including assigning several of the navy's most capable other warships to guard it. Paul H. B. Godwin argues that 'Three carriers would overwhelm the [PLA] navy's ability to defend them' (Godwin, 1996, p. 480).

A strength of the PLAN is its submarine force. Again, most of the 63 active boats are aging, but this is offset by the lack of sophisti-cated anti-submarine capabilities among most states in the region. The PLAN is purchasing from Russia several of the Kilo class boats, which are among the best diesel-powered attack submarines in the world. The Chinese launched the Han, a diesel-powered attack submarine of their own design, in 1994; this is a promising potential replacement for the numerous older Russian craft that currently make up the bulk of the force.

The Chinese defence industry reflects the traditional emphasis on self-reliance, which harks back to the *tiyong* attitude of nineteenth-century elites. *Tiyong* is a contraction of a slogan that meant 'Chinese learning for the essence, Western learning for practical usage'. The idea was that bringing foreign knowledge and technology into China must be limited to protect the Chinese way of life from corruption. The inclination toward self-help is also reinforced by the more recent influence of Marxist theory and the bad experience with over-reliance on the Soviet Union. China's massive military–industrial complex is one of the few worldwide that strives to produce all the weapons systems required by its armed forces. This desire to minimize reliance on foreign suppliers will likely continue well into the future, restricting the PRC's ability to keep up with the increasingly rapid advance of modern military technology.

Richard Bitzinger and Bates Gill contend that 'Military production in China is plagued by a fragmented, almost feudal system of defence industry fiefdoms, fraught with duplication, overproduction, undercapitalization, poor management and entrepreneurial skills, and the inability to access or to exploit available advanced technology'. The many parts of this complex are 'vertically isolated', which inhibits the sharing of knowledge and expertise both between defence firms and between the defence and private sectors, thus impeding innovation. The reform-era emphasis on competitiveness forces military industries to make themselves more viable economically by shifting their energies to commercial production. At the same time, decentralization throughout the Chinese state has worsened the problem of lack of coordination between the various industries involved in research and production (Bitzinger and Gill, 1996, pp. 19–24).

The result of all these characteristics in combination has been massive inefficiency in China's military production. According to one 1994 report from Western analysts, 40 per cent of China's defence industries were producing exclusively civilian goods, with that figure set to rise, and many other plants were idle or underused. Consequently, Chinese arms production was only operating at 10 to 30 per cent of its capacity (*Jane's Defence Weekly*, 1994, pp. 28–31).

China also lags behind the world leaders in weapons technology, with little prospect of bridging the gap. Up to now, the Chinese have relied heavily on incorporating foreign technology through reverse engineering. This method is becoming unfeasible, however, because the advantages built into state-of-the-art foreign weapons systems are increasingly found not in the hardware but in the software (i.e., sophisticated computer programming), which is not easily observed and copied. This limits the enhancement of Chinese military capabilities through the acquisition of advanced foreign weapons systems (Bitzinger and Gill, 1996, p. 21).

China's Nuclear Forces

In 1956–7, shortly before the severe deterioration in Sino-Soviet relations, the Soviets gave the Chinese nuclear weapons technology that would form much of the basis of China's atomic bomb programme. Soviet technicians got the Chinese started in mining uranium (of which China has its own deposits) and enriching it to produce weapons-grade uranium-235, helped them build a testing facility at Lop Nur in Xinjiang, and provided know-how for building the explosive mechanism. The Soviets discontinued their assistance to the Chinese nuclear weapons programme after the 1958 Taiwan Straits Crisis, by the end of which Krushchev became convinced that Mao had a dangerously flippant attitude toward nuclear war (Khrushchev, 1970, p. 261). Building on the foundation of expertise provided by the Soviets, including the painstaking restoration of documents torn to shreds by departing Soviet scientists in the fall of 1960 (Spence, 1990, p. 589), the PRC exploded its first atomic bomb in October 1964, following with a hydrogen bomb test in June 1967. The exact number of nuclear warheads in China's arsenal today is unknown to outsiders. The PRC's nuclear forces are even more secretive than other branches of the PLA, which in general is noted for its lack of transparency. A stockpile of 300 is probably a good approximation, although estimates vary from 200 to 650 (Johnston, 1995/96, p. 31).

China appears to have acquired nuclear weapons primarily for two reasons. The first is security. Without nuclear weapons of its own, China had no means of countering a nuclear attack by either of the superpowers. This gave them immense strategic leverage over the PRC, and Mao understandably spoke of his fear that the nuclear powers might practise 'atomic blackmail' against China (Lewis and Xue, 1988, p. 36). Indeed, the United States had repeatedly used nuclear threats against China as a diplomatic weapon in the 1950s. What China needed was the kind of 'deterrence' only a nuclear arsenal of its own could provide. Once this deterrent was in place, the PRC would have greater freedom of action. Washington, for example, could no longer use the threat of a nuclear attack to restrict PRC moves against Taiwan; if China could launch a nuclear counter-attack, the Americans would have to be willing to sacrifice Los Angeles to save Taipei, which of course lacked credibility. Interestingly, Chinese strategists have only recently incorporated the term 'deterrence' into their discussions of PRC nuclear strategy. Previously, this term was considered inappropriate for two reasons. First, it was ethically repugnant, associated with hegemonistic countries that used the threat of force to coerce weaker countries, and therefore unbefitting a principled and exemplary country such as China. Second, Chinese analysts understood that deterrence requires strong capabilities, which China originally did not have, to make the threat of retaliation credible (Nan, 1996, p. 451). Even today, some Chinese analysts prefer to use the terms 'defence' or 'self-protection' (Johnston, 1995/96, p. 11).

The second major reason China developed nuclear weapons is the belief that they confer major power status. Mao observed that 'In this present world, if we do not want to be bullied, we cannot afford not to have that thing [the atomic bomb]. . . . [I]f you do not have it, others will count you for nothing'. On another occasion he said that 'If we are not to be bullied in this world, we cannot do without the bomb' (Huang and Wang, 1992, p. 602). Deng expressed a similar view in 1988: 'If China did not make efforts to develop atom bombs and neutron bombs in the 1960s and if China was not able to launch satellites, then China would not have such a high position in the world today. These things *reflect the capabilities* of one nation and are a sign of [the] strength of one nation' (my emphasis) (Gao, 1992, p. 8). It is significant that Deng describes nuclear weapons as 'reflecting' rather than generating major power status. Contemporary Chinese strategic analysts, as well, concur that nuclear weapons command respect, and that this alone justifies keeping them. In the words of one analyst, 'If [China] did not have strategic nuclear power, people would look down upon us and our country's major power status would be hard to establish and preserve' (Su, 1992, p. 566).

Before China acquired nuclear weapons, its defence against a nuclear attack was a strategy of denial: even a nuclear strike would not allow a foreign power to conquer the PRC. Thus, the pre-nuclear Mao made public statements denigrating atomic bombs as 'paper tigers', and boasting that his country would survive a nuclear bombardment (Lewis and Xue, 1988, pp. 36–7). From the time it developed the bomb until recently, China's basic nuclear posture was to maintain a minimum second-strike capability. During the last decade, however, Chinese military planners have come to doubt the power and credibility of such a modest deterrent, and a consensus has developed that China's nuclear forces should be capable of supporting a somewhat more robust doctrine of limited nuclear deterrence (Johnston, 1995/96, pp. 5–42). In the case of minimum deterrence, the only use conceived for nuclear weapons is in a retaliatory counter-attack on the territory of an enemy state that had first used nuclear weapons against China. Since the targets are major enemy cities, only a relatively small number of warheads is needed, and the delivery system need not be highly accurate. A limited deterrence strategy, however, enlarges the role of nuclear weapons. While minimum deterrence threatens to use nuclear weapons only in the final, most drastic stage of nuclear war (destroying the enemy's civilian population), limited deterrence covers the lower levels of nuclear conflict, or 'limited nuclear war': nuclear attacks on the enemy's nuclear missile bases, and tactical nuclear warfare (the use of smaller-yield nuclear weapons on the battlefield).

By developing capabilities in these areas, a country hopes to be able to respond in kind to *any* form of nuclear attack, and therefore to deter such attacks. To implement this strategy, China needs a large arsenal of both strategic (targeted at the enemy's homeland) and tactical (for use on the actual battlefield) nuclear weapons. The missiles that deliver nuclear warheads must be accurate enough to destroy the enemy's missiles in their silos, and numerous enough to overwhelm the enemy's ballistic missile defences. China's nuclear forces in the 1990s do not have these capabilities. The Second Artillery Corps (the common English term for the *Dier Paobing*, which is more properly translated as 'Second Artillery Army'; Lewis and Xue, 1988, p. 213n), which operates China's strategic rocket forces, currently has only 17 intercontinental ballistic missiles (ICBMs), about 70 medium-range ballistic missiles, and 12 submar-ine-launched ballistic missiles (SLBMs) in its inventory. (By comparison, in 1997 Russia had 800 ICBMs and 540 SLBMs, and the United States had 580 ICBMs and 408 SLBMs [IISS, 1996/97]). About half of China's missiles are still liquid-fuelled, and require two hours to prepare for firing. Chinese missiles are suitable for 'countervalue' purposes (targeting the enemy's civilian population), but most are not accurate enough for 'counterforce' missions (targeting the enemy's strategic weapons; to destroy an enemy missile in a silo buried deep in the ground, a warhead must explode very close to it).

If the PLA is committed to enlarging the strategic role of its nuclear forces beyond the level of minimum deterrence, an expansion of both the size and sophistication of the nuclear forces is necessary. Upgrading along these lines is indeed taking place. Chinese technicians are working to perfect a new generation of smaller and more accurate warheads, which is a major reason for China's continued nuclear testing and delayed signing of the Comprehensive Test Ban Treaty. Another improvement the Chinese are attempting to implement is the multiple independently-targeted re-entry vehicle (MIRV), which allows a single ballistic missile to carry several warheads to as many different targets. China is improving the survivability of its missiles by making them more mobile and converting them to solid fuel, which permits quicker launching. A new ICBM tested in 1995 can reportedly carry an 800 kg payload far enough to strike anywhere in the United States, and with greater accuracy than its predecessors. Along with these qualitative improvements, the number of ICBMs is to be expanded as well, to 30 by the turn of the century (Shambaugh, 1994b, p. 56).

Like all parts of the PLA, however, the Second Artillery must cope with limited funding. International arms control agreements, which China has an interest in supporting because it is a weaker nuclear power than the USA and Russia, will also constrain the development of China's nuclear forces.

The Effect of Entrepreneurship on the PLA

The PLA's commercial activities have several potential effects on PLA involvement in China's foreign policy-making. Indirectly, PLA entrepreneurship changes the set of interests the armed forces bring into the bureaucratic bargaining process. As PLA-owned firms develop profitable economic links with foreigners, some PLA officers might become less supportive of PRC policies that are likely to raise tensions with China's neighbours. More directly, extensive commercial activities have the potential to erode the PLA's professionalism and combat readiness. If this occurs, China's military effectiveness is reduced, which might in turn limit the PRC's future capability to project force in the region.

The PLA has always been involved in the civilian economy, but in the early decades of CCP rule it was in different ways and for different reasons. Typical of the Mao era was Beijing's 196th Infantry Division, which sold its surplus bean curd to local civilians and used the proceeds to buy ping-pong paddles and balls for the soldiers and their families (Hollingworth, 1994/95, p. 30). Troops helped peasants raise crops and livestock and participated in irrigation and disaster-relief projects to maintain the common people's support for the PLA and to help defray the economic cost of feeding the vast soldiery (Joffe, 1995, p. 28).

In contrast, the primary purpose of the PLA's economic activities in the 1990s is to make money. Deng has encouraged, and given licence to, the PLA to raise more of its own revenue to reduce its dependence on the state central budget. The PLA has responded enthusiastically, clearly beyond the expectations or even the desires of the CCP leadership. The PLA's personnel and assets have effectively been divided into a military sector and a commercial sector. The latter is involved in a wide variety of activities ranging from agriculture (much of the PLA's food is produced by PLA soldiers), to construction projects, to manufacture of thousands of different types of consumer goods, to investment in private sector businesses, to overseas arms sales. The PLA Air Force has released its airfields, aircraft and pilots for civilian, revenue-generating activities. The PLA Navy has done the same with its ports, ships and sailors. PLA construction troops now accept private contracts to build roads, bridges and tunnels. The involvement of soldiers in business has produced absurdities that seem drawn from Joseph Heller's war satire *Catch-22*: from the Second Artillery franchising Baskin & Robbins ice cream outlets, to a PLA-run shooting range near Beijing where fee-paying foreign tourists can fire selected weapons.

The full extent of the Chinese military's business activities is perhaps impossible to assess; the officers involved conceal many of their dealings to evade taxes or avoid disciplinary action. Officially, PLA units are the registered owners of some 20,000 companies, although the actual number is undoubtedly much higher (Hollingworth, 1994/95, p. 30). Not all PLA businesses are profitable; many suffer the same inefficiences as the rest of China's state-owned industrial sector. Some PLA-run commercial activities are illegal: smuggling stolen cars and other consumer durable goods into China, speculating in real estate, and running prostitution rings. Off-duty PLA troops were blamed for the 1994 robbery and murder of a boatload of Taiwanese tourists on Qiandao Lake in Zhejiang Province (Shambaugh, 1996a, p. 277).

PLA entrepreneurship has the possible benefit of supplementing the military's available funds, which of course was the original objective. The profits earned by PLA firms, however, do not necessarily go toward fulfilling what are supposed to be the PLA's primary missions. Instead, much of this money undoubtedly goes into the pockets of well-placed officers, who use it for their own private purposes. Yitzhak Shichor judges that on balance, the PLA loses more than it gains: 'much, if not most, of the additional income is not used to promote military modernization, and by no means compensates for the loss of professional training, morale, and fighting effectiveness'. These commercial activities obviously pull PLA personnel away from strictly military activities, including combat-related instruction, exercises, maintenance of equipment, and the myriad individual assignments required to keep the PLA functioning. An important mitigating factor in this process is that few of China's actual core military resources have been converted to civilian activities. The civilianized assets have mostly been 'fictitious and useless military resources', the transfer of which would scarcely degrade the PRC's defence capabilities (Shichor, 1995, pp. 17, 23).

A more subtle consequence is the erosion of the officer corps' professionalism, the PLA's 'corporate spirit', and the enlisted man's ethic of duty (Joffe, 1995, pp. 39–41). The PLA leadership is fully aware of the debilitating effects of commercialism on PLA combat readiness. Liu Huaqing and Zhang Zhen, vice-chairmen of the Military Affairs Committee, warned in 1993, 'many armies in China and abroad have lost their fighting capacity and been defeated by peace or by themselves' (*Renmin Ribao*, 26 July 1993; in Segal, 1994a, p. 26). In 1994, the CMC banned commercial activities by PLA units below the group army level. Yet it is difficult for the PLA leadership to undertake a serious crackdown on PLA commercialism, for three reasons. First, PLA business activities are too widespread and unregulated for any attempted constraints imposed by the high command to be completely effective. Second, given the number of PLA officers who have a stake in these activities, such a crackdown would risk triggering massive opposition. Finally, the benefits of military commercialism are immediate and tangible, while the dangers are distant and vague (Joffe, 1995, p. 38).

China's Changing Military Strategy

Under Mao's leadership, the basic defence posture of the PRC was encompassed by the passive doctrine of 'people's war'. Essentially a strategy of the weak, people's war borrowed heavily from a well-developed Chinese tradition of guerrilla warfare. Sun Zi's *Art of War*, which is to China what Carl von Clausewitz's *On War* is to the West, extolled 'indirect' warfare; pitched battles, Sun Zi wrote, should be fought only as a last resort, or when one has superior strength, while 'to win without fighting is the acme of skill'. Mao's famous notion of guerrillas depending on the support of the local civilian population as much as fish need water is also borrowed from pre-modern Chinese history (Spence, 1990, p. 178; Segal, 1985, p. 29).

Maoist guerrilla warfare strategy is succinctly summarized in the guidelines drawn from his famous treatise 'On Guerrilla War', These include: retreat when the enemy advances; advance when the enemy retreats; attack only where there is a local superiority of numbers great enough to ensure success; subsist on the spoils taken from defeated enemy troops; and armies must maintain a harmonious relationship with the local population.

In its early decades, the PRC's principal security concern was defeating an invasion from the United States or (later) the Soviet Union. China's basic military strategy, which was designed to meet this contingency, drew on Mao's guerrilla warfare guidelines, and also recognized China's strategic weakness (a lack of modern weaponry) and strengths (vast territory and a huge, well-mobilized population). The strategy had three phases: defensive, stalemate, and counter-offensive. Rather than making an early stand in an attempt to repel the invaders, the Chinese defenders would strategically withdraw to 'lure the enemy in deep'. Chinese cities, which had little economic development and therefore offered little benefit to the enemy if captured, were to be abandoned; the people would disperse into the vast countryside, forcing the enemy to venture out in pursuit. The Chinese strategy intentionally sought to drag out the conflict into a war of attrition. With the enemy overextended throughout rural China and the PLA and militia forces able to rely on supplies and intelligence from local residents, who were expected to commit themselves totally to the war effort, Chinese soldiers could use guerrilla tactics to isolate and annihilate pockets of invading troops. Only after the enemy had been severely weakened by months of harassment would the Chinese counter-attack and seek a decisive victory. This strategy was not substantially different from that which the communist troops employed against the Japanese and the Guomindang.

The CCP Central Committee concluded in 1978 that the USSR was no longer an immediate threat to Chinese security, although the Soviet Union remained China's most compelling potential adversary, and protecting against a Soviet invasion into China's heartland was still the PLA's primary mission. Further strategic reassessment in Beijing continued into the 1980s. Gorbachev's ascension to power led to a lasting rapprochement with China, for which his Vladivostock speech in July 1986 paved the way. Perhaps even more significant, however, was the Reagan revolution in the United States. With Reagan's rejuvenation of the US armed forces, China's strategists concluded that the United States had become more formidable in both its military capabilities and its determination to block the expansion of Soviet influence. This, the Chinese believed, would constrain the Soviets from making aggressive moves toward China (Godwin, 1991, p. 650). In the long term, this stalemate would drain the resources, and in turn the global influence, of both superpowers, eventually creating new opportunities for China to improve its relative position.

In an address to the Central Military Commission in 1985, Deng announced that the PLA need no longer expect 'an early war, major war and nuclear war'; instead, it should prepare for the more likely event of a 'limited war'. The PLA had already begun reorganizing to improve its combat efficiency. The previous total of 35 field armies was converted to 24 'group armies', each of which had about 50,000 soldiers in three divisions that combined a variety of types of combat and support units (infantry, armour, engineers, etc.). In 1985, the leadership moved to make the PLA leaner as well, reducing the number of military regions from 11 to seven and announcing that the number of troops in the PLA would be reduced by one million. The PLA did indeed demobilize about a million troops over the next two years, although many of these were shifted into the People's Armed Police (PAP) or given new duties as government-employed labourers rather than being laid off.

Retooling the PLA for limited war instead of total or major war would become one of the two fundamental changes from Mao's era to China's present defence policy. As the Chinese understand 'limited war', the goal is not to destroy or conquer the enemy state, but rather to 'assert one's own standpoint and will' on a particular diplomatic issue – e.g., to coerce the enemy government to change a policy or to acquire control of natural resources. The states involved are not likely to use all their available force and resources in the conflict; how much they choose to invest is based on political rather than strictly military considerations (Jiao and Xiao, 1988, p. 49). A military conflict over the disputed Spratly Islands, for example, would clearly fit into this category. A closely related concept is local or regional war *(jubu zhanzheng)*, envisioned as a geographically-contained conflict on the PRC's periphery, which is also identified by many Chinese strategic analysts as a likely contingency of the future. Some analysts even combine the two terms as 'limited, regional war' *(youxian zhubu zhanzheng)*.

The second fundamental change in Chinese defence policy has been the abandonment of Mao's passive posture of large-scale guerrilla warfare in favour of a more offensive-oriented strategy that would seek to stop the enemy at or even beyond China's borders, even if this required pre-emptive strikes. Of course, the PLA had conducted 'defensive' military operations outside of the PRC proper prior to the 1980s; the difference was that carrying out such operations was now explicitly recognized as the PLA's core doctrine. This new doctrine was originally labelled 'people's war under modern conditions', which deceptively suggested it was no more than a minor modification of Mao's strategy. Later, Chinese strategic discourse coalesced around the term 'active defence' *(jiji fangyu)*. This term had appeared in previous Maoist writings, but now it was given a new meaning (Shambaugh, 1996a, p. 280).

Besides the decline in the possibility of invasion by a major power, another consideration explaining China's shift from 'people's war' to a more maritime-oriented, power-projecting 'active defence' strategy is improved relations with its traditional continental adversaries (Russia, India, Vietnam) combined with the persistence of many potential political problems off China's east and southeast coast: the Spratly and Diaoyutai Islands, Taiwan, tensions on the Korean peninsula, and ongoing disagreements with Japan and the USA (Bitzinger and Gill, 1996, p. 8).

The new doctrine includes an emphasis on the importance of developing rapid-reaction or 'fist' (*quantou*) units, which are supposed to be deployable anywhere in China within 24 hours. Eventually, each group army aims to maintain one of its divisions as a rapid-reaction unit (Shambaugh, 1996a, p. 284). The PLA Marines, founded in 1953 and dissolved in 1957, were also re-established in 1980. Based on Hainan Island, they are evidently intended for deployment to the South China Sea islands.

The PLA Navy's strategy has gone through a similar change. Although China was an accomplished maritime power during part of its pre-modern history, Mao had no interest in naval power projection. His concept of naval warfare was essentially an offshore extension of 'people's war': Chinese vessels were to be hidden in caves dug into the coastline (the maritime counterpart to hiding infantry in tunnels, a tactic of which Mao had grown fond during the Korean War), from which they would emerge at the opportune moment to conduct guerrilla warfare in coastal waters. In sharp contrast to Mao, Admiral Liu Huaqing, who has been to the PLA Navy what Alfred T. Mahan was to the US Navy, argued that China could not afford to neglect its maritime interests, and that the PLAN's mission should be enlarged beyond mere coastal defence to include power projection into the East and South China Seas out to the 'First Island Chain' (the Japanese island of Kyushu, the Ryukus, Taiwan, the Philippines, and Borneo). In a 1986 article in the Party's authoritative journal *Hong Qi (Red Flag)*, Liu called for 'a considerable number of advanced warships and aircraft equipped with modern weapons including all kinds of missiles and nuclear weapons; [and] talented human resources . . . who are well-versed in modern sea combat theories, strategies and tactics and are able skilfully to command and master sophisticated weapons and equipment' (Liu, 1986, pp. 17–21). Under Liu's leadership, the PLAN has adopted an 'active green water strategy' – i.e., employing naval forces offensively and at moderate distances from Chinese shores (Jun, 1994, pp. 181, 183–9, 192).

The lessons the PLA leadership drew from the Gulf War reinforced the conclusions many PLA officers and Chinese strategic analysts had already reached: in modern war, a quick victory is possible; mobility and strong C3I capabilities are essential; striking pre-emptively has advantages; a numerically smaller force can prevail with superior training, tactics and equipment; and the combatant with higher-technology equipment has an edge that may be insurmountable (Nan, 1996, pp. 456–8). Jiang told military commanders in Hunan Province in March 1991, 'China and its military modernization must depend on the progress of science and technology. The practice of every limited local war, especially the most recent war, tells us that modern warfare has become high-tech warfare. It is a multi-dimensional war, electronic war, missile war. The backward one is beaten'. In the year following the Gulf War, the buzzwords among the top military leadership were 'qualitative construction'. Liu, PLA logistics director General Zhao Nanqi, and *Jiefangjun Bao's* 1992 New Year house editorial all called qualitative construction the PLA's new 'guiding principle' and 'guiding philosophy' *(Jiefangjun Bao*, 20 March 1991; 9 December 1991; 17 December 1991, and 27 January 1992; cited in Chu, 1994, pp. 189–90). China's vicarious Gulf War experience is probably the greatest single reason why most PRC analyses of Chinese defence strategy now describe it as 'limited war under high-technology conditions' (Shambaugh, 1996a, p. 280).

Indeed, modernization has become a pressing concern for the PLA, and one that affects Chinese foreign relations. While the armed forces were told in the 1970s and 1980s that their modernization had to wait until the country as a whole made further economic progress, the PLA leadership has recently argued that military modernization could facilitate national economic development (mainly through enhancing the PRC's international prestige) rather than the reverse (Shichor, 1995, p. 6; Liu, 1993, p. 1; Xie *et al.*, 1992, p. 5). PLA leaders have also told the government with a 'sense of urgency' that 'without the support of high technology, the army can hardly win a war fought under modern conditions' *(Jiefangjun Bao*, 26 March 1993; Bitzinger and Gill, 1996, p. 10). High-ranking PLA officers seem to accept the view of many strategists worldwide that the high-tech 'Revolution in military affairs' (RMA) requires major military powers to develop the capacity to wage 'information warfare', integrating sophisticated systems of sensors, computers, and communication networks. This explains why the Chinese government reportedly established an organization of some 100 computer technicians in April 1997 charged with developing viruses to disable the computer systems of the USA and its allies (Dawnay, 1997, p. A8). The PLA brass also recognizes, however, that the

RMA exacerbates China's disadvantages relative to the other major powers (Pillsbury, 1997, pp. 249–420). Some of the impediments to PLA modernization arise from the quality of its personnel. Lack of education has long been a major problem, but the National Defence University (NDU) and other staff training institutes have improved military education. By 1994, over half the PLA officer corps held college degrees (Shambaugh, 1996a, p. 282). Generally, however, the military is a low-status occupation, just as it was in pre-modern China. Business is a better way to make money, and the PLA's reputation was badly damaged by Tiananmen. Thus, the ranks tend to be filled by uneducated young men from rural areas, or even convicts. Furthermore, thanks to the 'one child per family' population control policy, one result of which has been a generation of over-indulged children, many of the PLA's new recruits are reportedly proving unusually difficult to train (Wang, 1994, p. 30).

While there is much China can do on its own to improve the PLA's capabilities, the PRC needs foreign components and expertise if it is to fufil its ambition of building a first-class military. As Liu Huaqing says, 'Without advanced science and technology and people armed with advanced science and technology, modernization is empty talk' (Xie *et al.*, 1992, pp. 503–4). The PLA therefore has a stake in maintaining favourable relations with the developed countries, which are the sources of cutting-edge technology. Yet this does not restrain the PLA from promoting anti-US policies, because it is Russia, not the United States, that is the most important foreign partner in Chinese modernization efforts. Since the fall of the Soviet Union, China has recruited hundreds of former Soviet defence technicians, paying them far more than they can now earn in their economically strapped homeland. China also buys advanced Russian arms off the shelf, and is negotiating licences to produce some hi-tech Russian weapons in China.

The evolution of the PRC's basic defence strategy reflects the changing circumstances of the country as a whole from 1949 to the present. In its early years, the PRC was poor, technologically backward and relatively vulnerable. Now that China has become wealthier and better developed, with substantial economic assets to protect, the potential costs of 'luring the enemy in deep' are much greater. Yan Xuetong, one of the pioneering PRC scholars conducting original analysis of their country's national interests, notes that 'a consensus has basically been reached . . . [that] in order to ensure the safety of the country's economic achievements against war damages, the Chinese army must commit itself to engaging the enemy outside China's territory'. This requires 'a navy and air force strong enough to engage the enemy outside the country so as to ensure that the flames of war would not spread' to the PRC's economic centres, especially the relatively developed east coast provinces (Yan, 1995, pp. 8, 5).

With the nation's political maturation and healthy economic growth, China's military concerns have moved offshore, from defending China proper against invasion to challenging the status quo by enforcing Chinese claims to disputed territory. A growing core of its military is equipped with modern weapons systems and trained in modern tactics. China need no longer expect to be militarily inferior to its likely adversaries (its naval and air forces are still substantially inferior to those of the USA and probably Japan, but not to those of the ASEAN countries that dispute China's claims in the South China Sea). Mao's strategy of attrition and delaying decisive battles was a matter of necessity rather than choice. With the PRC growing stronger and more confident, however, most of today's military strategists prefer a strategy that seeks to 'fight a quick battle to force a quick resolution' and to overwhelm the enemy with concentrated firepower (Nan, 1996, pp. 452–3). Maoist strategy envisaged mobilizing the entire population, with local militias joining PLA regulars in combat. But with the country semi-industrialized, most of the urban populace can contribute more to national defence by remaining in the factories than by forming bands of guerrillas, while the PLA relies increasingly on the idea of 'winning victory through elite troops'. A famous principle of Mao-era PLA chief Marshal Zhu De was *You shenma wuqi, da shenma zhang* ('What weapons you possess [determine] what kind of war you fight'). Many contemporary Chinese strategists would now reverse the relationship – *Da shenma zhang, zao shenma wuqi* ('What kind of war you fight [determines] what kind of weapons you make') – and are in a far better position to do so than their predecessors of a generation ago (Nan, 1996, pp. 451, 459).

In sum, today's PLA mirrors China's changed circumstances: from people's war to active defence, from revolutionary army to professional army, from austerity to the corrupting effects of entrepreneurship. Yet some features of the old PLA persist, most importantly manifest in its hyper-nationalism and its continuing role as the ultimate guardian of regime security.

7

China and Global Politics

If China had a truly global political role during the Cold War, it was Beijing's position in the 'strategic triangle' with the two super-powers. Chinese officials angrily observed that with the collapse of the Soviet Union, the PRC's status and importance in Washington was immediately downgraded (Wang, 1996, p. 149). The end of the Cold War has left the Asia-Pacific region devolving from bipolarity to multipolarity. Instead of two great powers ('poles'), each controlling a tight bloc of allies, the new regional power structure sees four large states of more equal capabilities (the USA's pre-eminent military power is mitigated somewhat by its distance from East Asia) and much greater flexibility in alliance-making. The Gulf War of 1991 dramatized the implications of the post-Cold War era for China. Russia cooperated with NATO in the use of force against Iraq, a former Soviet client. From Beijing's standpoint, this was a sobering departure from the Cold War status quo, when there was never a serious possibility of Russian–American alliance against Beijing. 'The new world order advocated by the United States and other Western powers is nothing more than a revised expression of power politics', wrote one Chinese analyst. 'The ultimate goal is a world completely dominated by capitalist countries' (Du, 1991, p. 5).

Thus far, the post-Cold War era has seen something of a reversal of the triangular relationship of the latter stage of the Cold War: a notable improvement in Sino-Russian relations, and a notable deterioration in Sino-US relations.

Russia

From Beijing's standpoint, Russia is perhaps best understood as a perennial rival and potential foe that is presently in remission.

Russia's weakness resulting from its preoccupation with serious internal problems has cleared the way for Sino-Russian relations to improve to their best state since the early 1950s. Gorbachev's ascension to leadership of the Soviet Union ended the threat of an invasion of China from the north even before the breakup of the Soviet empire. Since then, Moscow and Beijing have taken steps to clarify their border and reduce the numbers of troops stationed along the Sino-Russian frontier. The visit of Russian President Yeltsin to China in April 1996, a set of new economic agreements and booming Russian arms sales to the Chinese have some observers wondering if China and Russia have become quasi-allies against the West (Forney and Chanda, 1996, p. 17).

Chinese analysts maintain that Gorbachev acted unwisely to give away the Soviet empire. Although China and the West benefited, Russia harmed its own national interest and hurt countries such as North Korea that heavily depended on Soviet aid. Gorbachev and Yeltsin invited chaos by implementing both economic and political liberalization simultaneously. Gorbachev was also duped by promises of massive Western aid if he made strategic concessions to NATO. While he did his part, Western aid proved disappointing, and in any case insufficient to compensate for what he lost (Shi, 1995, pp. 4–5).

Although the Russian armed forces are currently demoralized and financially strapped as a consequence of the country's political and economic disarray, Russia still has 'hard power', or the infrastructure of a militarily powerful nation. A minority of Chinese analysts, especially those who believe economic cooperation and Japanese pacifism will prevail in Sino-Japanese relations, see Russia as a greater long-term threat than Japan.

Most Chinese believe Russia is now in a period of transition, and that it will eventually achieve greater political stability and economic productivity than it demonstrated in the 1990s. Yan Xuetong's view represents that of many Chinese analysts: 'Russia is in need of a long period of time to stabilize its domestic political order and to extricate itself from its present economic crisis, and so has neither the will nor the strength to exercise military expansion in East Asia' (Yan, 1995, p. 2).

From the PRC's point of view, it is best that Russia does not recover too well, nor too quickly. Continued political turmoil and economic imbalance in Russia confirms the claim of CCP officials that they are doing it right (continued one-party rule and protection of inefficient state-owned industries from market forces), and Moscow is doing it wrong (multi-party system and economic 'shock therapy'). As Chen Qimao observes with unusual candour, this 'borrows time for the Chinese leadership in its effort to . . . consolidate political stability' (Chen, 1993, p. 240).

Furthermore, if Russia's rejuvenation efforts are highly successful, China will face new security threats. First, if a renewed Russia fell under the control of a Zhirinovsky-type nationalist leader, Moscow might re-energize its military forces and seek to reincorporate the former Soviet republics and expand Russian influence in Asia. This might generate a new Sino-Soviet cold war, requiring the Chinese to build up their northern armies and reopening old disputes over the ownership of certain frontier areas. Second, an economically more dynamic Russia might become a competitor to China in common overseas markets and among overseas investors. Third, if Russia enjoyed noticeable improvements in its standard of living under a relatively liberal government, demands for political liberalization by the CCP would grow stronger (Glaser, 1993, p. 256).

In the mid-1980s, Sino-Soviet relations remained stagnant over what Beijing called the three major obstacles to improved relations: Soviet troops in Afghanistan, large numbers of Soviet forces stationed on the Sino-Soviet border, and Moscow's assistance to Vietnam, which had invaded Cambodia to depose the Pro-Chinese Khmer Rouge. Faced simultaneously with an assertive NATO and an economic crisis that forced a re-evaluation of Soviet efforts to project influence abroad, Soviet leader Mikhail Gorbachev expressed a willingness to address these obstacles in key speeches in 1986 and 1988. The Soviets soon met China's demands on these issues, and additionally reduced Soviet troops in Mongolia and signed the 1987 Intermediate Nuclear Forces Treaty, which eliminated 100 Soviet SS-20 missiles based in the Soviet Far East. Gorbachev's visit to Beijing in May 1989 began a period of considerable upgrading of Sino-Russian relations, including new trade agreements, stronger military ties, visits between the two countries by high-level leaders, and further progress in the settlement of outstanding border disputes. On the Chinese side, the primary impetus for an improved relationship with Russia was Beijing's need for a powerful supporter in the wake of the post-Tiananmen economic and political backlash from the West. China also stood to gain from trade and technology transfer from the

Russians and from a reduction in tensions along the Sino-Russian border. Although China's official policy remains standoffish – 'neither confrontation nor alliance' with Moscow (Wang, 1996, p. 148) – it is somewhat remarkable that Sino-Russian relations have continued to improve through the breakup of the Soviet Union and the administration of Boris Yeltsin given the degree to which China and Russia have grown apart ideologically. Russian Foreign Minister Andrei Kozyrev, for example, criticized China's human rights record when he visited China in March 1992 (Dittmer, 1994, p. 109). Chinese officialdom also publicly scorned Yeltsin for his capitalist reforms. In the view of Chinese leaders, Russia should have learned from the East Asian NICs, which maintain a strong state and emphasize the importance of political stability during economic growth, instead of trying to emulate the liberal Western model. Finally, to the Beijing regime, Boris Yeltsin's commitment to 'democracy' meant an internally unstable and pro-Western Russia. China's initial misgivings were ameliorated, however, by subsequent events: Yeltsin's visits to China, the resurgence of conservatism in Russia's 1993 parliamentary elections, and Yeltsin's replacement of his reformist prime minister Yegor Gaidar with former Soviet bureaucrat Victor Chernomyrdin (Moltz, 1995, pp. 172–3, 166).

Increased Sino-Russian cooperation appears largely based on the two countries' common apprehension toward the United States. The Chinese want a partner to help them balance against the sole remaining superpower, while the Russians are concerned about NATO's recruitment of some of the Soviet Union's former Eastern European allies. At the same time, the Chinese do not appear seriously worried about the prospect of cooperation between Washington and Moscow contrary to China's interests; the perceived differences between Russia and the USA remain great, even under the more democratic and market-oriented Yeltsin regime. A similar judgment applies to Japan–Russia relations, where the inability to resolve the dispute over ownership of Sakhalin and the Kuril Islands remains a seemingly irremovable barrier to a real reconciliation (Lampton, 1995, pp. 88–9, 99). Beyond the united front against a powerful USA, China and Russia have a common interest in containing ethnic nationalism and Islamic fundamentalism in Central Asia. Moscow also espouses a 'one-China' policy and recognizes Beijing's sovereignty over Tibet, while China supports Russia's military campaign against separatists in Chechnya and has joined

Moscow in criticizing the North Atlantic Treaty Organization's recruitment of countries formerly allied with the Soviet Union. As China has grown richer and Russia has grown more desperate for revenue, mutual economic interests have provided a sound potential basis for amicable Sino-Russian relations. For the Chinese, trade with Russia allows further diversification of their economic links, which lessens the potential harm of being shut out of the US market due to protectionism or sanctions (Lampton, 1995, p. 86). Economic ties and joint ventures with the Russians have the particular advantage of giving China's northeastern provinces an economic boost. Chinese trade with Russia, however, is still comparatively small-scale, about $7 billion in 1997, and comprised only around 2 per cent of the PRC's total trade in the mid-1990s (compared to about 15 per cent held by the USA). China's place in Russia's trade is more significant: between Gorbachev's 1985 ascension to the leadership of the Soviet Union and the mid-1990s, China rose from Russia's 17th-largest to second-largest trading partner.

China's border dispute with Russia is close to settlement. Ninety-three per cent of the Sino-Soviet border was demarcated prior to the demise of the Soviet Union, and in any case the easing of tensions since the Cold War has greatly reduced the anxiety that previously surrounded this issue. In April 1997, Jiang and Yeltsin signed an agreement to limit the number of regular army troops (as opposed to border guards) within 100 kilometres of the Sino-Soviet border to 130,400 on each side. A few small disputed areas remain, but Moscow recently announced it accepts China's current borders (Quinn-Judge, 1997, p. 16). Russia has also withdrawn all its soldiers from Outer Mongolia (Dittmer, 1994, pp. 107–8).

Sino-Russian military cooperation, especially Russian arms sales to China, greatly expanded in the 1990s. China has become the largest single buyer of Russian arms, purchasing $1.8 billion worth in 1992 alone (Jencks, 1994, p. 72). For China, Russia is an attractive supplier because it offers top-of-the-line equipment at favourable prices (the Russians are even willing to accept partial payment through barter), and because the Chinese enjoy relatively free access to Russian weaponry, whereas some political restrictions still apply to China's arms trade with the Western countries. Co-production of a new fighter for the Chinese air force similar to the advanced Russian MiG-31 is under discussion. Russian weapons systems are also relatively easy to integrate into China's order of battle, which is based largely on Soviet equipment and designs. Furthermore, thousands of Russian technicians and scientists have come to China to assist in the design and production of various defence-related systems, including avionics, missiles and nuclear technology.

Russian arms sales to China, however, are not necessarily a guarantor of continued good relations. First, this is likely to be a short-term phenomenon, a stopgap measure for a Chinese leadership that is working to establish its own capacity for advanced weapons production. Second, there may be little correlation between arms sales and a favourable political relationship. China reportedly spent four times as much money on Russian arms as on US arms in 1982 – 6, when Beijing–Moscow relations were still strained but Chinese relations with Washington were relatively relaxed (Yuan, 1995, p. 82n).

Several bilateral problems persist, of course, some of them possibly serious. Although Moscow has promised Beijing not to formally recognize Taiwan or to sell objectionable weapons systems to the ROC, some Russian politicians openly favour greater diplomatic recognition of Taiwan.

Like Japan, Russia is victimized by Chinese pirates. In 1993 Moscow stationed a cruiser in the South China Sea to protect Russian cargo ships, which had suffered more pirate attacks than those of any other nation the previous year (Whiting, 1995a, p. 20). The Russians also frequently charge Chinese fishermen in the Ussuri and Amur Rivers with taking fish during agreed no-fishing seasons (Moltz, 1995, p. 178).

Many Russians complain about the influx of Chinese labourers and traders – both legal and illegal – into the Russian Far East. The Russian defence minister recently called this a 'peaceful invasion' (Johnston, 1996, p. 20), expressing the widespread Russian fear that their underpopulated Asian territory is vulnerable to falling under foreign control. Indeed, an estimated 150,000 more Chinese enter Russia each year, and there are now as many Chinese as Russians in parts of Russia's Maritime Province (Kim, 1995, p. 474). Structural forces drive this 'invasion'. While the Russian Far East is chronically short of labour, China's huge population includes millions who are unemployed or underemployed, and working in Russia offers the prospect of much higher pay than the average Chinese wage (Menon, 1997, p. 106). Deep-seated racial prejudices combined with transnational organized criminal activities give rise to Russian complaints that the Chinese are a corruptive influence on Russian society and Chinese complaints that their nationals are being abused on Russian soil. Chinese analysts also see Russian concerns about an alleged Chinese expansion into Siberia as fodder for Russian 'extreme nationalists' who have 'openly exaggerated that "the development of China has constituted threats to Russia"' (Shi, 1996, p. 15).

Most importantly, perhaps, Russia remains a latent security threat to China, subject to 'rising nationalism and increasing outcries of great Russia mentality', and 'determined to return to the international arena with the new image of an independent great power' (Shi, 1995, p. 5). The combination of resurgent Russian nationalism and a revitalized Russian economy would probably mark the end of China's post-Cold War era of relative external calm. Short of this development, political instability inside Russia might weaken Moscow's ability to control Russia's nuclear forces or the flow of people across the Sino-Russian border. Dangerous scenarios might also arise from the former Soviet republics. If Central Asian states fell into conflict with each other, they might involve China by recruiting fellow ethnics living on Chinese territory or by maintaining sanctuaries across the Chinese border. Worse, Russian troops might come to the aid of these republics in the event of disputes with China.

The geopolitical incentive for Sino-Russian amity is presently strong, but could quickly disappear with a reassessment of perceived threats. Economic interdependence is a potentially powerful bond, but remains underdeveloped. Culture and history are more likely to be divisive than unifying factors between the Russians and Chinese. In many respects, Sino-Russian relations in the 1990s are similar to Sino-Russian relations in the 1950s, which does not engender great hopes for the long-term stability of the relationship.

The USA

If Japan is the PRC's greatest long-term threat, the chief short-term threat comes from the United States, which Chinese analysts recognize as the world's sole remaining superpower, at least for the time being. As the most powerful country in the system, America is the most blatant practitioner of power politics, utilizing not only military force but also international law and economic and cultural relations to maintain its dominant global position and to suppress potential challengers.

In China's view, the basic US objective is to maintain its dominant position in the region, which allows America to control the region's politics and create a favourable climate for American business. This larger goal dictates the presumed main objectives of the US government's China policy, which are to divide the PRC, overthrow the CCP, and prevent China's emergence as a challenger to US hegemony.

Fortunately for China, America is increasingly unable to fulfil its wish for world domination because of a contracting economic base and growing social problems demanding a greater share of limited funds. One CCP official aptly summarizes mainstream Chinese thinking: 'The major developed countries of the West are preoccupied with a host of domestic problems and economic recession. Although the superpower has not forsaken its schemes for exporting its values and political–economic system or for interfering in other countries' affairs, its abilities very often fall short of its ambitions' (Ren, 1995, p. 104). Another points to the difference between the Korean and Vietnam Wars, which the USA financed by itself, and the Gulf War, for which the Americans relied on subsidies from its allies, as evidence of how much 'the American economy really has declined' (Yuan, 1994, p. 114). This decline, however, will not immediately threaten America's global political and military power, which remain pre-eminent. 'For a certain period of time', Foreign Minister Qian Qichen told a domestic audience, the USA 'will create much trouble' and 'the major obstacle to our foreign relations will come from the United States' (Qian, 1994, p. 113).

While the possibility of direct US military attacks against Chinese territory is now minimal, the presence of strong US military forces in the Asia-Pacific limits a relatively weak China's strategic options. Most importantly, since 1950, the United States has prevented the PRC from forcibly recapturing Taiwan, a position reaffirmed during the March 1996 Taiwan Straits crisis. The Chinese also see the United States as an 'arrogant' country that 'has always been apt to believe that only the moon shining over the United States is the roundest and tried to reshape the world according to its own values' (Shen, 1992, p. 8). The Americans have tried to force their own legal and political systems upon the rest of the world, including China, violating the norms of sovereignty and tolerance. Most seriously, many Chinese believe the USA is committed to keeping the PRC poor and weak. It is for all these reasons that a March 1997 report prepared for the CCP Central Committee General Office and the State Council General Office concluded that 'China and the United States will eventually go to war' (Bodansky, 1997, p. 12).

Like Japan, America offers China potential benefits as well as potential dangers. Its large and wealthy domestic market voraciously consumes Chinese exports, and it could provide the technology and investment capital China needs to fulfil Deng's goal of achieving the status of a developed nation by the year 2050. On the other hand, denying the Chinese access to this American treasure-house slows China's enrichment, forcing it to find other markets, suppliers and investors that are for various reasons less attractive. Similarly, the United States can use its diplomatic and political power to limit China's other opportunities to benefit from the international economy. Even in a more multipolar world, Washington retains enough influence to significantly punish China, as was seen in the 1989 Tiananmen sanctions, Beijing's unsuccessful bid to host the 2000 Olympics, and American blockage of China's early entry into the World Trade Organization.

China therefore has two main goals *vis-à-vis* the United States. The first is to resist American attempts to employ its unmatched global influence in ways the Chinese perceive as harmful to PRC interests. Specifically, Beijing wants Washington to accept China's emergence as a great political and economic power. This requires US policy to demonstrate proper 'respect' for China and to acquiesce to a diminution of American leadership in the region. Secondly, China works for increased access to US wealth, which is as vast as America's global influence. To access this wealth, the Chinese encourage the investment of US capital in China, strive to obtain favourable terms for the sale of Chinese exports in the American domestic market, and attempt to get the United States to transfer the high-technology goods and expertise the Chinese need.

Sino-US relations were comparatively constructive from the rapprochement in 1972 until 1989. The end of the Cold War, however, also saw the end of the consensus on US China policy among the two major American political parties and between the White House and Congress. There were several reasons for this change in the American approach to relations with Beijing. The collapse of the Soviet threat took away the strategic rationale for the Sino-US alliance. This made it more difficult to continue suppressing the substantial political and economic disagreements between Washington and Beijing. The Tiananmen Massacre, moreover, shocked Americans into the realization that political liberalization would not quickly follow economic liberalization in China, and that the man who shook hands with local crowds and donned a Texas ten-gallon hat during his visit to the United States was capable of brutality against his own young people. Finally, largely as a result of the above developments, the US government's commitment to a one-China policy has become uncertain, a fact not lost upon Beijing.

Consequently, Chinese elites often complain that the central problem in recent Sino-US relations is uncertainty, due to conflicting signals from the Clinton administration, over whether Washington views China as a potential enemy or a potential friend (Barnett *et al.*, 1996, pp. 4–5). Clinton's policy of 'engagement', announced in July 1993 by then-Assistant Secretary of State for East Asian and Pacific Affairs Winston Lord, points up this problem. The US government clearly hoped to make its approach sound non-adversarial (in contrast to a policy based on 'containing' China, which many American commentators have called for). The Chinese, however, have reacted coolly. In their view, America's move to 'engage' them implies that China is a troublemaker or pariah to be brought into line with international standards of behaviour (President Ronald Reagan's policy toward the apartheid government of South Africa was also known as 'constructive engagement'). This is offensive to a nation that sees itself as more principled than the United States.

The Chinese believe they are too often accused of being disruptive or irresponsible for doing some of the same things the other major powers have done, such as testing nuclear weapons, generating massive environmental pollution in the course of economic development, selling arms on the world market, and driving a hard bargain on international trade issues. Many Chinese therefore see engagement as an attempt by the United States to force China to abide by a set of rules the Americans themselves are not willing to follow (Wang, 1996, pp. 151, 152). Moreover, engagement may be a euphemism for containment – as in Foreign Minister Qian Qichen's blunt formulation, 'As they are unable to crush us, they must establish and maintain contacts with us' (Qian, 1994, p. 112). Engagement 'is not a friendly gesture', says PRC foreign affairs analyst Wang Jisi, 'but rather an attempt to pervade China with US economic, political, cultural and ideological influences' (quoted in

Forney and Holloway, 1996, p. 16). Another Chinese analyst writes, 'Engagement and containment are . . . identical in reality. America's concept of the term engagement means to participate in some activity so as to develop it according to one's own will. . . . [We should] not feel completely relaxed when we hear "engagement" or fly into a rage when we hear "containment" ' (Wei Yang, quoted in Cossa, 1996, p. 18).

Through frequent Sino-US political disputes, the PRC has built and maintained an economic pipeline that pumps an increasing flow of American wealth into China. Along the way, Beijing has made significant concessions when necessary, including agreements to protect US intellectual property rights and not to export products made through forced prison labour to the USA (both inadequately enforced, many Americans would contend). Sino-US trade has grown at an average annual rate of about 25 per cent during the 1990s. The USA takes in more Chinese exports and invests more money in China than any other nation. Despite the desire of Chinese authorities to diversify their markets as a means of reducing the PRC's potential vulnerability, China's dependence on trade with the USA is steadily increasing.

Indeed, China has been so successful exporting to the United States that by the mid-1990s, the US trade deficit with China was about $30 billion annually, second only to that with Japan, and was becoming a political problem in its own right. Many Chinese elites believe, like their Japanese counterparts, that their trade surplus with the United States is largely due to their superior competitiveness; the Americans who demand retaliatory measures are merely seeking to punish the Chinese for outplaying the USA by its own rules (Qian, 1994, p. 114).

China won a notable victory in its trade relations with America when Clinton announced in 1994 that he would no longer condition the PRC's Most Favoured Nation (MFN) trading status on human rights progress. The Chinese government had itself entered America's MFN debate, asserting that US exports to the PRC supported 250,000 American jobs – a pitch that seemed to be aimed directly at one of Clinton's chief concerns. During the Asia-Pacific Economic Cooperation (APEC) summit in Seattle in 1993, Jiang held a news conference with the US media during which he implicitly appealed to the American business community to help avoid US economic sanctions toward China. The de-linking of human rights from MFN not only made China's access to American markets more secure, it also affirmed China's growing influence, in this case as an economic power. The PRC has been less successful, of course, in gaining early membership in the World Trade Organization (WTO). The Chinese view the USA as their principal opponent on this issue, although some of America's allies in the developed world also see merit in Washington's case against China; consequently, Beijing's efforts to drive a wedge between the Americans on the one hand and the Europeans and Japanese on the other over this issue have met with little success. In China's view, the US government used Beijing's desire to join the WTO as a founding member to squeeze an excessive list of trade concessions from China, then in the end opposed China's membership anyway.

In general, both the Chinese and US governments have not only driven hard bargains in trade negotiations, but also used political issues to gain leverage in economic matters, and vice-versa.

There are two general views among Chinese elites on how best to deal with the United States. The more moderate of these two views holds that China has more to gain from a harmonious relationship with the Americans and should therefore avoid confrontation whenever possible. Most Chinese strategists prefer US hegemony in the Asia-Pacific over a hypothetical Japanese hegemony (Garrett and Glaser, 1994, pp. 22–3). In an unusually generous assessment, one accomplished Chinese scholar calls the USA 'the most benign [major] power since the Industrial Revolution', and says America's 'international behaviour is similar to [ancient] China's rule of the East' (quoted in Wang, 1996, p. 136). An authoritative 1991 essay by senior PRC foreign affairs analyst He Fang argued that since 'the US really does possess all-round superiority in political, economic and military affairs, and in science and technology', China should attempt to avoid antagonizing the USA for the time being. His analysis was followed by significant PRC concessions to the United States on trade relations, the Missile Technology Control Regime (MTCR), and Chinese prison labour (He Fang quoted in Johnston, 1996, p. 23). China's acquiescence to the American-led offensive against Saddam Hussein was another example of Beijing compromising its preferences for the sake of good relations with the sole superpower. Despite their stated opposition to a military campaign against Iraq, the Chinese abstained rather than vetoing Resolution 678, which authorized the forcible ejection of Iraqi forces from Kuwait.

The other view of how to deal with the United States is the 'hard-line' view, which calls for China to take a confrontational posture with the USA and to demand concessions from the Americans for every instance of Chinese cooperation with Washington's agenda. Hardliners point to several cases during the 1990s that might be interpreted as evidence of America's 'high-handed' unwillingness to treat China as an equal (Chu, 1996a, pp. 3, 4) or, worse, a US commitment to repress the growth of Chinese power and prestige. On top of the economic sanctions that followed the Tiananmen Massacre, the US government added insult to injury by producing annual reports criticizing China's human rights record and by meeting with the Dalai Lama and his representatives. In 1992 the Bush administration approved the sale of 150 F-16 fighter aircraft to Taiwan. In 1993, as the International Olympic Committee (IOC) deliberated over which city should host the 2000 Olympic Games and Beijing was thought to be one of the top contenders, the US Congress passed a resolution calling on the IOC to reject the Chinese bid because of the CCP's human rights violations. The IOC criticized Congress for meddling, but Beijing lost the Games to Sydney. The same year, the US Navy mounted surveillance on an Iran-bound Chinese cargo ship that American intelligence suspected was carrying raw materials for chemical weapons. US and Saudi officials eventually boarded and searched the ship but did not find the suspected chemicals. In October 1994, the PRC scrambled jets to confront US aircraft from the carrier *Kitty Hawk* that were tracking a Chinese submarine in the Yellow Sea. The Chinese government later said it considered the incident an intrusion into Chinese territorial waters and warned that Chinese pilots would shoot if it happened again. At about the same time Chinese negotiators were working desperately to hammer out a deal that would allow China to join the World Trade Organization as a founding member when it went into effect in January 1995, but their effort would fail due to American opposition. Later in 1995 Washington allowed ROC President Lee Denghui to visit the USA, and in 1996 US warships took up positions to defend Taiwan in response to PRC military coercion aimed at discouraging Taiwanese independence.

Both Chinese nationalism and antipathy toward the United States rose in the 1990s, expanding the appeal of the hardline approach. Nearly 90 per cent of respondents to a large poll conducted in China in 1995 identified the USA as the country most unfriendly to the PRC (Si, 1996, p. 13). In 1996 a US-bashing book called *China Can*

Say No became a Chinese bestseller. Even relatively liberal Chinese intellectuals are increasingly irritated by US policies, while ordinary Chinese believe Beijing should take a stronger stand against American pressure. Many Chinese elites privately say they share America's stated goals of more democratization and respect for political and civil liberties in China, but that they resent what they consider overbearing US tactics aimed at achieving these goals. Although Western analysts generally blamed the PRC succession crisis for tough, nationalistic Chinese policies and attitudes in the 1990s, Wang Jianwei says this factor is overstated. Rather, the main reason has been that 'Chinese leaders and their constituencies are fed up with American pressure on one issue after another' (Wang, 1996, p. 141). It is this attitude, evidently, that moved the PRC Politburo Standing Committee to release its 'four nots' policy statement on 1 September 1993: China did not desire confrontation, and would not provoke confrontation, but would not back down if confronted, and was not afraid of sanctions.

Rising support for a tougher approach to the United States is visible in the issue of American troops in Asia. In the past, Chinese officialdom tacitly accepted the US military presence in the Western Pacific as a restraint on Japanese military expansion. The logic here is as follows: Japan has relatively weak armed forces, clearly insufficient to repeat the campaign of conquest seen in the Pacific War, because Japan relies on the United States for defence. American bases in Japan and Korea make the US commitment credible. If US military forces left Asia, Japan would feel insecure. Tokyo would therefore be compelled to take responsibility for its own defence, building stronger armed forces and probably acquiring nuclear weapons as well. So the choice is between a militarily strong and independent Japan or a militarily weak Japan plus 100,000 US soldiers based in the region. For the Chinese, and most other Asians, the latter alternative is greatly preferable. This arrangement is also consistent with the age-old Chinese principle of using barbarians to control other barbarians. In the 1990s, however, as China grew closer to realizing its own potential as leader of the region, many Chinese elites openly questioned the desirability of US military bases in Asia. A semi-official study by PRC academic Wu Xinbo, for example, argued in March 1997 that 'America's military presence in East Asia should have been phased out with the end of the cold war'. There is still a range of opinion on the issue. At one end of this range is the view of a Chinese analyst who says 'people here [in China] want to see the United States reduce its forces in the Asia-Pacific so that if China ends up fighting with Taiwan the US fleet will be far away' (Glaser, 1993, p. 261). At the other end, a senior PRC academic says, 'I think a limited American military presence is not a bad thing, especially when Japan may one day become a threat to Asian nations once again' (McGregor, 1996, p. 6). The Chinese attitude toward forward-based US forces is thus left to fluctuate along with the general state of Sino-U.S. relations. The direction in which Chinese opinion is evolving, however, suggests the PRC will probably be a strong opponent of US Asian bases in the first decade of the twenty-first century.

How do these two views of dealing with the United States interact in Chinese foreign policy? Chinese Taoist philosophy holds that all natural phenomena stem from interaction between two opposite forces, the Yin and the Yang. Among other things, the Yin represents submission, and the Yang aggressiveness. These two forces simultaneously repel and attract each other, keeping nature in proper balance. This provides a useful metaphor for understanding the interaction between the two contending views in the PRC on proper relations with America. In Yin and Yang fashion, each of these views exerts influence on particular events, keeping Chinese initiatives and responses from being either too conciliatory or too provocative. Even after the Lee Denghui visit, for example, the PRC was careful to avoid damaging Sino-US economic ties. Yet there is little doubt that Beijing would sacrifice good relations with Washington rather than acquiesce to what it perceived to be a severe affront to Chinese sovereignty or status.

The Taiwan Issue in Sino-US Relations

In the three important communiqués issued in 1972, 1979 and 1982, the US government stated it 'acknowledges' the PRC's position that 'there is but one China and Taiwan is part of China'. Each US presidential administration since then has publicly reaffirmed that Washington pursues a one-China policy. On several occasions, however, Beijing has charged the United States with violating this policy. The Chinese were deeply embittered by the Taiwan Relations Act of 1979, which they perceived as a virtual restoration of the diplomatic and military relationship with Taiwan that Washington had already agreed to give up as a precondition for upgraded Sino-American relations. After Congress passed the Act, Chinese commentators complained, 'the United States despised China's importance and thought China was not qualified to be treated on an equal basis as an ally' (Xie, 1989, pp. 37–8). The PRC was similarly critical of President George Bush's 1992 decision to supply the ROC with F-16s, which the Chinese charged (with considerable merit) was inconsistent with Washington's commitment to phase out arms supplies to Taiwan.

The United States government had also maintained a policy of forbidding high-ranking ROC officials from entering the United States, lest Beijing complain that Washington was tacitly recognizing Taiwanese statehood. But this policy, too, changed when ROC President Lee Denghui was invited to visit Cornell University in New York state, where he had earned his doctorate degree. Beijing warned there would be serious consequences if the visit transpired. The Clinton administration initially heeded this warning, and Secretary of State Warren Christopher informed Beijing that Lee would not be granted a visa to enter the United States. In Congress, however, there was strong support for Lee's efforts to enlarge Taiwan's 'diplomatic space'. In September 1994, Assistant Secretary of State Winston Lord told the US Senate Foreign Relations Committee it would be a 'mistake' to allow Lee to visit the USA, and that the Clinton administration 'strongly opposes Congressional attempts to legislate visits of top leaders' from the ROC (Barnett *et al.*, 1996, p. 19). Undeterred, Congress passed nearly unanimously (the vote was 360 to 0 in the House and 97 to 1 in the Senate) a non-binding resolution that Lee should be allowed to make a 'private' visit to Cornell. Congress also threatened further steps, such as amending the Taiwan Relations Act in Taipei's favour. Under this pressure Clinton was forced to grant Lee his visa. Washington tried to limit the damage by insisting Lee's 1995 visit was 'unofficial', but Taiwan politicians and journalists celebrated the event as a political coup. The PRC's reaction was strong: Beijing recalled its ambassador from Washington, suspended cross-Straits dialogue, conducted military exercises and missile tests in the Straits area, and arrested former political prisoner Hongda Harry Wu, a naturalized American citizen who had a high profile and many friends in Washington. From China's point of view, Clinton had both broken his promise not to allow Lee's visit and disregarded the general unwritten Sino-US agreement on keeping ROC representatives at arm's length.

Tensions from Lee's visit carried over into what became the third

Taiwan Straits Crisis. In March 1996, Taiwan was scheduled to conduct its first direct presidential election, and Lee was expected to win, allowing him another term to continue his campaign to raise Taiwan's global diplomatic status. In a crude attempt to frighten Taiwanese voters away from supporting Lee, China conducted more missile tests off the Taiwanese coast a few days before the election. The United States responded by sending two aircraft carrier battle groups to the waters off Taiwan (one carrier might have been dismissed as a mere symbolic gesture, but two suggested Washington meant business). Lee was re-elected; indeed, polls showed he got additional votes as a result of China's sabre-rattling.

The recent tensions in the Taiwan Strait renewed interest in the question of what the United States would do in the event of hostilities between the PRC and the ROC. Officially, the US government practises 'strategic ambiguity', a tactic whereby governments attempt to maintain deterrence of the adversary without losing any of their own freedom of manoeuvre. By declining to publicly state how it would respond to a war across the Taiwan Strait, Washington avoids either provoking Beijing and dangerously emboldening Taiwan, or giving Beijing the 'green light' to invade and thereby abandoning Taiwan. Most strategic analysts who have studied US Taiwan policy believe the American military probably would intervene if China launched an unprovoked attack, but probably would not if China invaded in response to a declaration of independence by Taiwan.

US Opposition to PRC Missile Sales

China started selling ballistic missiles to Saudi Arabia, Iran and Iraq in the 1980s. Concerned that these missiles might increase the chances of conflict in the volatile Middle East, Washington convinced China in 1992 to accept the guidelines of the Missile Technology Control Regime (MTCR), which restricts the transfer of missiles capable of delivering a warhead of at least 500 kg over a distance of at least 300 km. China's commitment to observe the MTCR was a bilateral agreement with the USA, not an international agreement, and the Americans rather than a United Nations agency had to take responsibility for verification and enforcement.

Washington soon concluded that China had violated the MTCR by selling technology for the M-11 missile to Pakistan. In 1993 the USA levied punitive sanctions against China, blocking the transfer of $1 billion worth of high-technology. China in turn retaliated by conducting a nuclear test in defiance of a specific appeal by Clinton.

During a visit to Beijing by US Defense Secretary William Perry in October 1994 the Chinese government signed a statement reaffirming its commitment to obey the MTCR, but reports from the American press and CIA in 1995–6 indicated China had again sold M-11s to Pakistan. Throughout this period, the Chinese have either denied that the sales in question took place or maintained that they were not covered by the MTCR.

For the Chinese, the arms transfer problem represents both another instance of US hegemonism and an opportunity to force concessions from the Americans. The Chinese have complained that the MTCR exemplifies the United States' penchant for using its influence to make the rules of the international system suit American interests. Pakistan enjoys a long-standing strategic partnership with Beijing, just as Israel, Japan, South Korea and other states have had access to advanced US weaponry for decades. China happens to have a comparative advantage in the export of ballistic missiles. The United States has decreed these missiles to be destabilizing and has moved to constrain their trafficking. Yet the Americans freely export strike aircraft such as the F-16, which carries a larger payload than the M-11 over a greater distance. On the other hand, while financial profit is probably the prime motivation for sales of sophisticated Chinese weapons, Beijing has also found this a potential bargaining chip with Washington and a means of promoting the PRC's desired image as a great power (Segal, 1994c, pp. 165–6). Restraining the proliferation of weapons of mass destruction remains one of the key strategic areas in which Washington needs China's cooperation (the others are managing political tensions on the Korean Peninsula and in Cambodia; securing the passage of US-sponsored resolutions in the United Nations Security Council, where China holds a permanent seat and veto power; and managing the emergence of China itself as a potentially dominant regional power).

The Challenge of Globalization

Besides its relations with the two former Cold War superpowers, China's chief impact upon global politics is manifested through its relations with international organizations and regimes. Prior to

1970, the PRC's participation in international organizations was close to zero. Since Mao's death, however, Beijing has joined hundreds of international inter-governmental and non-governmental bodies in order to facilitate the drive for economic development (by gaining access to technical assistance and economic aid through various organizations) and to enhance China's international influence and reputation. Beijing has thus accepted limited 'globalism', but as a tool rather than an ideology. 'Globalization' implies the erosion of the political power and authority of national governments; indeed, adherents of globalism, the ideological arm of globalization, would argue that breaking down the sovereignty of states is desirable because states are outmoded institutions that often generate unnecessary conflict and obstruct the efficient movement of goods and services across political boundaries. The CCP leadership, however, views globalism as a means of facilitating the growth of Chinese economic power, political influence, and international prestige. Essentially, globalism is another strategy for protecting China's state sovereignty and other national interests.

The challenge of globalization for Beijing is to utilize the new avenues for pursuing its interests offered by a plethora of new foreign contacts, while at the same time preventing foreign governments, organizations and influences from pulling China in directions the regime considers undesirable. Now a participant in the global system rather than an outsider, China is increasingly compelled to pursue its interests by working within the strictures of international rules and structures. The UN and other non-governmental organizations have changed China, forcing the Chinese to make adjustments to gain the benefits of membership, and even socializing China to certain international norms. Having secured access to global fora, Beijing presents arguments on behalf of its position to an international audience that is usually more demanding than the CCP's domestic audience. On some issues, such as human rights, Beijing has enjoyed considerable success getting foreign governments to accept its point of view. On others, such as arms control, the Chinese have been pushed into compliance, or at least feigned compliance, with international norms. Capitalism is dramatically transforming Chinese society and politics as 'flies' enter through the open door. Yet even as they realize the danger of global influences, Chinese politicians find their freedom of action constrained by expectations of continued rapid growth within China that can only be met by continued economic interdependence.

The United Nations

In the 1960s, the Beijing regime derided the United Nations as a 'dirty international political stock exchange in the grip of a few big powers' (*Renmin Ribao*, 10 January 1965, p. 1) and called for the formation of a 'revolutionary United Nations'. But since regaining its UN seat in October 1971, Beijing has found the organization a useful forum for the peculiarly communist Chinese practice of 'dramatizing [China's] moral righteousness and shaming its principal enemy' (Kim, 1994b, p. 408). Its permanent seat and veto power in the UN Security Council, ironically a legacy of Chiang Kai-shek's alliance with the United States during the Second World War, has given the Chinese disproportionate influence (especially during the 1970s and 1980s, when the PRC had little to recommend it as a strategic player of global significance), which explains why despite growing international support for the proposal to give Germany and Japan permanent seats on the Security Council, Beijing opposes expanding the Council membership, as this would reduce China's share of power, and may ultimately lead to a reconsideration of the veto system.

A fundamental Chinese objection to the United Nations is that it attempts to undermine the sovereignty of individual state governments. As conveyed through Qian Qichen, Beijing's view is that the UN 'should contribute to maintaining the sovereignty of its member states' and that 'The maintenance of state sovereignty serves as the basis for the establishment of the new international order' (Qian, 1992, pp. 4–8). With the end of Cold War bipolarity and US President George Bush's vague yet ominous statements about a 'new world order' Beijing proposed a 'New International Political and Economic Order', an idea attributed to Deng, based on the Five Principles of Peaceful Coexistence with their reaffirmation of sovereignty for individual states (Xi, 1991, p. 7). On the North Korean nuclear weapons issue, for example, Beijing repeatedly objected to the Security Council and the International Atomic Energy Agency (IAEA) even becoming involved, saying this was a dispute that should be worked out between the US and North and South Korean governments. For largely the same reason, Beijing was critical of the general notion of UN peacekeeping until the 1980s. The Chinese attitude changed as they saw support for peacekeeping as a means of promoting China's reputation as a responsible major power with a global vision. This tactic took on even greater importance after the

Tiananmen incident in June 1989. Later that year, the PRC went from a supporter of UN peacekeeping to a participant, sending military observers to the Middle East and civilian monitors to Namibia under UN auspices. During the Gulf War and its lead-up the Chinese voted in favour of 11 Security Council resolutions against Iraq.

Nonetheless, Beijing has consistently opposed sending troops into battle under the UN banner. Qian told the UN in 1994, 'No peace-keeping operations or humanitarian aid programmes should be permitted to interfere in the internal affairs of any country, still less to use force and get embroiled in a conflict between the parties' (Qian, 1995b, p. 5). In its first involvement as a Security Council member with a peacekeeping issue in December 1971, the PRC set a precedent it has frequently followed ever since: the Chinese delega-tion stated that since it was opposed in principle to the intervention of UN troops, China would not participate in the vote (i.e. they would abstain). This tactic allowed the Chinese to claim that they had upheld their principles, while at the same time sparing them the anger and criticism that would have resulted had they used their veto power to block the proposed UN operation; in Samuel Kim's words, abstaining offers 'a face-saving exit' in cases of 'conflicting Realpolitik geopolitical interests and Idealpolitik normative con-cerns for international reputation' (Kim, in Robinson and Sham-baugh, 1994, p. 421; Kim, 1996, p. 23). The one Gulf War Security Council resolution the Chinese did *not* support was Resolution 678, which authorized the forcible ejection of Iraqi forces from Kuwait. Again, however, the Chinese chose to abstain rather than veto the resolution.

Despite its frequent use of international fora to proclaim itself as a champion of the rights of politically weak and economically less developed countries, China has consistently remained aloof from Third World organizations such as the Non-Aligned Movement, the Group of 77 and even the Organization of Petroleum Exporting Countries.

International Arms Control Regimes

Through the Mao era, Beijing's position was that arms control agreements were a tool of the Western governments designed to lock the poorer countries into a state of permanent military inferiority by preventing them from closing the gap with the industrialized great powers. In recent years, however, China has dramatically reversed its policy from aloofness to active involvement, mirroring its shift in orientation toward the world economy. There are several reasons for the change. First, Beijing desires to influence international rule-making and discussions of important issues. Second, the Chinese are concerned with their country's international prestige, which would suffer if Beijing chose to avoid or openly obstruct arms control regimes. Third, some arms control regimes give the Chinese access to advanced technology used in verification operations. Finally, although there is lingering suspicion that arms control is primarily designed to preserve a status quo disadvantageous to China, some Chinese elites have accepted one or both of the premises that arms control can contribute to global peace and can sometimes constrain rivals while allowing the Chinese to 'free-ride'.

Participation in arms control regimes carries serious risks for the Chinese. Their sovereignty may be undermined, with some agreements raising the possibility of foreigners setting limits on Chinese defence capabilities or even asking to inspect some of China's most sensitive installations and research facilities. Limitations on China's nuclear forces, which Beijing sees as crucial to PRC security, are a particularly serious matter.

With all these factors in mind, China's approach toward arms control indicates its underlying objectives to (1) use arms control regimes and discussions to promote China's desired self-image as a visionary and principled great power; (2) secure arms control agreements that provide maximum restrictions on the other major powers; and (3) minimize compromise of Chinese defence capabilities or sovereignty.

Critics charge that the result has been a pattern of Chinese violations of arms control regimes followed by 'denial, double-talk, and responsibility shifting'; when confronted with undisputable evidence that they have broken their agreements, Chinese officials recite their previous commitments to keep the rules (suggesting there is no real problem, since China always keeps its promises), attempt to reinterpret these rules to justify their behaviour, insist that their arms transfers were for legitimate or 'peaceful' purposes, or argue that responsibility for keeping the peace lies with foreign buyers and international monitors rather than with Chinese suppliers (Kim, 1996, p. 29).

Officially, of course, China takes a principled stand on nuclear arms control: 'China has always stood for the complete prohibition and thorough destruction of all weapons of mass destruction' and for 'ushering in a nuclear-weapon-free world' (Qian, 1995b, p. 6). Beijing has also pledged never to use nuclear weapons first in any conflict ('no first use', or NFU) or to use nuclear weapons against a non-nuclear weapons state (commonly known as a 'negative security assurance', or NSA), and regularly challenges the other nuclear powers to make the same commitments. Unofficially, some Chinese strategists believe that 'the complete destruction of nuclear weapons is already impossible' (Zhang, 1987, p. 52) and that China's nuclear NFU promise puts the PRC at a strategic disadvantage (Johnston, 1995/96, p. 21).

During the Cold War, the stockpiles of nuclear warheads amassed by the superpowers dwarfed China's, allowing the Chinese to argue that the onus of nuclear disarmanent was on the Americans and the Russians. In 1982, Chinese Foreign Minister Huang Hua committed China to begin reducing its own nuclear weapons after the super-powers had cut their arsenals 'by 50 per cent'. But after a 50 per cent reduction became the basis for US–Soviet negotiations in 1986, Chinese spokesmen changed their prerequisite to more vague wording such as 'substantial reductions' or 'drastic cuts' (*Beijing Review*, 21 June 1982, pp. 15–17, and 21 April 1986, pp. 14–15; *Heping*, December 1992, pp. 2–5; Malik, 1995b, pp. 5–7). Even the cuts the Americans and Russians are carrying out under the Strategic Arms Reduction Treaty, which will shrink the two countries' arsenals to about a quarter of previous levels, have not elicited a change in Beijing's position.

After years of criticizing the first (1968) Nuclear Nonproliferation Treaty (NPT), which they refused to sign, the Chinese acceded to the renewed NPT in March 1992, and despite expressing some reservations, submitted to the international consensus in favour of an indefinite extension of the NPT in 1995. China has also been a member of the International Atomic Energy Agency (IAEA), which monitors compliance with nuclear nonproliferation guidelines, since 1984. Yet China is often accused of transferring nuclear- weapons-related technology, often to states in sensitive regions such as the Middle East, in violation of Chinese commitments. A recent incident was typical of many in the last decade: the US government accused China of selling to Pakistan 5,000 ring magnets, which are components in the equipment used to produce weapons-grade enriched uranium. Qian Qichen told US Secretary of State Warren Christopher in May 1996 that the Chinese government was unaware of the alleged sale, and that in any case this would not happen in the future (Wallerstein, 1996, p. 64). Beijing officially acknowledges that it has had cooperative nuclear technology agreements with over 40 countries since the 1980s (Malik, 1995b), contributing to the belief of many analysts that China has been the single greatest source of illegal nuclear technology transfers worldwide. In their defence, the Chinese complain that Washington is quick to accuse China of nuclear proliferation while the Americans wink at the transgressions of US allies.

Of the 1963 Partial Test Ban Treaty signed by the USA and USSR, Beijing said, 'The central purpose of this treaty is . . . to prevent all the threatened peace-loving countries, including China, from increasing their defence capability, so that the United States may be more unbridled in threatening and blackmailing these countries'. Thirty years later, feeling the sting of international opprobrium over continued Chinese testing despite a 1992 commitment by the USA and Russia to halt all types of nuclear tests (including underground tests, which were not forbidden by the 1963 treaty), Beijing agreed to accede to a Comprehensive Test Ban Treaty (CTBT) by the end of 1996, although it would continue testing until then. Indeed, the Chinese drew worldwide condemnation for conducting a test in May 1995 only three days after the conclusion of the conference on extending the Nuclear Nonproliferation Treaty (NPT), during which Beijing had joined the other four declared nuclear powers in promising to exercise 'utmost restraint' in nuclear testing.

As the CTBT deadline drew near, The Chinese stalled negotiations on the formulation of the treaty by introducing new preconditions that were certain to be rejected by some of the other parties, including requiring all nuclear weapons states to take a NFU pledge and allowing them to continuing to conduct 'nuclear explosions for peaceful purposes' (Sha, 1995, p. 20). At one point the Chinese even raised the possibility of an asteroid heading for a collision with earth to justify the need for continuing 'peaceful' nuclear tests (Tyler, 1996, p. 4). The Chinese clearly intended to delay the treaty until they completed their latest round of tests, which Beijing considered essential to its nuclear modernization programme. In particular, Chinese technicians are striving to perfect smaller, more powerful warheads that are suitable for MIRVs. Many Chinese officials and strategists also seem to believe less strongly than their Western counterparts that a halt to testing is an important step toward denuclearization (Garrett and Glaser, 1995/96, p. 54). Generally speaking, China's involvement with the CTBT has been a case of acquiescence to foreign pressure.

China acceded to the Biological Weapons Convention (BWC) in 1984, but has not joined the Australia Group, the organization designed to control the export of chemical weapons technology and precursors. US officials have accused the Chinese government of frequently violating the BWC (which Beijing denies) and of working behind the scenes to crush initiatives to add new provisions for on-site inspections and disclosures of past biological-warfare-related exports (Frieman, 1996, p. 19). Beijing signed the Chemical Weapons Convention in 1993, but has not yet ratified it (nor has the United States). As with nuclear weapons, Beijing's official stand is that all countries should eliminate chemical weapons, but that the major military powers such as the United States should take the lead.

Human Rights

After joining the United Nations in 1971, the PRC evidenced an ambivalent attitude towards international efforts to safeguard human rights. Beijing supported UN resolutions condemning racial and gender-based discrimination, and went along with sanctions against South Africa. But the Chinese did not support resolutions criticizing human rights abuses in Libya, Cuba, El Salvador, and Chile. China evidently wanted to maintain a minimally controversial middle course: neither drawing attention to itself as an opponent of the campaign to promote human rights, nor committing itself to a position that would increase its vulnerability to outside criticism of its own domestic practices (Kent, 1993, p. 101). Generally, public statements by the Chinese government on human rights vigorously condemned the Soviet Union and the former colonial 'imperialist' powers and emphasized the importance of socio-economic rights for the Third World (China was much less vocal about civil and political rights), closely paralleling China's political agenda of the time.

Later, during the 1980s, China became more involved in UN committees and conventions on human rights, signalling a greater willingness to accept the idea of a universal minimum standard of human rights. At the same time, however, the Chinese maintained the principle of non-interference in the domestic affairs of sovereign states. China's position has been that international law has jurisdiction over states, but not over individuals within those states; individuals are subject only to the laws of the land in which they reside. Therefore, China maintains, international organizations have no authority to regulate or enforce human rights within sovereign states. This view implicitly rejects the concept of a minimum international standard of human rights protection, which commands a consensus within the UN.

As in other aspects of its international involvement, Beijing has sought to preserve its sovereignty while maintaining the image of a responsible nation that supports internationally accepted norms. These twin goals, however, invariably come into conflict. Although it has signed some important UN human rights initiatives, China has declined to endorse others, including the International Covenant on Civil and Political Rights and the International Covenant on Economic, Social and Cultural Rights. Nevertheless, as a UN member, China is subject to monitoring by the UN's Commission on Human Rights. This body's investigative subcommittee has twice recommended resolutions condemning China – over Tiananmen in 1990, and over Tibet in 1991. On both occasions, however, China managed to block the passage of these resolutions by mustering support from like-minded states such as Iraq, Iran, Libya, Cuba and Pakistan. Beijing has frequently impeded investigation of its human rights practices by foreign journalists and non-governmental human rights organizations such as Asia Watch, Amnesty International and the Red Cross.

The end of the Cold War increased China's susceptibility to American criticism over human rights. During the latter stage of the US–Soviet confrontation, when China was a *de facto* American ally, the US camp was willing to overlook a few warts to preserve this delicate but important strategic relationship. But with the diminution of the Soviet/Russian threat, the 'friendly dictators' lost their special status. While the principal political fault-line during the Cold War was that between pro-Soviet and pro-US (whether democratic or despotic) states, the main dichotomy in the 'New World Order' was the liberal versus the authoritarian countries – hence Washington's post-Cold War conflicts with Iraq, North Korea, Cuba, the Cedras junta in Haiti, etc. Recast as one of the villains of international politics, China became fair game for critics of human rights abuses, especially given Beijing's new economic openness, its obvious desire for recognition as an honourable member of the international community, and its aspirations to join the WTO.

From the standpoint of many Chinese elites, the human rights issue has become the spearhead of America's peaceful evolution strategy. This conclusion is supported by the fact that both private US-associated organizations, and the US government publish annual reports describing and condemning Chinese human rights performance. For the CCP, the real issue is the survival of Party rule. 'If we lose the battle on human rights', Deng said in 1992, 'everything will be meaningless to us. . . . [T]he human rights issue, in substance, is the crux of the struggle between the world's two social systems' (*Tang Tai*, 1992, p. 16). The real goal of American and other critics of the Chinese government 'is not to protect human rights, but to force China to be "Westernized" and "decentralized"' Human rights provides the 'pretext' for foreign enemies to 'meddle in the internal affairs of other countries' and weaken states such as China that might obstruct America's global domination project (*Straits Times*, 1994, p. 1). Seen in this light, the strength and hostility of China's reaction to international human rights pressure is not surprising.

After years of answering criticisms over Tibet, Tiananmen, and a general lack of protection for political and civil rights throughout the PRC, the Chinese government has a well-developed position on human rights that its official and unofficial spokespeople now aggressively market internationally. The basic points are as follows:

1. Human rights are an internal affair. Criticism of another country's domestic policies is unjustified interference. We don't tell you how to handle your dissidents; please show us the same courtesy.

2. It is hypocritical of the United States to criticize China over human rights given America's failure to protect so many of its own citizens from crime, poverty and racial injustice. (Here the Chinese apparently violate point no. 1, but only in self-defence: Washington struck first, and for several years the Chinese held back from criticizing America by name.)

3. Despite challenging circumstances, China has made great strides in extending many human rights, including basic socio-economic considerations such as access to food, education and employment, while under CCP rule. These kinds of rights are at least as important as the political rights Americans emphasize. The good results, demonstrable in the decline of undernourishment and

illiteracy and the increase in the average Chinese life-span, prove the CCP's methods are correct. In a recent public relations tour of Europe, Premier Li Peng said, 'If some Western politician claims he is in a position to use the normal Western methods to feed and clothe 1.2 billion Chinese, we would be happily prepared to elect him as the president of China' (*Straits Times*, 1994, p. 1).

4. China has no political prisoners. People are imprisoned in China only for criminal acts any reasonable government would consider dangerous to public safety and order.

5. Economic relations between China and other countries should not be linked to the human rights issue.

The 1989 Tiananmen Massacre made Chinese human rights a long-term global political issue. Many foreign observers understood the event as a sclerotic and tyrannical government's slaughter of college students peacefully expressing their discontent with monopoly rule by the Communist Party. The Chinese government vigorously counter-attacked overseas criticism. In Beijing's official version of the event, trouble-makers hoping to overthrow the government and profit from the ensuing disorder, many of them receiving funds and encouragement from the United States, used the student demonstration as the springboard for a violent attempted insurrection, and the real victims were the brave PLA soldiers killed by mobs of hooligans. Chinese officials argued that foreigners, principally the Americans, were once again guilty of interfering in other countries' domestic affairs, that they hoped to promote chaos in China, and that America's professed concern with human rights was a smokescreen. 'The US berates us for suppressing students', said Deng. 'But when they handled domestic student unrest and turmoil, didn't they send out police and troops to arrest people and cause bloodshed?' (*Beijing Review*, 1989, p. 17).

The G-7 countries punished the Chinese with economic sanctions. Within Washington, however, there was a debate over how severely to retaliate, with the business community and some Asia hands arguing that economic interchange was an effective means of promoting positive change in China and that economic sanctions would most severely hurt the entrepreneurial class that America hoped to develop as a force for Chinese political liberalization. Clinton dabbled with a tougher line on Chinese human rights early in his presidency, announcing that China's Most Favoured Nation (MFN) trading status with the USA, reviewed annually, would be partly conditioned upon Beijing's human rights progress. Eventually, however, Clinton too accepted the logic of constructive engagement. When China's MFN status came up for review in 1994, there was little support elsewhere in Asia for American human rights activism. Many Asians, especially in Southeast Asia, openly denounced Washington's 'arrogance' in attempting to force its own values upon such a proud, venerable civilization as China. They argued further that America's economic coercion of China would do little if anything to help political prisoners in China, while the economic and political costs to the entire region would be great: all of Asia would suffer indirect financial losses, and the Chinese government would take a more angry and vengeful view of the West, with ominous future consequences.

Most important, perhaps, was the warning by US businesspeople that denying MFN to China would seriously undermine the economic recovery Clinton had said was his top priority. Donald Anderson, president of the United States–China Business Council, trotted out alarming figures in his testimony before Congress. '[W]ithdrawing or conditioning MFN would be a recipe for disaster for US workers, for US consumers and employers', he said, 'and it could lead to the loss of over 150,000 [US] jobs, $8 billion in lost exports, and at least $14 billion in higher import prices for American consumers' (Committee on Foreign Affairs, 1993, p. 10). US business interests noted further that important ally-competitors such as Germany and Japan would trade with China without regard for issues such as prison labour or the torture of dissidents. Significantly, many Chinese human rights activists, including Tiananmen ringleader Wang Dan, also supported a renewal of MFN status, saying economic liberalization would help hasten democratization. Clinton reversed his China policy, not only granting MFN, but removing human rights improvements as a consideration for renewal of MFN for China in the future.

Nevertheless, human rights pressure has coaxed Beijing into making certain significant concessions. On several occasions the Chinese government freed groups of political prisoners, totalling several hundred, prior to the US government's annual MFN decisions. Beijing also signed agreements with Washington in 1992 and 1994 not to export products made with prison labour to the USA, although Chinese compliance has been problematic.

Even with economic pragmatism rather than moral idealism in command, however, China's human rights performance will not soon disappear as an international political issue. Increasing numbers of foreign traders recognize that human rights violations are another manifestation of one of the basic difficulties of doing business in China: absence of the rule of law (Friedman, 1995, p. 4). Some human rights abuses themselves also have an economic dimension. For example, the employers of forced labourers, of which there are untold thousands in PRC prisons and labour camps, need only provide workers with enough food, shelter, and medical care to remain productive. By contrast, in the capitalist democracies, safety standards are relatively high; wages must be lucrative enough to attract workers who are free to choose other jobs; labourers can join independent organizations and bargain collectively for better pay and benefits; and many employers must provide insurance and pensions for their employees. The result is that Chinese export industries enjoy lower overhead costs, giving them a competitive advantage in the world market. As China seeks even greater integration into the liberal international economic regime, including membership in the World Trade Organization, it faces complaints that its trading partners are forced to compete with state-sponsored 'slave labour'. Finally, periodic, high-profile Chinese retribution against dissidents, such as the detention of Harry Wu, a former PRC political prisoner turned human rights activist, and the imprisonment of well-known dissidents Wang Dan and Wei Jingsheng, inevitably mobilize political outrage among some foreign polities, particularly the democracies, as not everyone fully accepts the logic of constructive engagement.

If China's human rights record is less a concern in its immediate region, a variety of other issues pose equally complicated challenges in China's relations with its Asian neighbours.

8
Regional Relationships

The PRC has no apparent 'Asia policy'. Chinese policy toward the region is a collection of distinct bilateral relationships with a highly diverse group of countries. In each case, there are incentives for cooperation, such as economic opportunities and a common interest in resisting US pressure, as well as divisive issues such as territorial disputes and security fears. In some aspects of its relations within the region, China is a supporter of the status quo; in other aspects, a challenger.

Sino-Japanese Relations

China's relationship with Japan is itself ambivalent. As Samuel S. Kim observes (Kim, 1995, p. 471), China is simultaneously attracted to and revolted by the Japanese: on the one hand, Japan represents a successful economic model and a source of capital, technology and expertise for China's own development; on the other hand, Japan was China's most cruel and destructive enemy this century, and a Japanese relapse into a militaristic and imperialistic foreign policy cannot be ruled out. While some Chinese analysts believe Japan is already scheming to take over the role of Asian hegemon from a declining United States (Glaser, 1993, pp. 257–8), others are hopeful that the logic of mutual economic interest will ensure that Japan remains content to be 'civilian' power and an engine of regional economic growth – or, as Chinese scholar Lu Zhongwei puts it, 'The international community hopes that . . . a kind and beautiful bride will unveil herself and bring peace rather than a calamity to Asia and the World' (Lu, 1995, p. 12). (Japan as the 'bride'; China as the groom?) Fears of a potential Japanese military threat are tempered by the realization that Japan has important structural weaknesses and that in the near future both domestic and international political circumstances preclude any possibility of Tokyo pursuing its goals through military coercion of its neighbours. Lu sees in Japan an outbreak of ' "the disease of the developed countries" with symptoms like a bloated bureaucracy; an ever-mounting social welfare bill; an overcommitted financing system and a dwindling productivity. Admittedly, the case of Japan pales before what we see in the Western countries, yet it is still a serious hidden danger in the nation's vitals' (Lu, 1995, p. 4).

Chinese relations with Japan therefore reflect the tension between two phenomena: growing Chinese economic interdependence with Japan and Beijing's fear of Japan as a potential adversary. The latter stems not only from historical animosity, but also from the present distribution of power, with China and Japan in contention for the role of the region's dominant country.

The main goals of the PRC's Japan policy are to: prevent a resurgence of the Japanese armed forces that would give Japan the capability to harm, challenge or coerce China by military means; discourage Tokyo from aspiring to leadership of the region or taking on a greater global or regional political role; acquire as much investment, economic assistance and advanced technology from the Japanese as possible; and get Tokyo to follow a one-China policy, minimizing Japanese diplomatic contact with Taipei.

The common ground for Sino-Japanese cooperation is predominantly in the economic rather than the political realm. The political aspects of the Sino-Japanese relationship serve mainly to complicate their economic cooperation. These political problems include the unhealed wounds of Japan's invasion and occupation of China during the Pacific War; Japanese discomfort with China's growing political and military power; the aspiration of both nations to regional and global leadership; and the unresolved status of Taiwan. Tokyo and Beijing might be able to combine their efforts in resistance to aggressive trade policies by the USA aimed at penetrating Asian markets, and there is a hypothetical possibility of future Sino-Japanese security collaboration against a resurgent Russia. In the main, however, political cooperation between China and Japan is weak. Although the PRC might wish for it (one PRC commentator writes that post-Cold War 'contradictions between Japan and the US have grown in intensity' and that 'Japan perceives Sino-Japanese relations as a "trump card" to counter US pressure' [*Beijing Review*, 1992c, p. 21]), there is no 'triangular' relationship here comparable to the USA–USSR–China relationship during the latter part of the Cold War. Rather, when America has good relations with China, usually Japan does as well (EAAU, 1996, p. 16).

Nevertheless, Japan has sometimes acted as a moderating influence on American policies toward China, encouraging Washington to avoid or limit confrontation. Tokyo's post-Tiananmen China policy provides a suitable illustration. In response to Tiananmen, Tokyo suspended a loan package due to begin in April 1990. But the eventual result was merely a three-month delay, as the programme recommenced in July. Japan was the first of the G-7 countries to lift economic sanctions against China, and Tokyo also encouraged its allies to quickly resume normal trade and political relations with China. Japanese Prime Minister Kaifu Toshiki's visit to China in 1991 was the first by a head of state or government of one of the industrialized countries since Tiananmen. While this brought criticism of Japan from the West, Beijing appreciated Japanese efforts to sustain the relationship, and Japanese relations with Beijing were exceptionally good from 1991 through to 1994. (Relations worsened again in 1995, mainly over Japan's protest, accompanied by a partial suspension of economic aid, of PRC nuclear testing; and public support of many Japanese politicians for greater political recognition of Taiwan.)

Sino-Japanese Economic Relations

In line with Neoliberal theory, China and Japan have maintained strong economic links into the post-Cold War era despite the potential political and military threat the two countries pose to each other. After several political disputes destroyed Sino-Japanese trade relations in the 1950s, Beijing sought to rebuild them in the 1960s as part of a strategy of diversifying China's foreign economic links. The Long Term Trade Agreement (1978) ushered in a series of contracts for China's purchase (partly through barter, using Chinese oil and coal in lieu of cash) of Japanese equipment and technology. Sino-Japanese economic interdependence grew rapidly in the mid-1990s. In terms of bilateral economic relationships, the China–Japan partnership is the presently the world's fourth largest (USA–Canada is first, USA–Japan second). If present trends continue, China–Japan trade will be as large in about the year 2015 as USA–Japan trade is today (EAAU, 1996, pp. 25, 36). The favourable Sino-

Japanese economic match creates an irresistible attraction: China desperately needs high-technology equipment and expertise but enjoys vast territory and resources and cheap labour; Japan lacks the hinterland to produce sufficient food, energy and raw materials to meet its needs, but is bursting with wealth, skills and high technology. Moreover, the complementarity of China–Japan trade is increasing. Initially, China traded primary goods for Japanese manufactures and high-tech products. By the early 1990s, however, Chinese exports to Japan were dominated by products with value added by Chinese labour or capital. To put the concept in more concrete terms, the Japanese are now buying Chinese VCRs and computer components in addition to Chinese oil, coal and agricultural products. Many observers believe this economic interdependence is the best hope for precluding serious future Sino-Japanese conflict.

In Neorealist fashion, however, the relative gains problem often introduces severe tensions into the relationship. From the Chinese point of view, Japan often seems an arrogant, unfair and unprincipled trading partner with no commitment to the official PRC guideline of 'equal benefit' in economic relations. The Japanese appear happy to sell high-end consumer goods in China, but are uninterested in or even opposed to assisting China's economic development. Japan's trade surplus with China was a major point of Chinese dissatisfaction until it was alleviated in the early 1990s, and the Chinese still demand more importation of Chinese goods, more investment, more economic assistance and more technology transfer from Japan. Japanese loans to China under Tokyo's overseas direct assistance (ODA) programme reached nearly $2 billion per year in the late 1990s. Nevertheless, the Chinese have often suggested that Japan's wartime misbehaviour obligates Tokyo to make a more generous ODA contribution, especially since the PRC did not require Japan to pay war reparations under the terms of the 1972 agreement that normalized Sino-Japanese relations. Deng said in 1987, for example, 'Japan is indebted to China more than any other nation in the world. At the time of diplomatic normalization, we did not raise any demand for war reparations. From the viewpoint of Asian people, Japan should make a much greater contribution in order to assist China's development' (quoted in Ijiri, 1990, p. 642).

In fairness to the Japanese, China has not always maintained an attractive environment for Japanese investors. In 1981, for example,

Beijing cancelled its order for a Japanese plant to be constructed at the huge Baoshan steelworks, apparently due to a budget shortfall. This and other incidents created strong doubts among the Japanese business community about the desirability of dealing with China, limiting in turn the level of Japanese investment. At the end of the decade of the 1980s, China's wealthy neighbour had supplied only 8 per cent of all the direct foreign investment in China (Ono, 1992, p. 17). (Japanese investment greatly increased, however, in the 1990s.) In response, many Chinese argued that Japan was once again economically exploiting China as it did during the Century of Shame; indeed, this was a major cause of large anti-Japanese riots in China during the 1980s.

Japan as a Potential Military Threat

Chinese strategists expect Japan to be China's most threatening potential adversary within a decade or two after the turn of the century (Whiting, 1995a, p. 9). Most Chinese elites seem convinced Japan is in the midst of a gradual restoration of its military power. Despite the fact that according to its postwar constitution Japan 'renounce[s] . . . the threat of use of force' and commits that 'land, sea and air forces as well as other war potential will never be maintained', the Chinese have seen Tokyo breach its previous guideline not to spend more than 1 per cent of GNP on defence; accept the responsibility, urged on Japan by Washington, to provide surveillance and defence of the waters within a radius of 1,000 nautical miles from Tokyo (encompassing most of the East China Sea, over which the PLA Navy also claims jurisdiction); send Japanese soldiers abroad as part of United Nations peacekeeping operations; discuss joint military exercises with several other Asia-Pacific states (excluding China); and build up the most capable navy of any Asian country. While fielding only a limited number of troops in uniform and weapons systems, Japan continues to improve the technological and economic base from which it could generate a formidable military machine on short notice. Japan's lead over China in hi-tech research and development currently seems insurmountable, a considerable worry in the age of information warfare.

Japan is presently an 'unbalanced' country – very strong economically, but relatively weak militarily and politically – that most Chinese analysts expect will seek to become a 'normal' country by increasing its international political power and, in turn, its military capabilities. Chinese analysts frequently suggest Japan is drifting toward a repeat of the Pacific War (for example, Da, 1995, p. 5). If it is sometimes difficult to distinguish real from manufactured fears, most Chinese strategists would agree at minimum that Japan is the PRC's most serious potential long-term adversary (Jencks, 1994, p. 67).

While many Chinese are willing to accept Japan's alliance with the USA as a necessary evil, they object to what they perceive as US efforts to push Japan into a greater military and political role in the region. Throughout the Cold War, many PRC analysts believed postwar Japan continued to harbour plans to establish a sphere of influence in East Asia. The first steps of this suspected plan were Japanese economic penetration of South Korea, which was allegedly the opening move in a process that would lead to political control over the Korean peninsula, and the cultivation of economic and cultural ties with Taiwan to pull the ROC away from reunification with China and into an alliance with Japan. In a reversal from the Pacific War era, the United States and Japan had formed an 'evil alliance', giving Tokyo the assistance of the world's strongest power in achieving its objectives (Whiting, 1975a, p. 36).

This background inevitably colours Chinese interpretations of the alliance today. Non-Chinese analysts typically saw the revision of the US–Japan security treaty in April 1996 as a guarantee that Japan would remain a second-rate political and military power into the foreseeable future, but Chinese commentators interpreted the treaty's modest expansion of Japan's responsibilities as another step in Tokyo's quest for mastery over Asia: America and Japan were 'working hand-in-hand to dominate the Asia-Pacific region', and 'there is no doubt that the aim [of the revised treaty] is to keep a close watch on China' (Zhang, 1996, pp. 3-4; Yu, 1996, pp. 4-5; Yang, 1996). A May 1997 article in an official PRC newspaper described the revised US-Japan agreement and the US-Australia alliance as 'two pincers . . . intended to pin down China'.

Despite its remilitarization, Japan's current military capabilities do not allow for power projection beyond the defence of sealanes in the waters surrounding the Japanese home islands. Japan's defence budget of $47 billion (1997) is substantial, but the high yen and low dollar inflate the figure's apparent value, and over half of this funding goes toward salaries, food, and maintaining American bases in Japan. Chinese fears, therefore, seem to exceed Japanese capabilities. An obvious reason is the psychological baggage from the

Pacific War the Chinese still carry – some 20 million Chinese died in the war, according to Beijing. Some Chinese analysts also believe Japan's ethnic and cultural homogeneity makes Japan more likely than a hetergenous country (such as the USA) to generate the kind of nationalism that might lead to jingoism (author's interviews in Beijing, October 1995). Less obvious, but also important, is Chinese exploitation of history to gain advantages in its relations with Japan.

In the early 1990s, the Japanese emperor, prime ministers and other high officials offered direct apologies to China for Japan's wartime aggression. Emperor Akihito visited China in 1992, the first time in history any Japanese emperor had set foot in the Middle Kingdom. From the Chinese standpoint, however, these gestures were cancelled out by the periodic statements from right-wing Japanese public figures defending Tokyo's Pacific War record. In a typical incident, Japanese Minister of Justice Shigeto Nagano said publicly in 1994 that he believed the Nanjing Massacre was a 'fabrication'. (The Japanese right wing excepted, most historians accept that after invading Japanese troops captured the Chinese city of Nanjing in 1937, they went on a rampage of rape, pillage and murder among its civilian population, killing 200,000 according to Chinese sources.) The intense reaction from China and Korea that followed forced him to resign. Japanese Prime Minister Yasuhiro Nakasone also visited the Yasakuni Shrine, built to honour Japanese soldiers killed in war, in 1985, which the Chinese criticized as legitimizing Japanese aggression and atrocities. Visits to the Yasakuni Shrine by Japanese officials remain a touchy issue; Prime Minister Ryutaro Hashimoto's visit on the anniversary of his soldier cousin's death in July 1996 may have contributed to the latest flare-up of the Diaoyudao Islands controversy (see below).

Along with Korea, China has been a severe critic of Japanese attempts to 'sanitize' the Pacific War: teaching Japanese schoolchildren a version of history that obscures their former government's aggression and atrocities. Efforts by the Japanese Ministry of Education to amend textbooks along these lines came to light in 1982 and 1986, drawing strident charges from China that Tokyo still harboured militarism. Ironically, the Beijing regime has evidently been conducting some sanitization of its own. The mid-1995 survey of the foreign affairs views of Chinese young adults (referred to in Chapter 1) conducted by the *China Youth Daily* produced results some outsiders might find startling. Over three-quarters of the respondents said the leadership of the Chinese Communist Party was the main reason for China's victory over Japan during the Pacific War, while only 2.8 per cent thought Japan was beaten by 'international support'. (The dominant interpretation in the West is that CCP and Guomindang forces were capable of little more than harassing the invading Japanese forces, which, while unable to subdue all of China, controlled the key cities in the east. Japanese forces were ejected from China only after the American campaign in the Northwest Pacific and the entry of Soviet forces into Manchuria forced Tokyo to surrender and yield up its remaining conquests.) The respondents, which numbered 100,000, were not ignorant peasants; half had some university-level education, and a quarter were CCP members (Xinhua News Agency report, 24 July 1995). They represented, in other words, a large chunk of the PRC's future leadership.

While Chinese fears of a resurgence of Japanese militarism are understandable, Beijing clearly plays the 'guilt card' as a political tactic in its relations with Tokyo. China's criticism of Japanese 'militarism' or failure to atone for past sins tends to grow more intense when Beijing is unhappy with other, often unrelated, Japanese policies (EAAU, 1996, p. 12). Chinese authorities adjust the level of such criticism through their control of content in the Chinese press and by alternatively promoting or disallowing public anti-Japanese demonstrations. For instance, prior to Prime Minister's Morihiro Hosokawa's visit to China in March 1994, during which the Chinese planned to press for more Japanese loans and investment, Chinese police rounded up and detained hundreds of elderly Chinese who were peacefully protesting against Japan's wartime atrocities and demanding compensation from Tokyo (Kim, 1994d, p. 15).

Piracy

China, of course, also poses actual and potential security challenges to Japan. Piracy is perhaps the most immediate problem. Incidents of Japanese shipping being robbed and/or fired upon rose through the 1990s. While the identity of the perpetrators is not always clear, the evidence suggests that most have been based in the People's Republic. According to the International Maritime Bureau in London, the majority of the world's incidents of piracy occur in the South China Sea; the bulk of these are carried out by Chinese using government-issued equipment (Kyodo news report, Tokyo,

19 October 1993; Whiting, 1995a, p. 20). PLA vessels, uniforms and weapons figure prominently in the reports of these incidents. These PLA-associated pirates may be carrying out a subtle campaign of asserting PRC sovereignty over the area under high-level orders, while Beijing maintains plausible deniability. The more likely explanation, however, is that these are rogue activities, a by-product of an increased Chinese naval presence combined with uncontrolled PLA entrepreneurism. Japan has frequently lodged official complaints about these attacks. In some cases, Beijing has apologized and blamed the incidents on mistaken or overzealous efforts to suppress smuggling, an explanation Japanese authorities find not entirely convincing. Whatever the cause, Chinese attacks on merchant shipping are a disturbing phenomenon, especially given Japan's economic dependence on sea-borne trade, the growing strength of the PLA Navy, and the lack of cooperation or coordination among the navies of the Northeast Asian states.

Japan and Taiwan

Although Tokyo officially supports the one-China principle, Beijing continues to find reasons for accusing the Japanese of supporting Taiwanese independence. One such case followed Japan's invitation to ROC President Lee Denghui to attend the 1994 Asian Games in Hiroshima. The Japanese response to Beijing's knee-jerk protest was stiffer than the complete backdown many observers expected. Tokyo 'encouraged' Lee not to attend the Games, but instead hosted Taiwan's Vice-Premier Hsu Li-teh. Hsu also heads the organizing committee for the 2002 Asian Games, which Taiwan is scheduled to host, allowing Japan to argue that Hsu was invited as a sporting figure rather than a political official. After Lee's Cornell visit, many Japanese politicians also demanded, ultimately unsuccessfully, that he be allowed to visit his undergraduate alma mater Kyoto University as well.

As a country that relies on international commerce for its very survival, Japan was particularly alarmed by the interruption of sea and air traffic around Taiwan caused by PRC military exercises in 1995–6. The Japanese Foreign Ministry offered more public support than most other governments in the region for the US response to the PLA missile tests and war games in March 1996, saying it considered the dispatch of American warships an expression of Washington's 'strong interest in peace and security'.

In some respects, the PRC authorities consider Japan's relationship with Taiwan more threatening than America's. As with the United States, Taiwan has strong economic links with Japan and many friends in the Japanese government. But in addition to this, many native Taiwanese politicians have pointedly asserted that they feel stronger cultural and historical bonds with Japan, which controlled Taiwan from 1895 to 1945, than with mainland China. Sentiment among Taiwanese, especially the older generation, toward Japan is more positive than in most other parts of Japan's former imperial empire. ROC President Lee, who studied in Japan and speaks Japanese fluently, epitomizes his country's historical ties with Japan, which provides PRC propagandists with a ready explanation for the Lee government's alleged lack of Chinese patriotism.

The Diaoyudao (Senkaku) Islands Dispute

The Diaoyudao (Chinese) or Senkaku (Japanese) Islands are a group of five small uninhabited islands (the largest is about three square miles) and three rocks (i.e., outcroppings without flora or fauna) about 100 miles northeast of Taiwan. (Since this book focuses on China rather than Japan, I will hereafter refer to the islands as the Diaoyudao.) Japan currently controls them, but the PRC and Taiwan also claim ownership. China's claim is based on what the Chinese describe as a long history of unchallenged control. Chinese authorities named the islands Diaoyudao ('Fishing Islands') in the fifteenth century. Pre-modern Chinese historical and maritime records refer to the islands as a Chinese possession. The famous Qing Dynasty Empress Dowager, Ci Xi, reportedly gave three of the islands to a Chinese official so he could supply his pharmacies with Daioyudao herbs (Park, 1972, p. 47).

Although the Japanese would later call the islands part of the nearby Ryukyu chain, the Ryukyu kingdom of antiquity recognized the Diaoyudao as Chinese territory. Tokyo says it effectively inherited the islands when it annexed the principal Ryukyu island of Okinawa in 1879. China says the Japanese government tacitly accepted Chinese ownership until 1895, when Japan formally took over the islands, along with Taiwan, as part of the Treaty of Shimonoseki settlement of the Sino-Japanese War. Japan did not change the islands' Chinese names until 1900, when an Okinawan schoolteacher came up with the collective name Senkaku ('Pointed House') Islands. Japanese names for each individual island did not follow until 1972. Japan currently controls the islands because after the Second World War they were lumped together with the Ryukyus – first placed under US administration, then returned to Japanese control along with Okinawa. China points out that the Daioyudao are geographically distinct from the Ryukyu chain. The Okinawa Trough forms a natural dividing line between the Ryukyus and the Diaoyudao. The waters between the Diaoyudao and the Chinese coast are a comparatively shallow 100–200 yards deep, indicating that these islands are just within the East Asian continental shelf; the seabed east and south of the Diaoyudao plunges to depths of over 2,000 yards before rising again to form the base of the Ryukyus.

Like the South China Sea islands, the Diaoyudao Islands offer substantial economic resources, even if they lack the strategic significance of the Paracels or Spratlys. The seas around the islands are prime fishing waters, and some of the flora covering the islands have medicinal value. Under the United Nations Law of the Sea, the owner of the islands also has economic rights to about 20,000 square miles of the surrounding waters and seabed. A 1969 UN report said offshore oil and natural gas deposits in this area might be among the world's largest, although subsequent exploration has scaled down these hopes. Finally, like all territorial issues, the Diaoyudao invoke powerful nationalist sentiments.

There have been several minor confrontations between the Chinese (both the PRC and the ROC) and the Japanese over ownership of the islands. In 1970, Taiwan signed a deal with Gulf Oil Company for oil exploration within an area whose boundaries included the Diaoyudao. Tokyo challenged the concession, and in response a group of Taiwanese journalists travelled to one of the islands and planted the ROC flag before Japanese police dragged them away. Beijing weighed in by issuing a strong reaffirmation of Chinese ownership. In 1978 and again in 1979, dozens of PRC fishing boats sailed to the islands to protest against Tokyo's attempts to solidify its claim. Chinese survey vessels have occasionally entered Diaoyudao waters, eliciting Japanese complaints.

In 1990, Japanese conservatives seeking to steal a march on the Chinese secured Tokyo's permission to renovate a lighthouse on one of the islands. Taiwan retaliated by announcing plans to run an Olympic-style torch relay through the islands and dispatching two boatloads of dignitaries and athletes. Japanese ships and helicopters waiting near the islands stopped the Taiwanese boats and forced them to turn back. Beijing then released another statement criticizing Tokyo and insisting that the islands were rightfully China's. Public anti-Japanese protests erupted in China. Nevertheless, the PRC's official reaction was notably underplayed, evidently because the Chinese were courting Tokyo's favour to help lift Beijing out of its post-Tiananmen isolation (for a good summary, see Ji, 1994).

A reprise of the 1990 incident occurred in 1996, when conservative Japanese activists erected a lighthouse-type beacon and placed a flag and two memorial markers honouring Japanese war dead on the islands. A few weeks later Tokyo gave members of the right-wing Japan Youth Foundation permission to repair the beacon, which had been damaged in a typhoon. Again protesters from Taiwan and Hong Kong sailed to the islands and were confronted by Japanese coastal defence vessels, while Beijing's official response was limited to a formal protest and cautionary remarks from the PRC ambassador to Japan. Several boatloads of Chinese activists from Taiwan and Hong Kong made another attempt in 1997 to land on the Diaoyudao and dismantle the Japanese-built beacon, but some 60 Japanese patrol craft turned them back, resorting to ramming several of the Chinese vessels that crossed into the islands' 12-nautical-mile territorial zone.

Significantly, the recent incidents were instigated by private groups, while the Beijing, Tokyo and Taipei governments all seemed to favour containing the controversy and preventing the issue from damaging relations between the Chinese and Japan. For the PRC's part, Deng recommended in 1978 that the sovereignty issue be shelved and that the claimants jointly develop the islands. Any Chinese approach to resolving the ownership issue is complicated by the possibility that the Diaoyudao might be linked with the territorial dispute in the South China Sea. As with the Spratlys, the PRC has claimed 'indisputable' sovereignty over the Diaoyudao. Thus, if Beijing reaches a compromise settlement with Japan, the other Spratly claimants might demand a similar deal, putting the Chinese leadership in an awkward position both at home and abroad. In the meantime, even if the Chinese and Japanese governments tacitly agree to shelve the matter, it remains subject to a blowup driven by public opinion or political factions seeking to pressure or embarrass the ruling government.

Problems such as the Diaoyudao, Taiwan, and mutual security fears help us frame the most important question in Sino-Japanese relations: whether the incentives for peace and cooperation generated by economic interdependence can overcome the tensions arising from historical legacies, the geostrategic landscape of Northeast Asia, and the strains stemming from interdependence itself.

China and South Asia

India principally represents to China a budding regional rival. As with Vietnam, tensions between China and India in the 1990s have been relatively low. One Chinese strategist noted, 'We still regard India as a threat because they still occupy Chinese territory, though not as ominously as a few years ago' (Cheung, 1992, pp. 29–30). Tensions will probably increase in step with India's economic growth, because the Chinese expect India to try to establish a sphere of influence in South Asia and the Indian Ocean, and they interpret increases in Indian military capability in this light. Many Chinese elites favour an active policy to prevent India from becoming too influential. General Zhao Nanqi, director of the Chinese Academy of Military Sciences, was quoted in 1993 as saying the Chinese would step in to prevent what they saw as an attempt by India to 'dominate' the Indian Ocean. 'We are not prepared to let the Indian Ocean become India's Ocean', Zhao said ('China's Plan to Build Up Navy', *The Hindustan Times*, 13 January 1993, p. 14; cited in Malik, 1995a, p. 328). To these suspicions is added the conclusion of many high-ranking Chinese based on their interpretations of past experience that the Indian government is duplicitous in negotiations and responds favourably only under the threat or use of force (Garver, 1996, p. 343).

China and India are in state of rapprochement that began to develop in the late 1980s. China was already amenable to improved relations with India as part of Deng's general strategy of establishing a peaceful and stable external environment to facilitate China's economic development (Foot, 1996, p. 65). The fallout from Tiananmen provided further impetus for China to improve its neglected relations with the Third World. India broke the ice with a conciliatory gesture: New Delhi dropped its previous precondition that the Sino-Indian border dispute must be resolved before the two countries' heads of state could meet. This prepared the way for Indian Prime Minister Rajiv Gandhi's visit to China in December 1988, during which several agreements were signed and both sides expressed a commitment to greater bilateral cooperation. Several other high-level visits have followed.

The Sino-Indian relationship is more cordial than a decade ago, but remains superficial. Diplomatic cooperation between the two countries has increased (e.g., both oppose pressure from the developed countries over some human rights issues, including the notion of universal minimum labour standards; India supports WTO membership for China, and China supports APEC membership for India), but there is little economic or security cooperation. Economically, the two economies are largely competitive rather than complementary (Garver, 1996, p. 326). India's economy is growing only about half as fast as China's. Both are heavy textile exporters, and both offer low labour costs and a large potential domestic market as attractions for foreign investment. While Sino-Indian trade is growing at about 25 per cent annually, it amounted to a modest $1.2 billion in 1995 (Mapes, 1996, pp. 16–17).

In the security sphere, geopolitical rivalry between China and India seems inescapable, and would seem to leave the relationship with little common ground. Fundamentally, China seeks to prevent India from dominating South Asia, which could otherwise limit China's potential leadership role in Asia as a whole. J. Mohan Malik concludes that this rules out 'a genuine post-Cold War detente' between Beijing and New Delhi, and that 'Over the next decade, a serious contest both in the military and economic spheres will develop between China and India' (Malik, 1995a, pp. 321, 330). More specifically, New Delhi tends to view any military relationships between its neighbours in South Asia and countries outside the region as fundamentally threatening to India. Beijing, on the other hand, claims the right to have whatever relations it wishes with whomever it chooses, and asserts that India's attitude smacks of 'hegemonism' (Garver, 1996, pp. 344–5). This makes China's relationships with Pakistan and Myanmar particularly serious problems between the PRC and India, as we shall see below. Tibet and the lingering Sino-Indian border dispute are additional complications.

India did not welcome China's incorporation of Tibet, which can now serve as a base for Chinese troops and nuclear missiles. Since the rapprochement, New Delhi has publicly affirmed Beijing's position that Tibet is part of China. At the same time, however, the Chinese are irritated that India allows the Dalai Lama and a community of Tibetan exiles to reside in the Indian city of Dharmasala, where they conduct a public relations campaign advocating Tibetan independence. Some Indian politicians also openly support Tibetan separatism. The Chinese complain that these activities constitute a breach of New Delhi's policy on Tibet; the Indian government maintains that as a pluralist democracy it cannot suppress discussion of political issues. In March 1994, a conference on Tibet held in New Delhi produced the first public PRC criticism of India in several years of improved Sino-Indian relations. Participants in the conference called for Tibetan independence, and a collective closing statement demanded that Beijing begin a dialogue with the Dalai Lama to settle Tibet's status. To the Chinese Foreign Ministry's bitter complaints, the Indian government responded that the offending statements arose from a privately sponsored academic assembly and did not represent official policy.

Two segments of the 2,500-mile Sino-Indian border are disputed: the southeastern Himalayan Mountains, now administered by India, and the Aksai Chin plateau, through which runs a major Chinese highway linking Tibet and Xinjiang. India still claims the territory China seized in 1962. Border tensions increased to dangerous levels again in 1986–7. US Secretary of State Caspar Weinberger warned New Delhi on China's behalf that continued territorial 'nibbling' would force China to 'teach India a lesson' (Mansingh and Levine, 1989, p. 32; Foot, 1996, p. 63). India responded with a large military exercise near the Himalayan border. This near-repeat of the 1962 war sobered both sides and helped set the stage for rapprochement. Yet as recently as Jiang's visit to New Delhi in November 1996, the two sides could agree only to promise not to settle the dispute by force and to move an unspecified number of troops back from the 'line of actual control' (LOC) by an unspecified time. Many observers expect the two governments will eventually accept the LOC as the *de facto* border, with China getting what it wants in Aksai Chin while acquiescing to India's claim in the southeastern Himalayas.

The Sino-Pakistani security relationship began in 1964, when Beijing firmly supported Pakistan in the Kashmir dispute. The mostly-Muslim Kashmir region is presently under India's control, but many Kashmiris object, and Pakistan maintains Kashmir is mistreated by India and should have the right to secede from India via plebiscite, which India opposes. During the 1964 Kashmir dispute, the Chinese said they would back Pakistan militarily if it was attacked by India. China took a more neutral position on Kashmir through the 1980s. Beijing still suggested it would defend Pakistan militarily during the Kashmir crisis of 1990, although

Chinese statements were significantly weaker than in the past due to the reconciliation with New Delhi which was then under way. (China no longer supports Kashmiri self-determination, fearing this would set an undesirable precedent for Muslims in Xinjiang.) Nevertheless, PRC military support for Pakistan, including transfers of Chinese weapons, Chinese assistance to Pakistan's defence industries, and exchange visits by military officers, has continued or even increased through the period of improving Sino-Indian relations. China has, for example, reportedly sold up to 40 M-11 ballistic missiles to Pakistan. (Although Beijing persistently denies these reports, they are widely believed in India.)

Interestingly, while in other cases rapprochement with one country has led to a deterioration in Chinese relations with that country's adversary (as with the United States and Vietnam, respectively), the improvement in Sino-Indian relations did not weaken the Sino-Pakistan security relationship (Garver, 1996, pp. 324, 328–32). Beijing's relationship with Pakistan thus remains the most serious problem in Sino-Indian relations, and one that brings their fundamental geopolitical differences into sharp relief: Beijing supports Pakistan *because* Pakistan is India's most troublesome adversary. Consequently, Beijing appears committed to maintaining its relationship with Pakistan even if this prevents better relations with India (Garver, 1996, p. 346).

China's Relationship with Myanmar

Like Pakistan, China's relationship with the buffer state of Myanmar (formerly known as Burma) has unfavourable strategic ramifications for India, and thus represents another potential strain in the Sino-Indian relationship. Relations between the Indians and Myanmarese are historically poor, and there is inherent antipathy between democratic India and authoritarian Myanmar. Yangon (Rangoon) and Beijing, on the other hand, found a new common cause in the early 1990s as both suffered international ostracisim for their violent suppression of anti-government demonstrators. Beijing defends Myanmar's interests in the United Nations, including helping it fend off human rights pressure. Furthermore, the State Law and Order Restoration Council (SLORC) government of Ne Win and other top generals abandoned Myanmar's neutralism and autarkic socialism, giving China unprecedented opportunities for political and economic penetration (Selth, 1996, p. 214). China has secured special trading and investment privileges, and several thousand Chinese are helping the Burmese repair and build roads, bridges and railways.

China has been virtually the sole arms supplier to Myanmar since the imposition of sanctions in 1988 as punishment for the Yangon regime's violent crackdown on pro-democracy activists. The Chinese are passing on some of their obsolete military stock to Myanmar as the PLA acquires newer Russian equipment. Besides small arms, the supplies include heavy weapons such as fighter aircraft, tanks, and patrol boats, plus training in how to use this equipment. The total value of these transfers through 1994 was estimated at $1.4 billion (Hollingworth, 1994/95, p. 31).

The Sino-Myanmar relationship is not without tensions. Many Myanmarese view the Chinese as a new crop of colonialists – arrogant and conspicuously consuming businessmen who drain Myanmar's raw materials, force rural Myanmarese to relocate, and accelerate the erosion of traditional values. For its part, Beijing is unhappy with the Yangon regime's inability to curtail the flow of narcotics and AIDS into Yunnan Province. Nevertheless, the PRC's military and diplomatic assistance and strong economic ties with Myanmar give Beijing vast potential to exercise influence over certain SLORC policies. Malik observes that Chinese arms transfers and economic ties 'have turned the non-aligned state of Burma into China's client state' – ironically, 'an objective which three decades of Beijing-supported insurgency and the Burmese Communist Party's armed struggle failed to achieve' (Malik, 1995a, pp. 340–1).

One area where the PRC may be exploiting its influence, and an area of principal concern to India, is in developing Myanmar as a conduit for the projection of Chinese power into the Indian Ocean. Throughout the 1990s there were reports that the Chinese are constructing and/or upgrading naval facilities on Myanmarese territory accessing the Bay of Bengal and the western entrance to the heavily-trafficked Strait of Malacca. The PRC-backed Irrawaddy Corridor Project now under way encompasses a transportation network that will facilitate the movement of people and materiel by road from Yunnan's principal city Kunming to the Myanmarese port of Bhamo and from there down the Irrawaddy River to Yangon. Besides facilitating trade, this network could support PLA naval operations around the important Indian Ocean sea lanes.

Issues in China's Relations with ASEAN

The perceived threat from Communist China was one of several important impetuses for the formation of the Association of Southeast Asian Nations (ASEAN) in 1967. The deterioration of relations between Beijing and Indonesia after the latter's 1965 coup and destruction of the Indonesian Communist Party cleared the way for a formal organization composed of Southeast Asia's non-communist states. Accordingly, Beijing originally decried ASEAN as a manifestation of US 'imperialism' and part of a system of alliances designed to contain China and the other socialist countries. But the Soviets as well as the Americans sought to gain the cooperation of Southeast Asian states in opposing Chinese influence, as demonstrated in the USSR's 1969 proposal for an 'Asian Collective Security System'. To counteract these efforts by its superpower adversaries, Beijing attempted to improve relations with the ASEAN states. Washington's Nixon Doctrine and the withdrawal of US forces from Indochina created doubts in the region about America's will and capability to defend Southeast Asia from communism. China played upon the region's fears of the Soviet Union, warning Southeast Asia not to let the 'tiger' enter through the back gate while driving the 'wolf' out the front gate (Kao, 1990, p. 240). The US pullout was a major reason why the ASEAN states responded to Beijing's overtures. Malaysia normalized diplomatic relations with China in 1974, followed by Thailand and the Philippines in 1975.

The Indonesians were slower to respond to Beijing's suggestions that diplomatic relations be resumed. Indonesia had recognized Beijing in 1950, but the two countries broke relations in 1967 because Jakarta blamed the PRC for supporting Indonesian communists in their unsuccessful 1965 coup. The new Soeharto government was hostile to communism, and Indonesian Malay and Islamic interests wanted to avoid strengthening the economic position of Indonesia's ethnic Chinese. Many Indonesian elites feared recognition would also increase sympathy for the PRC among ethnic Chinese Indonesians and thereby facilitate subversion, which was Jakarta's greatest perceived security threat. An official rapprochement did not come about until 1990, after Qian Qichen had reassured Soeharto when Hirohito's funeral brought the two men together in Tokyo the previous year that China would not intervene in Indonesia's internal affairs. Even after the normalization, however, Soeharto and other high officials emphasized the need for 'vigilance' (Sukma, 1994, p. 38). Indonesia's reticence in turn delayed Singapore's recognition of the Beijing regime until 1990 as well, while ASEAN's smallest member Brunei was not an independent state until 1984 and established diplomatic relations with the PRC only in 1991.

A problem in the early years of PRC–ASEAN relations was China's insistence that even after Beijing had established diplomatic relations with a given Southeast Asian state, the CCP should be able to maintain its links with the local communist party. Under threat from PRC support to communist insurgencies in the region, the ASEAN countries wanted China to discontinue this support in exchange for diplomatic recognition. Singapore's Lee Kuan Yew, for example, asserted that 'every ASEAN government is convinced that its own communists are a threat only because of outside assistance and interference' (*Straits Times*, 12 August 1981; Leo, 1985, p. 129). Beijing, however, argued that the Chinese Communist Party is distinct from the Chinese government, and that the CCP's relationships with other parties are therefore independent and necessary. This tactic, as everyone foresaw, would allow Beijing to keep using local communist parties as a means of applying pressure on their home governments in support of Chinese foreign policy goals.

Leo Suryadinata argues the perceived correlation between Southeast Asian Chinese and local communist parties has been exaggerated. Chinese have not dominated the leadership or membership of most postwar Southeast Asian communist parties. When Chinese did cooperate with communists, it was sometimes because their local governments failed to provide due protection or services. If anything, the Chinese in Southeast Asia were inherently disinclined to support communism because they control a disproportionate share of national wealth. Finally, the ethnic Chinese are 'aware that their prosperity and safety depend largely on the local authorities rather than on Beijing or Taipei' (Leo, 1985, pp. 20–3).

In any case, the problem faded as worsening Sino-Vietnam relations moved China to make peace with ASEAN. While declining to sever party-to-party relations, Deng promised in 1978 that Beijing would not interfere in the domestic affairs of ASEAN states, and his Premier Zhao Ziyang reaffirmed in 1981 that CCP ties with local communist parties 'would not affect our friendship and cooperation with ASEAN countries' (quoted in Garver, 1993, p. 170). Through the 1980s PRC assistance to Southeast Asian communist parties practically disappeared, contributing to the capitulations of the Communist Party of Thailand in 1985 and the Communist Party of Malaya in 1989.

Today, China's relations with ASEAN reflect a combination of the general orientation of 'friendship and cooperation', which supports China's economic development efforts, and the age-old tendency to view Southeast Asia as part of the Chinese sphere of influence. China cooperates with ASEAN readily on ideological issues that unite Asia against the West, and less readily on efforts to build a multilateral security organization. At the same time, however, tensions result from the old problem of race relations between ethnic Chinese and indigenous inhabitants of Southeast Asia and the new problem of disputed sovereignty over the South China Sea islands.

Most importantly, current ASEAN–China relations are coloured by the expectation that within a generation China will grow into a power of such size that it will dominate Southeast Asia's international political and economic affairs.

United Front against the West

China and at least some of the ASEAN states have frequently formed an ideological united front in defence of 'Asian values' against 'Western values' (for a good overview of this debate, see Dupont, 1996). Politically, China and most of the ASEAN states have converged in their adherence to 'soft authoritarianism': free-market capitalism combined with a strong state dominated by a single party and committed to resisting Western-style liberalism. Economically, they share the confidence that comes from relatively high economic growth rates.

Chinese scholar Geng Huichang asserts that Western international relations principles and the 'new world order' brought about 'turbulence' such as the collapse of the Soviet Union and the war in the former Yugoslavia. 'In striking contrast' is 'the Oriental wisdom', which has produced a model based on 'peaceful coexistence and national amity' and preserved peace in the region. Geng's argument is similar to that of Singaporean official Kishore Mahbubani, who boasts that 'while the guns are almost silent in East Asia,

Europe is surrounded by conflict. . . . It is a result of the strategic incoherence in Europe's approach to its immediate environment. East Asia, meanwhile, is making relatively sound decisions' (Geng, 1992, pp. 2–3; Mahbubani, 1994). Thus, China's appeals to pan-Asianism and discussions of an 'Oriental international order' (Lu, 1992, p. 16) have considerable resonance in Southeast Asia. Most Asian governments, particularly in ASEAN, side with China against the United States on the human rights issue. Southeast Asia's reaction to Tiananmen was much more restrained than that of the West, and the ASEAN governments maintained high-level visits and economic ties with the PRC after the massacre, even inviting China to attend the ASEAN Post-Ministerial Conference in 1991. Based on their experiences with Chinese-supported communist insurgencies during the Cold War, Southeast Asian governments largely accept the view that isolating China drives Beijing to trouble-making, while multiplying economic and other ties encourages Chinese moderation and pragmatism. Many Southeast Asian officials also sympathize with the CCP's struggle to maintain its monopoly on political power amidst pressures for political liberalization. The 'soft authoritarian' city-state of Singapore has been an especially vocal defender of China against Western human rights pressure. 'You can't change a Chinese civilization of 4,000 years by an act of [the US] Congress', said former prime minister and current 'Senior Minister' Lee Kuan Yew. Singapore's current Prime Minister, Goh Chok Tong, defends the Chinese government's desire to 'maintain stability and order' even at the expense of civil liberties, adding, 'They do not want China to descend into chaos, and neither does the rest of Asia' (*Straits Times*, 1993, p. 3; Goh, 1993, p. 6) The reasoning of these Singaporean politicians is based, of course, on the dubious assumption that the choice is between 'chaos' on the one hand and the protection of human rights on the other, and that it would be impossible for the CCP to maintain order and progress under greater rule of law and without harsh punishment of peaceful dissidents or widespread torture of detainees.

ASEAN also accepts Beijing's position that the Taiwan problem is a Chinese domestic issue – not only because this is a prerequisite of official relations with the PRC, but also because most of the ASEAN states have separatist questions of their own, and concur with China's attitude that these should not become international issues that invite foreign interference into one's perceived internal affairs (Wanandi, 1996, p. 125).

Multilateral Security Cooperation

China has discouraged the construction of a multilateral security framework in the region mostly out of fear that it might facilitate international cooperation against Chinese interests: internationalizing the Spratly or Taiwan issues, marketizing the Asian communist countries, pressuring the Chinese military for greater transparency, or even containing China. The Chinese have seen both the Soviet Union and the USA attempting to use these mechanisms to build anti-China alliances. The PRC's stated position through the early 1990s was that a multilateral security framework is not desirable because of this region's diversity and because of the large number and variety of small disputes. Because each Asian state has a different view of national security and how to achieve it, attempting to settle these disputes multilaterally rather than bilaterally would complicate the process, making problems harder to solve, the Chinese have said. Moreover, the Asia-Pacific should not attempt to ape the multilateral security organizations used in Europe; European concoctions are doomed to unfeasibility in Asia because of this region's diversity in culture, geography, history, and security perceptions. Beijing has made it clear it favours bilateral rather than multilateral security discussions. Samuel Kim terms China's approach 'a triumph of unilateralism-cum-bilateralism over regionalism-cum-multilateralism' (Kim, 1995, p. 469). Beijing has successfully killed recent proposals for multilateral security frameworks proposed by Japan, Australia, Canada and the Soviet Union.

But with its ASEAN neighbours highly supportive of a multilateral security framework, Beijing has no choice but to join the consensus, while attempting to anticipate and undercut any moves that might restrict its desired course of future action. The only other alternative would be to appear obstructionist and be left behind. The Chinese have therefore recently accepted multilateralism in principle, although not to the exclusion of bilateralism. Qian Qichen, for example, proposed 'promoting bilateral and multilateral security dialogues' during the 1994 meeting of the ASEAN Regional Forum (ARF) in Bangkok.

Having joined the ARF, a multilateral discussion group formed in 1993 that includes 20 Asia-Pacific countries and the European Union, the Chinese expressed hope in its potential to break free of 'US dominance over political/security discussions in the Asia-Pacific region' – i.e., to take up China's position on issues such as Western human rights pressure on Myanmar, US–Japan efforts to build a theater anti-ballistic missile defence system, and the participation of Japanese soldiers in international peacekeeping missions (Ding, 1996, pp. 4, 7). In turn, however, Michael Leifer argues that the ARF 'appears to have had some moderating influence on China's assertiveness in the South China Sea', the price Beijing has paid to gain ASEAN's cooperation in debates with the United States and Japan (Leifer, 1996, p. 56).

Transparency was one of the prime thrusts of ASEAN multilateral security discussions in the 1990s, reflecting the very limited progress these discussions have thus far made. Yet even this rudimentary norm is a difficult one for the Chinese to accept, given the emphasis on deception that is so prominent in their traditional military thought. Deng's famous '24-character directive' on international relations, for instance, advises 'hide one's capabilities' (Qiao Shi, 1994, p. 135). PRC officials believe a 'weak' country such as China should not be expected to be as transparent in its military policies as stronger countries such as the USA and Japan. China has agreed to publish a defence White Paper every two years. Its first, published in 1995, was rather unrevealing. In fairness, however, so were those of ASEAN states such as Singapore, Indonesia or Thailand (Wanandi, 1996, p. 124).

The Overseas Chinese

Communities of ethnic Chinese, totalling about 24 million people, are well established throughout Southeast Asia. Hailing mostly from the commerce-oriented provinces of southeastern China, the Southeast Asian Chinese enjoy disproportionate economic power in their adopted homelands, which creates resentment among the indigenous population. In Indonesia, for example, ethnic Chinese make up only 3 per cent of the population, but control 70 per cent of the nation's wealth, while in the Philippines ethnic Chinese comprise 2 per cent of the population and own half the country's private capital. In Thailand the numbers are 10 per cent and 81 per cent, and in Malaysia 29 per cent and 61 per cent. There is also a common perception in Southeast Asia that ethnic Chinese are unwilling to assimilate into the local society, leading to accusations from the indigenous peoples that the Chinese are clannish, arrogant, and lack both loyalty toward their countries of residence and respect for local customs.

The Cold War brought the additional fear that ethnic Chinese were agents of the PRC's programme to sow communist revolution in Southeast Asia. After the Cold War, antipathy toward the ethnic Chinese persists. Before the 1997 Chinese (Lunar) New Year, for example, the governor of Jakarta warned his Chinese community not to celebrate in public, for fear this might spark yet another in a series of recent anti-Chinese rampages by Indonesian Muslims (*Straits Times*, 1997b, p. 15). Southeast Asia has witnessed a range of approaches to the problem of race relations. Vietnam sought to expel its Chinese community; Malaysia has implemented laws that discriminate in favour of Malays to help them catch up economically with the Chinese; Thailand, the Philippines and Indonesia have encouraged their Chinese residents to assimilate; and Singapore has embraced multiculturalism.

The problem of rich ethnic Chinese minorities in the individual states of Southeast Asia is writ large in the relationship between Singapore and the rest of the region. The tiny island nation is by far the wealthiest state (measured on a per capita basis) in ASEAN, and it is also the only one where Chinese comprise the majority race (79 per cent). Singapore's relations with the mainland Chinese reflect its awkward position. On the one hand, the cultural, linguistic, economic and even ideological affinities between Singapore and the PRC are irresistible. Both private and government-sponsored Singaporean investment in China is heavy, including the $3 billion transplantation of a Singapore-style township to the Chinese city of Suzhou. Singaporean 'Senior Minister' Lee Kuan Yew is an 'old friend of China' whose achievements and advice are highly respected on the mainland. The Singapore government promotes Confucian values and encourages Singaporean Chinese to learn Mandarin to take full advantage of opportunities to do business with China. On the other hand, the Singapore government has been at pains to get its Malay neighbors to view it as a fellow Southeast Asian state rather than a potential satellite of Beijing or a Chinese 'Trojan Horse' (Winterford, 1993, pp. 369–98). For this reason Singapore treats Malaysia with delicacy and Indonesia with deference. Singapore even held off on establishing diplomatic relations with Beijing until Indonesia did so first.

Various arguments have been made about how the overseas Chinese fit into China's foreign policy in Southeast Asia, including these: ethnic Chinese are a potential fifth column for PRC interests, including serving as liaisons between China and communist or pro-Beijing political parties; they may involve the PRC in another country's domestic affairs by appealing for protection when they are mistreated; Beijing can make their favourable treatment a condition for good relations between Southeast Asian governments and Beijing; conversely, they may be considered hostages ensuring China behaves well toward Southeast Asian governments (Leo, 1985, pp. 7–8). In fact, however, while assumptions and expectations about the role of the ethnic Chinese have been important factors in the politics of the Southeast Asian states, the ethnic Chinese have rarely been a major factor in the PRC's foreign policy.

Beijing originally considered all overseas Chinese its nationals and urged them to return to China. Since the 1950s, however, Beijing has sought favour with Southeast Asian nations by renouncing dual citizenship for overseas ethnic Chinese. This means when ethnic Chinese living abroad voluntarily take up foreign citizenship, Beijing will no longer consider them Chinese nationals, and in principle their welfare is no longer a matter of PRC concern. (Ethnic Chinese in Vietnam during the late 1970s were an exception because, according to Beijing, Hanoi systematically persecuted them, including forcing them to become Vietnamese citizens.) Despite its policy against dual citizenship, however, Beijing continued to manifest a sense of attachment to the ethnic Chinese in Southeast Asia. Prior to the late 1970s, PRC officials and media routinely referred to the ethnic Chinese in Southeast Asia as *huaqiao* ('Chinese sojourners', implying they will eventually return to China) or *Zhongguo ren* ('Chinese', the same term used for PRC citizens living in China). It was only after Deng visited three ASEAN countries in 1978 that the PRC leadership realized the Chinese in Southeast Asia preferred to be called *huaren, huazu* or *huayi* (all of which mean 'people of Chinese ancestry') (Leo, 1985, pp. 3–4).

Occasional statements of concern for overseas Chinese from the PRC government and press have upheld suspicions in Southeast Asian countries that Beijing has never completely relinquished its desire to use the ethnic Chinese as a means of manipulating local politics. When labour unrest turned into an anti-Chinese riot in Medan, Indonesia in 1994, for example, the PRC Ministry of Foreign Affairs made a public statement of 'concern'. Jakarta retorted that China was meddling in Indonesian domestic politics and 'had better mind its own internal affairs' (the quotation is from Justice Minister Utoyo Usman; Sukma, 1994, p. 36)

Ethnic Chinese communities in Southeast Asia have frequently been in peril during the PRC's history. On these occasions, Beijing has sometimes put pressure on Southeast Asian governments to protect their Chinese residents (through public protests, propaganda, withdrawal of aid, or even repatriation) and sometimes not. Although the Chinese government has affirmed in its various constitutions that it 'protects the just rights and interests of Chinese residents abroad', this principle by itself clearly has not been a high priority (Leo, 1985, pp. 25, 140). Robert S. Ross argues that Beijing has little intrinsic interest in protecting the overseas Chinese from abuse in the countries where they reside, but has reacted to such abuse only when it appeared to be part of a larger anti-China policy by a foreign government that affected the PRC's geostrategic interests (Ross, 1988, pp. 151–8).

Under its 1955 dual nationality treaty with China, Indonesia agreed to protect the legitimate rights of its ethnic Chinese inhabitants. In 1959 and 1960, however, Indonesia passed regulations restricting the commercial and residential privileges of ethnic Chinese. In addition, anti-Chinese rioting killed or injured thousands. Beijing accused Jakarta of violating the treaty and sent ships offering to transport Indonesian Chinese back to China. About 100,000 Chinese left Indonesia in these ships, damaging the country's economy and weakening Sukarno's position. At the same time, Soviet influence in Indonesia was increasing. In the interest of retaining Sukarno as an ally, Beijing stopped complaining and sending ships. When anti-Chinese riots broke out in 1963, Beijing blamed Indonesian 'reactionaries' (the Indonesian armed forces were anti-PRC) rather than Sukarno. Thus, protection of ethnic Chinese in Indonesia was sacrificed in the interest of preserving PRC–Indonesian relations. China responded weakly to anti-Chinese activities in 1973, 1974 and 1980 for the same reason (Leo, 1985, pp. 35–8), while Beijing's public response was stronger and more prolonged over the anti-Chinese violence in 1965–6, when the Indonesian government was unambiguously hostile toward China. In similar fashion, Beijing declined to criticize the Malaysian government for allowing hundreds of ethnic Chinese to be murdered by mobs in May 1969, when the PRC hoped to improve its relations with Kuala Lumpur.

The clearest example in this pattern of strategic neglect was Kampuchea (Cambodia), where the Khmer Rouge seized power in April 1975. Khmer Rouge leader Pol Pot's radical plan to implement his brand of socialism called for annihilation of all class 'enemies', including capitalists, merchants, professionals, and anyone else with wealth or education. By some estimates, the Khmer Rouge's campaign of murder reduced Kampuchea's population from seven to four million. The country's Chinese population suffered disproportionately because of its relatively high economic standing; perhaps 200,000 died (Ross, 1988, p. 159). The Khmer Rouge, however, were anti-Vietnamese and pro-Mao as well as murderous. China depended on Pol Pot to counter the influence of Hanoi, which was increasingly closely aligned with the Soviet Union. Despite the atrocities committed against ethnic Chinese in Kampuchea, Beijing refrained from condemning the Khmer Rouge, and even defended them, claiming they enjoyed popular Kampuchean support and challenging the notion they had committed 'genocide'.

Beijing took a different approach toward post-unification Vietnam, home of a million ethnic Chinese, where a pro-Soviet faction gained control of the government at the expense of pro-China leaders in 1976. Vietnam's post-reunification programmes of resettling city-dwellers in rural areas and restricting private enterprise were disruptive to many Chinese. After complaining about Beijing's support for the Khmer Rouge in neighbouring Kampuchea, the Vietnamese government began removing ethnic Chinese who held positions of authority. These developments contributed to an exodus of some 160,000 ethnic Chinese back to China by 1978. Most of the 300,000 'boat people' refugees from Vietnam in the 1970s were also ethnic Chinese. (Even ASEAN complained with uncharacteristic openness, as the arrival on their shores of refugees from Vietnam created a new economic burden and threatened to increase the proportion of ethnic Chinese in the local population.) Beijing publicly charged Vietnam with mistreating and expelling Chinese residents and cut most of its aid to Hanoi in apparent retaliation. China's poor relations with the Soviet Union, combined with the perception that the Soviets had strong influence in Hanoi, were clearly a major factor in the PRC's strong reaction (Leo, 1985, pp. 47, 48).

The South China Sea

The disputed sovereignty over the islands of the South China Sea has become ASEAN's chief security concern, and an issue that increasingly pits ASEAN against China. The Spratly Islands is the common collective name for some 230 small islands, rocks and reefs scattered west of the Philippine island of Palawan and north of Borneo. The largest is less than a mile long and 600 metres wide, and all but 26 are under water during high tide. China says it owns the entire Spratly group, which it calls the Nansha ('Southern Sands') Islands, a claim challenged by Vietnam, the Philippines, Malaysia and Brunei. Taiwan's claim is identical to Beijing's. Vietnam presently occupies 21 'islands', China eight, the Philippines eight, Malaysia three to six, and Taiwan one (Snyder, 1996, p. 5). Because the islands are not economically viable, none has ever been permanently inhabited, save for the garrisons recently placed on some of them. Thus none of the claimant governments has a particularly strong case for ownership. Beijing says official Chinese records cite the Spratlys as Chinese-administered territory as far back as the Song Dynasty (A.D. 960–1279), and that Chinese fishermen have used the islands as a base since then.

Vietnam, as well, claims to have administered the islands from pre-modern times. The United Nations Convention on the Law of the Sea, which came into effect in 1994, recognizes 'historic use and administration' as a possible basis for ownership, but this criterion specifies continuous control and governance of the territory in question, which neither China nor Vietnam can convincingly claim (Segal, 1996, p. 117). The Philippines' claim is based on the 'discovery' of the Spratly Islands (which the Philippines calls Kalayaan, or 'Freedomland') by Tomas Cloma in 1956. Malaysia claims the islands it says are part of the country's continental shelf, and Brunei claims those that are within its 200-mile exclusive economic zone.

Interestingly, Taiwan not only supports Beijing's claims, but even coordinates its South China Sea policy with Beijing. Beijing has tolerated the occupation of Itu Aba (Taiping) Island, the largest island in the Spratly group, by ROC troops since 1956. The ROC defence minister offered to assist the PRC during its 1988 battle with the Vietnamese in the Spratlys. The Taiwanese base on Itu Aba helped supply PLA marines during the operation. Representatives from Taiwan and the PRC have discussed cooperation in exploring the South China Sea and drafting a joint legal statement in support of the Chinese claim. On the Spratlys issue, the behaviour of a liberal democratic Chinese government has been identical to that of an authoritarian communist Chinese government.

The Spratlys are strategically located astride the heavily travelled sealanes between Northeast Asia and the Strait of Malacca, through which Middle East oil is shipped to the Far East. The islands and their surrounding waters are also prized fisheries, and the seabed beneath may hold large deposits of oil, natural gas and valuable minerals. How much oil and gas are contained in the disputed areas of the South China Sea is still uncertain. Estimates have ranged from one billion to over 17 billion tons (Valencia, 1995, p. 10; by comparison, Kuwait contains an estimated 13 billion tons). Russia's Research Institute of Geology of Foreign Countries estimated 6 billion barrels of oil and gas in 1995. China, on the other hand, has called the area the 'second Persian Gulf' and floated an estimate of 130 billion barrels (Snyder, 1996, p. 4). According to one calculation presented in an officially sanctioned PRC publication, the economic value of the various resources in the South China Sea is $1 trillion (Garver, 1992, p. 1027). It is significant, perhaps, that the PRC's estimates of the Sea's resource wealth are among the highest; the higher the perceived reward, the higher the acceptable level of costs that might be paid to secure ownership.

John Garver perceptively summarizes the economic aspect of the Spratlys issue for China: 'Control over the South China Sea will substantially enhance China's ability to provide prosperity for its people and achieve a position of global power in the future. It is not a question of oil, or gas, or fish, or manganese nodules, but all of these and other now unknown resources taken together and exploited . . . in 50 or 100 years' time' (Garver, 1992, p. 1020).

The political aspect of the dispute is equally salient for China. In Beijing's view, the challengers to China's long-established ownership of the Spratlys have taken advantage of Chinese preoccupation with domestic and superpower politics. It is another case of foreigners grabbing Chinese territory and property in a moment of Chinese weakness. Claimants other than China have, for example, drilled some 120 wells in the South China Sea. In the face of these perceived encroachments, Beijing has shown great restraint, despite having right and, increasingly, might on its side (Chen, 1994, pp. 893-4). The Chinese see the other claimants employing three tactics. The first is 'island snatching', or surreptitiously placing one's personnel on an unoccupied island claimed by another state, which is a relatively non-provocative way to increase the size of one's claim. Second, the other claimant governments link China's behaviour in the Spratlys to the 'China threat' issue – i.e., how China treats the other Spratlys claimants now is a barometer for how China as a superpower will treat its neighbours in the future – which makes it politically costly for the Chinese to defend their claims. Third, Beijing sees the other parties attempting to internationalize the Spratlys issue in order to get as many other nations as possible to join them in pressuring China for a compromise settlement. The Chinese observe bitterly that their sovereignty over the islands was not seriously disputed until scientific surveys in the 1960s and 1970s suggested the possible existence of oil and natural gas reserves. Some North Vietnamese government statements in the 1950s even acknowledged Chinese sovereignty over the Paracels and the Spratlys, and it was not until after Vietnam's reunification in 1975 that Hanoi asserted any claim of its own (Sheng, 1995b, pp. 3–4). In 1976–7 Hanoi claimed that the Paracel and Spratly Islands were within Vietnamese territorial waters and therefore belonged to Vietnam. PRC Vice-Premier Li Xiannian reportedly met secretly with Vietnamese Premier Pham Van Dong in June 1977. Questioned about the reversal of his country's position, Pham said Vietnam previously supported China's position in the interest of maintaining Sino-Vietnamese cooperation against the United States, but that circumstances had now changed (*Beijing Review*, 1979, pp. 17–22).

Vietnam's move brought severe criticism from Beijing, but the Chinese response to similar claims by the Philippines (which made its first claim in 1978) and Malaysia (1979) was low-key, subordinate to the more pressing goal of cultivating the ASEAN states as allies against Soviet influence in the region. Beginning in the late 1980s, however, Beijing's approach to the South China Sea islands disputes grew noticeably more assertive for three reasons. First, the post-Cold War reduction of US and Soviet military influence in South-east Asia gave the Chinese more strategic freedom of action (Hyer, 1995, p. 47). Second, rapid economic growth both increased Chinese confidence and underscored the need to secure new resources to meet increasing domestic demand. Third, the PRC perceived the ASEAN states were seeking to band together against China on the Spratlys issue.

China began stationing troops and building permanent installa-tions on the islands under its control in 1987. On Fiery Cross Reef (Yonshu Jiao), for example, the Chinese have built an oceano-graphic research installation, a pier and a helipad, and personnel stationed there enjoy postal service and telephone links to the mainland.

In March 1988 Chinese and Vietnamese naval forces clashed over Johnson Reef. The Vietnamese government said Chinese gunfire sank three of its supply ships and killed 72 sailors. In 1992 China contracted with the US oil firm Crestone to explore and drill in Spratly waters also claimed by Vietnam, and reportedly promised the company's president that the PLA would protect the Crestone operation if the Vietnamese tried to interfere. This was a crafty move by the Chinese, as Vietnam was then lobbying Washington for upgraded relations and an end to the American economic embargo, and thus had a strong disincentive to take action against an US corporation. Vietnam countered by organizing a seismic survey in the same area, but the foreign operators of the survey vessel backed out after the Chinese issued a warning. In response to the Crestone concession, ASEAN released a 'Declaration on the South China Sea' that included a call for claimants to forswear the use of force in settling the dispute. Nonetheless, in typical ASEAN style, the Declaration was reportedly rewritten four times to avoid language that might upset Beijing (Lee, 1995, p. 539).

Indonesia, which began in 1990 to sponsor annual, unofficial workshops on managing potential conflicts in the South China Sea, had considered itself a neutral party in the Spratly dispute until 1993, when China's delegates to the workshop produced a map outlining the PRC's claim. The map included a dashed line encompassing nearly the entire South China Sea, an area of about two million square miles (about a third of the land area China presently occupies) extending as far as 1,200 miles from the nearest undisputed PRC territory (Hainan Island). The dashed line also took in Indonesia's Natuna gas field, which is one of the world's largest reserves, with an estimated volume of 45 trillion cubic feet, and lies well within the 200-mile exclusive economic zone Indonesia claims under the Law of the Sea. The Exxon Corporation, with which Jakarta signed a $35 billion contract to develop the Natuna gas field, asked for confirmation that the area is not disputed territory. Indonesia in turn asked Beijing to clarify its position on the Natuna Islands, but for months thereafter the Chinese declined (McBeth, 1995, p. 28).

Among the many Spratlys incidents of the 1990s (confrontations at sea, complaints about one party placing buildings or markers on various islands, one claimant's detention of another's fishermen, the PLA Navy's temporary blockade of a Vietnamese oil drilling platform in disputed waters, etc.), the most noted was the Mischief Reef affair. Chinese officials had apparently accepted the ASEAN De-claration's principle against using force to change the status quo. Outside analysts had also become convinced that China would never challenge an ASEAN state over the Spratlys (Vietnam was not yet a member of ASEAN during the clashes of 1988 and 1974). Yet at the end of 1994, several PLA Navy vessels targeted Philippine-claimed Mischief Reef, only 135 miles from Palawan. When they arrived, the PLA personnel arrested and removed the Filipino fishermen they found there, then built structures (apparently military, although Beijing claimed they were shelters for Chinese fishermen) and stationed guards on the reef. This was widely interpreted as a Chinese probing action designed to cautiously test ASEAN and US reaction by challenging ASEAN's weakest member and a military ally of the United States. (A minority of analysts suggested that the PLA units carrying out the Mischief Reef operation acted without orders from the high command in Beijing.) Manila asked Washington if their defence pact committed America to defend the Philippines' Spratlys claims; the US government responded that it did not.

Mischief Reef galvanized ASEAN into a stronger and more unified stand against the PRC. In March 1995, Malaysian navy vessels fired on a Chinese fishing boat off the coast of Sarawak, injuring four crewmen, and Philippine forces detained 62 Chinese in four fishing boats around Half Moon Shoal near Palawan. ASEAN ministers reportedly expressed strong displeasure over the Mischief Reef action during an April 1995 meeting in Hangzhou, China. Beijing subsequently softened, agreeing in principle that it would establish (on a bilateral basis) 'codes of conduct' with Vietnam and the Philippines that would include a recommitment to resolve disputes peacefully. Qian Qichen also said China would honour the United Nations Convention on the Law of the Sea (UNCLOS) and that China's claim did not preclude freedom of passage through the South China Sea. Nevertheless, Chinese troops remain stationed on Mischief Reef, and many observers believe the Chinese intend to upgrade the flimsy structures there into a permanent, concrete-fortified military installation (Tiglao, 1995, p. 20).

The PLA now has the capability to seize the entire Spratly group by force. Holding on to islands hundreds of miles away from the Chinese mainland against a counter-attack, however, would prob-ably be too difficult for today's PLA, especially if the ASEAN states pooled their forces. A Chinese attack on Malaysian forces would invoke Malaysia's defence links with Australia, Great Britain, New Zealand and Singapore through the Five Power Defence Arrangement. The United States might also decide to intervene if it judged that China's actions violated the norm of peaceful resolution of disputes or threatened freedom of navigation through the South China Sea. More generally, perceived Chinese aggression would severely damage China's reputation and curtail its access to foreign trade, capital and technology.

The use of force is therefore an unattractive option for Beijing. You Ji is probably correct in arguing that 'military force is likely to be employed only as a last resort to defend direct threats to Chinese sovereignty or territorial integrity, and not as a means to expand Chinese presence. . . . [The] prospect of a PLA attack on islands already occupied by other claimants is very low' (You, 1994, pp. 391, 396). Instead, the PRC has relied on a set of more subtle tactics. To maximize its own leverage and preclude the other parties from forming a united front against China, Beijing has insisted each of the other claimants negotiate bilaterally with China and opposed both a multilateral approach to settling the dispute and bilateral talks among other claimants excluding China. The PRC has employed intentional ambiguity, exemplified by the unexplained 'u-shaped line' drawn around the South China Sea on Chinese maps. This has allowed the Chinese to effectually assert a vast, if vague, claim without having to defend it on the basis of international law (Valencia, 1995, p. 13). China has occasionally claimed it was acting under the auspices of international organizations while taking steps to strengthen its position. The Chinese said they built a weather station on one of the islands they occupy at the direction of the World Meteorological Organization; the WMO denied it supported construction of the station. Finally, Beijing has probed the vigilance and determination of its opponents through such means as the Crestone concession and the occupation of Mischief Reef.

Throughout the 1980s and 1990s the PRC proposed that the question of sovereignty be 'shelved' and that the other claimant countries begin joint development with Beijing of the islands and their surrounding waters. This approach seems to reflect a conviction among the Chinese that time is on their side, a plausible assumption given China's potential to develop into the region's dominant power. No joint development projects have yet come to fruition, not least because specific discussions have indicated that by 'joint development' the Chinese do not mean equal sharing of the resources in a disputed area, as the term is conventionally used, but rather foreign assistance in the development of resources China claims as its own (Valencia, 1995, p. 12).

With the near-universal acceptance of UNCLOS, which came into force in 1994, Beijing seems to have abandoned its attempt to legitimize its claim by unilateral legal means through the law on territorial seas passed by the Chinese government in 1992. The Chinese now seem prepared to argue their case under the terms outlined in UNCLOS, which they ratifed in May 1996. Along these lines, Pan Shiying, a strategist at a Beijing institute, observes that 'Possession of one small island or a piece of reef enables the country to claim a total of 1,500 square kilometres of territorial sea, or three times the size of Singapore . . . [and] 430,000 kilometres of special economic zone' (quoted in Tiglao, 1995, p. 20).

Another group of disputed South China Sea islands is the Paracels (Xisha, or 'Western Sands', in Chinese), which lie roughly equidistant from Hainan Island and the coast of northern Vietnam. Although Vietnam claims them, the Paracels are now occupied solely by the PRC. China took some of the islands from a war-weary Vietnam in 1956. In 1974, Chinese forces seized six islands and ousted the remaining Vietnamese inhabitants in a battle that saw a Vietnamese corvette sunk and two other Vietnamese warships damaged. This, as well, was an opportune time for the Chinese to strike. South Vietnam, then the custodian of the Vietnamese-held Paracels, had recently seen the departure of its US military allies; there was little chance of American intervention on Saigon's behalf over a few tiny islands in the South China Sea. Furthermore, the Saigon regime was clearly close to being conquered by North Vietnam, after which control of the islands would revert to Hanoi. China thus acquired territory from the Vietnamese without an open clash with its communist ally. The Chinese have built an airstrip on Woody Island (Lin Dao) that puts the entire Spratly group within range of Chinese B-6 bombers. Significantly, China has made no offers for jointly developing the Paracels, as it has with the Spratlys. Evidently Beijing feels less inclined to compromise when it is in full control of the territory in dispute (Valencia, 1995, p. 20).

China as a 'Threat' to ASEAN

Southeast Asia has great economic significance to China (and, of course, Japan): populous and resource-rich, it is a potential hinterland as well as a market for Chinese exports and, increasingly, a source of capital for investment in China. Trade between China and ASEAN reached nearly $20 billion in 1995 – still only 5 per cent of China's total trade, but a 42 per cent increase from the previous year. From time immemorial, the relatively small and weak states of Southeast Asia have faced the spectre of being drawn into a Chinese sphere of influence. Although most of these states are now prosperous and better able to defend themselves than at any other time in history, they still face the possibility that China will dominate their sub-region politically and economically.

Beijing, of course, wants Southeast Asia to 'bandwagon' rather than 'balance'. In international relations theory, these two terms describe the ways a weaker state might react to a powerful, potentially threatening state. 'Bandwagoning' is to befriend the powerful state, and perhaps even take its orders, to avoid being attacked. 'Balancing' is to join with other weak states to form a coalition against the powerful state. Thus high Chinese officials have continually assured the region that even a stronger China 'will never seek hegemony', and that anyone who says otherwise is attempting to drive a wedge between China and its neighbours. To Beijing's approval, in contrast to the United States and to a lesser extent Japan, ASEAN in general has taken an attitude of accommodation, even appeasement, toward the prospect of a Chinese superpower. Many analysts have complained that ASEAN demonstrates a lack of fortitude in its unwillingness to take a stronger position on untoward Chinese policies (Segal, 1996, p. 108; Lym, 1996, p. 1). Some of the ASEAN governments have publicly denounced the view that a stronger China may pose a potential threat to the region. Other than Singapore, ASEAN states are reluctant to host US military installations, or even to allow the United States to preposition military material stocks in their waters, out of fear of displeasing China or of appearing soft on 'Western imperialism'. The ASEAN states assert that they are dealing with China effectively 'the ASEAN way'. This includes emphasising informal, behind-the-scenes diplomacy and avoiding sharp public criticism of other governments, including Beijing. To speak publicly of a 'China threat' may become a self-fulfilling prophecy, while Southeast Asian governments are capable of taking united action against China if its moves become genuinely threatening, say ASEAN diplomats.

In fact, the ASEAN states have differing views on the extent to which China represents a potential 'threat'. Vietnam, the Philippines and Indonesia tend to support stronger measures to discourage or condemn Chinese misbehaviour. Vietnam lives in the shadow of Chinese hegemony, and most of its current leadership has lived through a PLA invasion. Hanoi is also a newcomer to the ASEAN norm of treating the PRC with deference. The Mischief Reef affair greatly increased the Philippines' apprehension toward Beijing. Besides its lingering antipathy toward the PRC based on deep-seated anti-Chinese and anti-communist sentiments, Indonesia aspires to the role of regional leader, and therefore has an incentive to play up the Chinese threat to limit China's competing influence. Jakarta is relatively under-sensitive to China's view of the Taiwan issue, as demonstrated by President Soeharto's meeting with Lee Denghui during the latter's 'private' visit to Indonesia in 1994, which Beijing strongly opposed. In contrast, Thailand has reached a relatively comfortable accommodation with the PRC, and in any case is more concerned about Vietnam than China as a potential security threat. The mostly-Chinese city-state of Singapore has an exceptionally strong business, cultural, and ideological partnership with Beijing. Malaysia's attitude is ambivalent; markedly conciliatory toward China in the early 1990s, emphasizing that they saw China as an 'opportunity rather than a threat', the Malaysians appear to have cooled towards China since Mischief Reef, although they remain in ASEAN's accommodationist wing (Denoon and Frieman, 1996, pp. 430–1).

Sino-Vietnamese Relations

From a long-term historical perspective, Sino-Vietnamese cooperation against the French and the Americans was a mere flash in the pan compared to the centuries of Vietnamese resistance against attempted Chinese domination. China directly ruled Vietnam for over a thousand years from 111 BC to AD 939, a period marked by several major Vietnamese uprisings. The Chinese, not surprisingly, have generally viewed their influence in Vietnam as generous and civilizing. A common Chinese attitude is that the Vietnamese are disrespectful *bai yan lang* ('white-eyed wolves', i.e. ingrates), having enjoyed substantial Chinese support during the wars against the French and the Americans, only to side with the Soviet Union, invade Chinese protégé Kampuchea and challenge Chinese ownership of the South China Sea islands soon after Vietnam's unification. From the colonization and tributary relationship of pre-modern times to the punitive invasion of 1979, China's relationship with Vietnam has been consistent with the traditional Chinese attitude toward smaller peripheral states, but it is also consistent with modern regional hegemony. In both cases, the powerful state demands influence in the smaller state's affairs and works to prevent it from growing too strong or from joining an adversarial coalition. Thus, China's fundamental interests toward Vietnam are to preclude it from challenging Chinese influence in Indochina and to prevent it from aligning with another major power or from developing into too strong an economic rival to China (Schultz and Ardrey, 1995, p. 131).

Sino-Vietnamese relations were close in the late 1950s and early 1960s as the two countries cooperated against the USA, but the relationship began to break down thereafter, mostly over differences of opinion on negotiating an end to the Vietnam War and over Vietnam's friendship with the Soviet Union. Relations worsened further in the 1970s with the conflicting ownership claims over islands in the South China Sea, Vietnamese hostility toward the Chinese client state of Kampuchea, and Vietnam's persecution and expulsion of its ethnic Chinese residents. From the recent low-point of the 1979 war and bitter quarrelling throughout the 1980s over conflicting claims in the South China Sea, China and Vietnam have found it in their mutual interest to reduce tensions and help preserve a favourable atmosphere in the region for the economic construction both desperately need. Beijing and Hanoi reached a rapprochement in the early 1990s. The collapse of communism in Eastern Europe, which drove the Asian socialist governments closer together, and a settlement in Kampuchea, with Vietnam withdrawing its troops and China halting support for the Khmer Rouge, cleared the way for Beijing and Hanoi to normalize their diplomatic relations in November 1991. Hanoi has promised it will maintain only economic relations, not official diplomatic relations, with Taiwan (which is Vietnam's greatest source of foreign investment).

Most of the contentious issues in the two countries' relations, however, remain unresolved. They have not reached an agreement on demarcating their borders either on land or at sea. Besides the South China Sea islands, China and Vietnam dispute sovereignty over the Gulf of Tonkin, which also contains oil deposits. In 1993 the two governments agreed not to use force in settling the issue, but incidents in the Gulf have continued since then, often sparking heated diplomatic exchanges. The PRC has been critical of Hanoi for spending too much on its armed forces and too little on economic development – another signal that Beijing cannot accept a militarily strong Vietnam. China also wants Hanoi to readmit some 270,000 ethnic Chinese who fled from Vietnam during the late 1970s.

Although PLA forces were less than impressive during their invasion of Vietnam in 1979, Vietnam is relatively unthreatening to China at present: (1) it is no longer a conduit for Soviet influence in the region; (2) it no longer occupies Cambodia; (3) it has no major power patron; and (4) it is well behind China and other countries in the region in economic development. Indeed, Hanoi faces the prospect of increasing strategic vulnerability *vis-à-vis* China. Since the 1979 campaign, Vietnam has lost the heavy Soviet military aid it enjoyed during the Cold War, while the PLA has become more efficient and modern. Most ominously, China's economic growth has far outstripped Vietnam's, even when measured per capita (Betts, 1995, pp. 66–9). To protect itself, Hanoi will probably seek a security relationship with another major power or with its fellow ASEAN members. (Vietnam has, for example, offered the US Navy use of Cam Ranh Bay.) Either avenue would bring new tensions with Beijing.

Vietnam is far from a major Chinese trading partner, but their trade is increasing. Official Sino-Vietnamese trade amounted to about $1 billion in 1995, double the previous year's total (Singh, 1996, p. 310). Vietnam is attractive as a market for Chinese goods and a site for Chinese investment (labour costs in Vietnam are lower than in China). Chinese-made goods are popular in Vietnam because they are cheaper and often higher in quality than their Vietnamese equivalents. The Vietnamese authorities have therefore tried to control trade to protect domestic producers. The result has been an explosion of 'unofficial' trade between Vietnam and the Chinese provinces of Yunnan, Guangxi and Guangdong, contributing to the possibility that economic relations will generate as well as mollify tensions in the relationship.

Although they did not say so publicly, Chinese officials were displeased to see Vietnam join ASEAN and the ARF, as this increased the possibility that these organizations would become more unitedly anti-China on issues such as sovereignty over the South China Sea. Since ASEAN has in general been relatively conciliatory toward China, Vietnam's membership automatically adds weight to the organization's hard-line wing. ASEAN membership makes the islands that Vietnam claims less vulnerable to seizure by China, as this would now be considered a violation of ASEAN norms, and Beijing could expect a reaction similar to what followed the Mischief Reef incident. Thus Vietnam benefits from joining ASEAN, China loses, and the organization itself takes on new challenges. ASEAN officials know that early membership for Vietnam is a 'gamble', but they supported it in the belief it would eventually improve Sino-Vietnam relations without damaging ASEAN–China relations (Hiebert and Schwarz, 1995, pp. 23–24). Since ASEAN's success has been in managing rather than solving disputes, there is reason for hoping that it might dampen possible future Sino-Vietnam conflicts, if little expectation that it will broker a long-term resolution.

The Taiwan Question

Beijing still considers Taiwan a renegade province that belongs to China and must eventually return to PRC control. However far Taiwan and the mainland grow apart culturally, economically and politically, Taipei's adherence to the principle that Taiwan is still part of China assures the CCP and its constituencies that the long-term goal of restoring Beijing's rule over all rightful Chinese territory is still within the Party's grasp. Conversely, a declaration of independence by Taiwan would destroy this hope, with shattering ramifications for the self-image of the Party and of China as a whole. (Not least among these ramifications is the possibility of Taiwanese independence leading to a 'domino effect' of separatism on the mainland [Yan, 1993, p. 6]). There is no reason to doubt that every member and faction within the top CCP leadership accepts the assumption that Taiwan cannot be allowed break permanently away from the mainland. Certainly no PRC leader who acquiesced to the 'loss' of Taiwan could remain in power. Thus, the broad guideline for Beijing's Taiwan policy is that reunification is desirable, temporary separation is tolerable, but Taiwanese independence is unacceptable. Day-to-day policy goals are to persuade Taipei to maintain good relations with the PRC and to prevent other governments from providing Taiwan with either arms or increased diplomatic status.

The PRC's initial approach to dealing with Taipei was predominantly military. Besides shelling Jinmen (Quemoy) and Mazu (Matsu), the PLA attacked and captured the ROC-held island of Dachen in 1955. Although there were no serious skirmishes in the 1960s and 1970s, Beijing's belligerent rhetoric indicated its basic policy toward Taiwan was to prepare for an invasion while working to isolate the island economically and diplomatically. With the rise to paramount leadership of the Deng regime, however, Beijing shifted to a policy of detente and peaceful overtures toward Taiwan. As the United States severed diplomatic relations with Taiwan in accord with its new recognition of the PRC, Beijing announced it would stop shelling ROC-held islands in the Taiwan Strait and enunciated a set of comparatively generous terms under which Taiwan and the PRC could peacefully reunify.

The PRC's position remains substantially unchanged since the 'Message to Compatriots in Taiwan', released by the Standing Committee of the Fifth National People's Congress on 1 January 1979. Reiterated in the Chinese government's 1993 White Paper on 'The Taiwan Question and the Reunification of China', the PRC position is that: (1) the issue is solely between the CCP and the Guomindang (i.e., Beijing opposes placing the matter on the agenda of any international or regional fora); (2) China supports 'peaceful' reunification; (3) in exchange for acknowledgment that Taiwan is part of the People's Republic, Beijing offers Taipei the same 'one country, two systems' deal it offered Hong Kong, which means Taiwan could retain its own armed forces and political, economic and legal systems for a long transition period; and (4) Taiwan and the mainland should immediately establish the 'three links' (direct air and sea travel, mail services, and trade across the Strait) and the 'four exchanges' (scholarly, cultural, athletic, and technological). These basic points were reiterated and sometimes elaborated upon in subsequent communications aimed at Taiwan, including Standing Committee Chairman Ye Jianying's 'nine-point' speech in 1981, Beijing's White Paper on Taiwan in 1993, and Jiang Zemin's 'eight point' speech in 1995.

Taiwanese reaction to the 'one country, two systems' proposal has been cool. Past attempts at cooperation between the CCP and the Guomindang prior to the Chinese Civil War and during the Japanese invasion have convinced many Taiwanese that the CCP's offer to allow Taiwan to retain its own system after reunification should be viewed with suspicion. Events preceding the transfer of Hong

Kong to PRC control in July 1997 did little to assuage Taiwanese scepticism. Hong Kong was much-discussed as a test case for the feasibility of the 'one country, two systems' idea; indeed, many analysts argued that good faith and good behaviour by the CCP in Hong Kong were ensured by the fact that Taiwan was watching intently. Yet the PRC began dismantling Hong Kong's political and legal systems even before the British administration left.

Taiwan's basic mainland policy has been the 'three no's': no contact, no negotiation, and no compromise with Beijing. For all practical purposes, however, Taiwan has already dropped the 'three no's' policy. The only significant remaining restrictions involve the circulation of mainland literature on Taiwan, direct air and sea travel between the ROC and the PRC, and the circumstances under which ROC and PRC officials may meet. Taipei was close to formally accepting the PRC's proposed 'four exchanges' and 'three direct links' before the latest Straits Crisis in 1995–6, but appeared to be holding out for a commitment from Beijing not to use force against Taiwan.

The 'no contact' proviso did not prevent the two sides from establishing a rudimentary framework for dialogue and technical negotiations. When the Asian Development Bank held its 1989 annual meeting in Beijing, Taiwan's Finance Minister Shirley Kuo made the trip, which represented the first contact between ROC and PRC officials on the mainland since 1949. In 1991 both sides founded organizations to facilitate negotiations that were officially 'unofficial'. Taiwan established the Straits Exchange Foundation (SEF), chaired by Koo Chenfu, a multi-millionaire and member of the Guomindang Central Standing Committee. The PRC counterpart was the Association for Relations Across the Taiwan Straits (ARATS) headed by former Shanghai mayor Wang Daohan. Wang and Koo met in Singapore in 1993, and ARATS' Vice-Chairman Tang Shubei visited Taiwan in 1994. These talks were a modest success. The two sides made progress on issues including the resolution of fishing disputes and the repatriation of illegal immigrants and hijackers from Taiwan back to the mainland. Broader political issues, however, were strictly ruled out by pre-agreement. Further progress in subsequent meetings was limited by Taiwan's perception that the PRC was trying to treat Taipei as a provincial government and to use the SEF–ARATS talks to persuade Taiwan to drop the 'three no's' policy.

Taiwan's mainland policy under President Lee Denghui has been a combination of peaceful gestures toward the PRC and gradual movement toward independent nationhood – a reasonable approach from Taiwan's point of view, but a contradictory or even duplicitous policy from Beijing's standpoint. Lee Denghui declared during his first term that Taiwan's 'period of national mobilization for suppression of the communist rebellion' was officially terminated and that his administration recognized the CCP had effective control over the mainland and would no longer be labelled a 'bandit regime'. Before cross-Straits tensions rose in 1995 over Lee's Cornell University visit, an official of the Lee administration had also made the ROC government's first public reference to China using its official name of 'People's Republic of China'. Nonetheless, his administration's responses to PRC overtures have set three difficult conditions for progress toward political reconciliation with Beijing. First, the PRC must accept the Taipei regime as an equal, the government of a 'sovereign state', and cease undermining Taiwan's diplomatic efforts. Second, the PRC must pledge not to use force against Taiwan. Finally, China must convert to a market-capitalist democracy. Other ROC government statements have added that the gap in living standards between Taiwan and the mainland would have to narrow greatly before Taiwan would assent to reunification. All this suggests, of course, that the ROC government is willing to maintain the status quo indefinitely. Even more disturbing, from Beijing's standpoint, is Lee's insistence that Taiwan needs more 'international space'. 'We have to stand up, we have to go out', says Lee. 'We must not let the Chinese communists completely cut off our space for survival' (Baum, 1996, p. 14).

Indeed, despite increased cross-Straits contacts of various kinds, Beijing has seen Taiwan drift steadily toward independence during the last decade. Until recently, advocating independence from China was illegal in Taiwan. This was one of two issues (the other being China's claim to sovereignty over the South China Sea islands) on which the ruling Guomindang and the CCP were in complete agreement. But in 1986, during the final months of martial law on Taiwan, a coalition of non-Guomindang activists and parliamentarians who represented the views and interests of the Taiwan-born Chinese (as opposed to the 'mainlanders' who fled to Taiwan after the CCP's victory in the Chinese Civil War) established the Democratic Progressive Party (DPP). An important plank of the DPP platform was the assertion that Taiwan should declare independence from the mainland and rename itself the 'Republic of Taiwan'. There are now three main political parties in Taiwan, each taking a different stance on independence. The DPP favours it most strongly, although some party members, reacting to public concern over PRC retaliation, no longer insist on an immediate declaration of independence. Lee's Guomindang appears to favour *de facto* independence while officially maintaining the principle of reunification sometime in the future. The New Party, founded by former Guomindang conservatives, is strongly opposed to independence and in favour of reunification. While Lee's view represents the mainstream of Taiwanese voters, there is little doubt that were it not for the PRC's sabre-rattling, Taiwan would have declared independence already, as only a minority of Taiwan's inhabitants wants to politically reunify with China. Most of Taiwan's population would accept separate statehood as appropriate for the island but is frightened of provoking the mainland. The threat to use force has deterred Taiwan from officially breaking away from China, and in this sense Beijing's policy has been successful.

Diplomatic Rivalry

The PRC has required that any country establishing normal diplomatic relations with Beijing must recognize the 'one-China principle', which means no diplomatic relations with Taiwan; foreign governments are thus forced to choose between recognizing Taipei and recognizing Beijing. Since the 1970s, when the PRC replaced Taiwan in the UN, it has not been much of a contest: only 29 countries, most of them small and poor, have diplomatic relations with Taiwan. But Taiwan still struggles for recognition where it sees an opportunity, and the PRC still tries to stop it. In June 1995, the ROC government bought full-page advertisements in two San Francisco newspapers calling for Taiwanese membership in the United Nations. Arguing that one nation can hold more than one UN seat, ROC officials cite the examples of North and South Korea, which occupy separate seats even though both profess a commitment to reunify, and the Soviet Union, which effectually held three seats ('independent' Ukraine and Belarus had their own seats). Beijing moved extraordinarily quickly to recognize twelve former Soviet republics in December 1991; apparently the PRC was rushing to establish relations with the new states before Taipei did (Kim, 1995, p. 470).

In January 1997, China vetoed a UN resolution to send peace-keepers to Guatemala because that nation has diplomatic relations with Taiwan. Ministry of Foreign Affairs spokesman Shen Guofang explained, 'Guatemala cannot expect on the one hand to do something that harms the sovereignty and territorial integrity of China while on the other hand requesting China to cooperate in peace-keeping' (Tyler, 1997, p. 5).

Beijing uses its diplomatic and economic power to prevent foreign governments from selling armaments to Taiwan as well. After France agreed to sell Taipei 60 Mirage fighter aircraft and 1,500 advanced air-to-surface missiles, Beijing evicted the French consulate from Guangzhou. Soon thereafter, Paris promised to halt further arms deals with the ROC.

The PRC complains regularly about Taiwan's practice of 'money diplomacy', or trying to buy itself greater international political status. Taiwan has publicly pledged to donate $1 billion to UN aid programmes for developing countries if allowed to rejoin the UN. The ROC recently got recognition from Gambia, for example, after agreeing to provide $35 million in aid. Indeed, some countries have tried to squeeze more cash out of Taiwan by threatening to recognize Beijing instead. Weary of this diplomatic extortion, ROC Foreign Minister John Chang said in November 1996 that his country would 'turn down those who want to profit from the situation and make unreasonable demands'. After South Africa decided to switch its recognition to Beijing in 1998, Taiwan cancelled 36 bilateral agreements, including a plan to invest $5 billion in a South African petrochemical plant (Healy and Eyton, 1996, p. 20).

Expanding Economic Interdependence

In contrast to the stalemate in Sino-Taiwan political relations, their economic relationship seems to affirm the liberalist image of market forces overwhelming political barriers. Here the forces of the international marketplace have worked in the interest of the PRC, which seeks to maximize links with Taiwan. Taipei, conversely, has feared that economic ties would make Taiwan vulnerable to political control by Beijing. To guard against this, Taiwan had for decades banned trade with the PRC. But through the 1980s, cross-Straits business flourished anyway, much of it using Hong Kong as an entrepot. Unable to stem the tide, Taipei capitulated, lifting the ban in 1988 and gradually reducing the remaining restrictions thereafter. The ROC government now admits that 'Taiwan's economic future depends largely on China' (Premier Lien Chan said this in 1995. Harris and Smith, 1996, p. 1). Attracted by the common language and culture, geographic proximity, cheap labour, and an alternative market to those in the protectionism-prone West (Lee, 1996, pp. 353–4), Taiwanese have set up thousands of factories on the mainland, mostly in Fujian Province. Taiwan–PRC trade reached a value of $29 billion in 1995 and is still rising quickly. Cumulative Taiwanese foreign direct investment in China was about $30 billion at the end of 1995. China has become the main recipient of Taiwan's foreign direct investment and exports.

To further facilitate trade, Taiwan's business community now pressures Taipei to drop its remaining restrictions on direct sea and air links. Taiwan already allows Hong Kong and Macau airlines to fly from the ROC to Chinese cities on the condition that the aircraft first land in Hong Kong or Macau and change their flight numbers. The Taipei government also recently agreed to allow approved ships to sail from an offshore shipping centre in the port of Kaohsiung directly to China if they fly the flag of a third country.

While the Taiwanese government originally lifted the ban on travel to the mainland in 1987 due to demonstrations by elderly mainland-born military veterans desiring a final visit to their home towns, it has been the business community that has pushed Taipei to drop the restrictions on mainlanders visiting Taiwan. Previously, PRC nationals desiring to visit Taiwan had to prove that they planned to participate in a business, athletic or academic meeting, attend a family funeral, or see a sick relative. As a consequence of these restrictions, the PRC has enjoyed a massive surplus in tourism revenue: visits by Taiwanese to the mainland outnumbered visits by mainlanders to Taiwan by 1.5 million to 50,000 in 1996, with the average Taiwanese tourist spending $2,000 during a trip to China (*Straits Times,* 1997c, p. 17).

Beijing eagerly welcomes cross-Straits business, even granting the Taiwanese special tax breaks and allowing them to invest in any mainland project they wish, while other foreigners must choose from a list of Beijing-approved projects. The PRC benefits from Taiwan's wealth and expertise, although not equally: since 1979, Taiwan has maintained a huge trade surplus with the mainland. But more important for the PRC, fostering cross-Straits economic interdependence binds Taiwan to the mainland, contributing surreptitiously to the goal of eventual reunification.

The Taiwan Straits Crisis of 1995–6

The PRC's more patient and conciliatory approach to Taiwan acquiesced to a limited increase in the ROC's international stature and freedom of action. This was thought necessary to check pro-independence sentiment, which would continue to rise if China overtly tried to smother Taiwan. At the same time, the Chinese hoped the economic, cultural and familial connections that would form in a more peaceful cross-Straits environment would gradually increase the pro-reunification constituency among the Taiwanese.

Lee Denghui's campaign to gain for Taiwan greater international diplomatic status, including his meetings with dignitaries while on 'vacation' in Southeast Asia and his interest in Taiwan's admission to the United Nations, convinced many PRC political and military elites that the patient and conciliatory approach begun in 1979 was not working. Some PRC officials were already inclined to believe that the longer Taiwan and the PRC were separated, the more difficult it would be to reunite them – not least because the remnants of the group of two million that emigrated to Taiwan from the mainland to escape communism were dying off, and the subsequent generations that were born and raised in Taiwan could not be expected to maintain the same commitment to reunification. Lee's visit to the United States confirmed to many Chinese that Taiwan was exploiting Beijing's restraint, that Lee had dealt with Beijing in bad faith, and that his government was indeed committed to independence in the absence of drastic action by the PRC. 'Lee', said the Chinese press, 'has cast off his disguise to reveal his splittist nature' (*Beijing Review*, 1995, p. 12). Lee (and Washington, which violated the gentlemen's agreement not to host high-ranking ROC officials) had exceeded Beijing's acceptable limits and had to be deterred from doing so again. Hence the PLA missile 'exercises' off the coast of Taiwan in the summer of 1995 and again during Lee's re-election campaign in March 1996.

The results of this tactic for the PRC were mixed. On the positive side, Beijing demonstrated a capacity to influence Taiwan's prosperity, sending the island's stock market into a dive and temporarily disrupting air and sea traffic near the areas where the missiles were being fired. Although Lee apparently got more votes as a result of the PLA's missile-rattling, the Taiwanese were clearly frightened. During these tensions, a book titled *T-Day August 1995: China's Violent Invasion of Taiwan* sold over 288,000 copies in the ROC in less than a year, a record for a Taiwanese-authored book (Baum, 1995, p. 26). The long-term result is that a Taiwanese declaration of independence is less likely than before the missile tests. Indeed, during his 20 May 1996 inauguration speech, Lee said Taiwan's independence was both impossible and unnecessary, and he offered to make a 'journey of peace' to the mainland – a significant concession, as previously he had said he would meet PRC leaders only in a neutral arena.

Unfortunately for Beijing, the use of military intimidation against Taiwan undermined its desired image as a peaceful and responsible power. For several years prior to the latest Taiwan Straits episode, the Chinese had emphasized the weakness and passivity of their armed forces in order to minimize fears throughout the region arising from the PLA's modernization campaign. In the months between Lee's Cornell visit and the ROC presidential elections, however, Beijing completely reversed this image. The chosen strategy of intimidation required a show of force, both on the ground and through the media airwaves, that sent belligerent signals: China had a modern and efficient military, including many high-tech systems, that gave it a significant power-projection capability; the PLA was well-trained in combined arms operations; and PLA personnel were anxious for combat. Whether or not these images were accurate, they supported the view of the 'China bashers' that China is predisposed to using force to achieve its political goals and that economic development has made the Chinese even more dangerous.

Would the PRC Attack Taiwan?

Despite complaints from Taipei and criticism from many other governments, Beijing has continually reaffirmed its right to use force against Taiwan. PRC officials have identified several scenarios that would trigger military intervention. The best known of these is a declaration of independence from China by the Taipei government. Others include: 'interference' in Taiwan's domestic affairs by another country; a breakdown of political and social order on the island; a refusal by Taipei to negotiate with Beijing; and an attempt by Taiwan to deploy nuclear weapons. The ethical justification Beijing offers for this threat to use force is that Taiwan is Chinese territory, and all states have the right to use force to defend their territory. The awkward implication is that in the event of a declaration of independence, the PLA would be dispatched to prevent the Taiwanese from invading Taiwan. High PRC officials have even been known to hint at the possibility of using nuclear weapons against the island. Speaking in 1990 to a group of overseas Chinese in Argentina about the PRC's refusal to renounce the possible use of force against Taiwan, Senior PLA figure Yang Shangkun said pointedly, 'we have nuclear warheads, ballistic missiles, submarines, many submarines' (*Shijie Ribao* (New York), 8 June 1990; Cabestan, 1995, p. 41). In 1996, China's chief arms control negotiator Sha Zukang said the PRC's pledge of 'no first use' of nuclear weapons applies to foreign countries but not to Taiwan. Recently PRC spokesmen have assured Taiwan that 'the Chinese will not fight the Chinese'; the threat to use force 'is not directed at Taiwan compatriots but at foreign interventionist forces and Taiwan independence elements' (British Broadcasting Cooperation, 1995, p. G/3). How this distinction between ordinary Taiwan 'Chinese' and 'Taiwan independence elements' would be worked out in the event of hostilities was not explained.

The disincentives to attempting to settle the Taiwan question through a use of force are strong. To begin with, the success of the operation itself could not be taken for granted, especially if Beijing attempted an amphibious assault, which is an extraordinarily difficult undertaking even for a fully modern military skilled in joint-service manoeuvres. Although the PLA has far superior numbers of troops and equipment, Taiwan's soldiers are better trained, have a higher proportion of advanced weapons, and enjoy the advantages of superior surveillance capabilities and bases nearer the battlefield. A war with Taiwan would expose some of the PRC's economically best-developed areas to retaliatory bombardment. The Chinese attackers would probably be unable to gain control of the seas and skies; without this, their soldiers would be highly vulnerable as their boats crossed the 100 miles of the Taiwan Strait. Even if the PLA managed to land sufficient troops on the Taiwanese coast, completely subduing the mountainous island would remain a formidable military and political task; as one analyst conjectured, Taiwan might become for China what Northern Ireland has been to Britain (Chen, 1996, pp. 461–2).

Regardless of success or failure on the battlefield, Beijing would pay a heavy political price for attacking Taiwan. Public opinion in the PRC might sour on the idea of China killing fellow Chinese, especially if the PLA was not able to win a quick victory or keep casualties low. Fear among other countries of China as a threat to regional security would increase, perhaps sparking arms buildups and anti-China alignments. China's trade links to the outside world would invariably be damaged, slowing down the PRC's development and modernization (Li, 1996, pp. 454–5).

Despite these risks and costs, Beijing could be expected to resort to military force to overturn a declaration of independence by Taiwan. 'For the majority of the Chinese population', explains Chen Jian, 'acceptance of Taiwan's independence would mean the continuation of China's division and humiliation. Consequently, no Chinese government, be it a democracy or a dictatorship, will or can accept Taiwan's independence' (Chen Jian, 1996, pp. 460–1). Besides Taiwan's vast material and symbolic value to the PRC, the ruling regime has so strongly and publicly committed itself to hanging onto the former province that the leadership could not escape giving the order to unleash the PLA.

What about the possible intervention of US military forces? The political significance of Taiwan raises the level of acceptable costs so high that the prospect of facing the superior US Navy is probably not a sufficient deterrent. As Chu Shulong writes, 'Taiwan is the last piece of territory that foreigners still endeavour to remove from China. This time the Americans are closely following in the wake of the Japanese, who took Taiwan away from China for half a century'. When a campaign to recapture Taiwan is placed in this context, Beijing can win even by losing, *à la* Saddam Hussein in the Gulf War: 'bravery in fighting a superpower when that power tries to bully China would itself constitute a victory; destroying two major ships would become a victory, no matter whether our opponents destroy eight or 10 of our ships at the same time. The Chinese still consider the Korean War as a Chinese victory because a year-old republic was brave enough to fight a superpower that had just won the Second World War and possessed nuclear weapons' (Chu, 1996b, p. 100).

If Beijing decided to take military action against Taiwan, immediately launching an amphibious assault would not be its most attractive option. More likely would be a longer-term campaign of gradually-escalating coercion designed to erode Taiwan's economic stability and force Taipei to rescind its declaration of independence. Conducting missile tests near Taiwan's major ports has proved an effective means of disrupting the island's air and sea traffic. The PRC might also launch false attacks, detain or harass Taiwanese commercial or fishing vessels, send boatloads of mainland refugees to Taiwan, or increase cross-Straits smuggling. To step up the pressure, China could attack one or more of the 85 smaller islands administered by the ROC, announce a naval blockade of all shipping entering or leaving Taiwan harbours, or bombard selected military targets on the main island. Such acts would be difficult for Taiwan to stop, and would interrupt Taiwan's trade, create panic in its stock market, and trigger the flight of capital from the island. At the same time, the United States would be unlikely to intervene decisively against such low-level, intermittent and long-term coercion (Nathan, 1996, p. 92).

The ideal outcome for Beijing, to paraphrase the famous ancient Chinese military thinker Sun Zi, is 'to win without fighting'. In any case, however, the PRC's Taiwan policy will be founded on the *capability* to capture the island by military means. The PLA understands that Taiwan's recent diplomatic assertiveness stems from the realization that the ROC armed forces presently constitute a formidable deterrent to a PRC invasion. This suggests China must therefore strive for the capacity to dominate Taiwan by military means. Once attained, such a capability will presumably elicit political concessions from Taipei even without military forces being sent into battle (Wang, 1995, pp. 7–10). This provides another important motive for modernizing the PLA, and makes Beijing unlikely to renounce the threat to use force against Taiwan as long as the island remains aloof.

China and the Two Koreas

China's traditional policy toward Korea has been to strive to control it or, at minimum, prevent it from falling under the domination of another power (Bedeski, 1995, p. 516). South Korea is no longer susceptible to direct control by foreign powers; a reunited Korea, roughly half the size of Japan and nuclear-capable, would be even less so. Modern China has had to settle for an alliance with the weaker half of the peninsula, with the stronger half hosting the military bases of a hostile superpower. Yet given the likely alternatives, this status quo is acceptable to Beijing. The most important objective of China's new policy toward Korea is stability. This means both reducing inter-Korean tensions that might lead to military conflict and also working to prevent a North Korean collapse, the disruptions from which could spill across the border into China. Beijing wants the North Korean regime to survive, but with communism on the wane and an improved Sino-South Korean relationship, this reflects a fear of regional instability more than a desire to preserve an ideological ally. China also seeks to maintain a friendly relationship with Seoul to exploit opportunities for political and economic cooperation with South Korea that would benefit China and to forge ties that will persist if Korea is reunified on South Korea's terms, as is expected in the near future. More specific Chinese goals are preventing the deployment of nuclear weapons on the peninsula and minimizing Chinese subsidies to ailing North Korea.

Beijing's Relations with North Korea

North Korea's greatest value to China has been as a buffer state. Summing up the PRC's decision to send troops to save North Korea in 1950, PLA commander-in-chief Zhu De said, '*Chun wang, chi han*' (When the lips are gone, the teeth get cold). This was a classical aphorism from the Warring States period (475-221 BC) that originally referred to the plight of the state of Guo after the Qin emperor had conquered the state of Yu, which was Guo's ally and buffer (Spurr, 1988, p. 62). The significance of North Korea as a Chinese buffer state, however, has greatly declined since the Cold War (Lee, 1994, p. 102).

Despite the veneer of socialist solidarity and 'blood' ties forged as a result of China's intervention to save Kim Il Sung's government during the Korean War, China's relationship with North Korea has often been difficult. The North Koreans have on occasion played off China and the Soviet Union against each other, turning to Moscow when they were dissatisfied with the assistance China was providing and refusing to abandon their relationship with the Soviets during the Sino-Soviet rift. Kim Il Sung was labelled a 'revisionist' in China during the Cultural Revolution, and the two countries fought border skirmishes in 1969. Chinese recognition of the South Korean government was a bitter disappointment for Pyongyang, which has retaliated by increasing its economic ties with Taiwan. China has had a security treaty with North Korea since 1961, but Beijing has made it clear Pyongyang could not count on Chinese military support in a scenario where North Korea is the aggressor. A Chinese Ministry of Foreign Affairs official, for example, said explicitly during a recent visit of Jiang Zemin to South Korea that China's security relationship with North Korea does not guarantee Chinese troops will defend the North in the event of hostilities. Some Chinese elites have suggested the PLA might not intervene even if South Korea attacked the North. Indeed, certain Chinese scholars have recently argued that PRC military intervention in the Korean War of 1950–3 was a mistake, and that Beijing should have negotiated with Washington to solve the problem instead (Garrett and Glaser, 1995, p. 540).

While Western analysts have often placed their hopes upon the Chinese talking sense into the North Koreans, Chinese officials emphasize that they have had only limited influence in Pyongyang, and even less since normalizing relations with South Korea. North Korea has always been an opaque and fiercely independent state, and Chinese leaders do not have the ties with Kim Jong Il and other younger elites that they had with Kim Il Sung.

Nonetheless, China's interest in maintaining stability on the Korean peninsula often leads to the Chinese using their influence to protect Pyongyang. Chinese officials describe North Korea as the weaker country on the peninsula and contend that its seemingly aggressive actions result from its sense of insecurity *vis-à-vis* South Korea and the USA, not from offensive intentions. The Chinese have encouraged other countries to pursue a conciliatory policy to reduce tensions and induce North Korea to increase its economic links with the outside world. The PRC strongly encourages direct North Korean–US dialogue and the establishment of diplomatic relations as soon as possible, especially since Beijing has already done its part by recognizing Seoul. China supports North Korea's call for renegotiation of the Armistice Agreement that ended Korean War hostilities, although unlike Pyongyang, Beijing does not want the armistice negated until a permanent peace framework is ready to replace it. China has also joined North Korea in criticizing the large US–South Korean 'Team Spirit' military exercises as provocative.

Beijing was highly condemnatory of the US military presence in South Korea until the 1970s, although it tacitly accepted the status quo thereafter, seeing American forces as a useful check on Soviet or, more recently, Japanese ambitions (Wang, 1997, pp. 3–5).

Sentiment against US bases has returned among some Chinese elites since the early 1990s. The key to the Chinese attitude is the perceived primary mission of the Korean-based US forces – whether it is to support an objective the Chinese share (e.g. preventing a Korean War or a larger Japanese military buildup) or to counter Chinese influence in the region.

Although Sino-North Korean trade has declined in the post-Mao era as the PRC has expanded its economic relations with Japan and the West, China remains Pyongyang's top trading partner, the principal supplier of North Korea's food and energy imports, and its only significant source of economic assistance outside of the recent emergency donations of grain and other survival essentials. Interestingly, the PRC–North Korea trading pattern has made North Korea look like a semi-peripheral state and China a peripheral state, with the North Koreans exchanging steel products and consumer manufactures for Chinese agricultural products and oil. This reflects the industrial foundation the Japanese laid in northern Korea during their occupation from 1910 to the end of the Second World War.

China increasingly views North Korea as an economic burden. After the end of the Cold War the Chinese insisted North Korea begin paying for Chinese goods in hard currency instead of through barter. China has also been phasing out 'friendship prices' for the North Koreans, although they still pay somewhat less than the world market rate for Chinese products. Beijing has encouraged North Korea to implement market-oriented economic reforms while maintaining one-party rule – i.e., the 'soft authoritarian' model the Chinese themselves have implemented. China has thus praised Pyongyang's modest efforts to develop links with the world economy, such as the Rajin-Sonbong Free Economic Zone (Wang, 1997, p. 8). The PRC is likely to provide whatever assistance is necessary to keep the North Korean economy from collapsing, but Beijing currently keeps this aid at a minimum to goad North Korea into accepting the need for economic reform and because China itself can ill afford a serious drain on its resources (Garrett and Glaser, 1995, pp. 539, 541).

Beijing's Relations with South Korea

The common observation that post-Mao China has abandoned communist ideology is reinforced by China's much improved relationship with South Korea during the last decade, which inescapably entailed a betrayal of Beijing's socialist ally North Korea. In pragmatic terms, China and South Korea are natural economic partners and have strong common political interests in containing Japanese power and resisting some items on America's hegemonic agenda.

Even in more philosophical terms, the China of today and the near future may share more common ground with South Korea than with North Korea. For example, Seoul's economic development strategy of the 1970s, which saw high growth while the state kept society under martial law, foreshadowed China's strategy of the 1980s and 1990s. Bruce Cumings asserts that 'Deng is really nothing more than the Park Chung Hee of China', referring to the authoritarian ex-general who presided over South Korea's rapid economic growth in 1961–79 (Cumings, 1996, p. 35). This point is not lost on Chinese scholars, who frequently discuss the applicability of South Korea's experience to China.

In 1988 the PRC made an important concession in agreeing to participate in the Seoul Olympic Games over Pyongyang's objection. Seoul wanted to join the United Nations, while North Korea argued that UN participation by either Korean regime would perpetuate national separation. The South Korean government got the Chinese to agree not to block its application for UN admission. Pyongyang was thereby forced to follow suit, and both Koreas entered the UN in September 1991. The culmination of the improving Sino-South Korean relationship was their diplomatic normalization in August 1992. Qian Qichen reportedly said this allowed Beijing to 'down four birds with one stone': (1) Taiwan would be further diplomatically isolated as Seoul broke relations with Taipei; (2) the way to greater economic cooperation between China and South Korea would be opened; (3) North Korea would be discouraged from asking for more economic assistance from China; and (4) China and South Korea could band together in opposition to US pressure to halt what Washington called unfair trade practices (Kim, 1994d, p. 17).

Sino-South Korean trade is increasing rapidly. From an estimated $30 billion in 1997 it is projected to reach as high as $56 billion early in the twenty-first century, by which time China is expected to be South Korea's largest trading partner (*Newsreview* (Seoul), 21 February 1994; Lee and Sohn, 1995, p. 35). South Korea mainly exports industrial equipment, building materials and high-tech electronic goods to China, while buying mostly Chinese raw materials (oil, minerals, etc.), agricultural goods, and fabrics. The Sino-South Korean economic relationship is complementary in ways similar to the Sino-Japanese relationship: China offers cheap labour (South Korea's average wage is 28 times higher than that in China), abundant natural resources, and a large domestic market, while South Korea, with few resources and a small market, has a relatively high technological and skill base. In another parallel with the Sino-Japanese relationship, the Chinese feel South Koreans do not invest enough in China, and transfer too little technology where they do invest. The Chinese are counting on Korean investment to put more pressure to Japan to increase its own investments before the South Koreans capture a larger share of the pool of Chinese labour and resources in desirable areas such as China's northeast, where average wages are lower than in southern China (Shuja, 1995, pp. 63–4). For their part, the South Koreans complain about China's trade surplus and about Chinese exports eating into South Korea's share of the US and Japanese markets, partly on the strength of China's undervalued currency.

Some points of political friction remain as well. Sometimes characterized as a 'shrimp among whales', Korea sees both of its large Asian neighbours as potentially domineering, leading to Chinese complaints about South Korean analysts buying into the 'China threat' argument. China and South Korea also dispute each other's operating rights in the Yellow Sea, which is bounded by China's east coast and Korea's west coast. Incidents in recent years have included PRC interference with South Korean offshore oil exploration, the detention of Chinese fishing boast by the South Korean Navy, and PLA warships firing on commercial vessels passing through the Yellow Sea.

China's Position on Korean Reunification

China's publicly stated position is that it supports efforts by both Koreas toward peaceful reunification. Most of the scenarios associated with reunification, however, would leave China worse off than the status quo. A collapse of North Korea's present political system, which now appears the most likely avenue to reunification, would create dislocation on China's border, which the Chinese fear. With a democratizing political system, a history of strong ties with the United States and heavy economic interdependence with America and Japan, the South Korean regime that became master of a reunified Korea would have closer ties with the West than with Beijing, reducing China's overall influence on the Korean peninsula. At worst, a united Korea might join one or more of the other major powers in an anti-China coalition. Despite the many areas in which the Chinese and Korean economies are complementary, the Koreans might also prove to be economic competitors in some sectors. Furthermore, Chinese-controlled Manchuria includes territory in which Korea has interests. A large number of ethnic Koreans live in this region, which is traditionally considered the birthplace of the Korean people. In 1994, Pyongyang claimed part of Chonji Lake, which lies within the Chinese border, and the North Koreans recently rejected China's request for the right to transit the Tumen River to the Sea of Japan. Some Chinese officials say they fear a united Korea might pursue territorial claims against China more forcefully (Glaser, 1993, p. 262). Finally, reunification would divert South Korean investment capital into North Korea and away from China, where its influx rose rapidly, from $260 million in 1992 to $1.67 billion in 1994 (Sheng, 1995a, p. 120). These potential disadvantages explain Beijing's interest in prolonging the status quo by attempting to extend the life of the North Korean regime through economic aid and selective diplomatic support, which realistically are Beijing's only means of influencing Korean reunification.

In the meantime, its relationships with Seoul, Washington and Tokyo on the one hand and Pyongyang on the other uniquely qualify China to play the role of mediator. China used its influence to encourage both sides to take steps to reduce tensions during the crisis over North Korea's suspected nuclear weapons programme in 1992–4. Early in the crisis Chinese officials began to pressure North Korea to cooperate with the International Atomic Energy Agency (IAEA), to which Pyongyang responded by accusing China of breaking the mutual security treaty and recalling its ambassador from Beijing. Chinese pressure on the North Koreans to accept a reasonable deal continued until Pyongyang signed the Agreed Framework, and then reportedly resumed when the North Koreans objected to the proposal that South Korea supply the light-water nuclear reactors promised them under the Agreed Framework. On the other side, Chinese officials urged the US government to negotiate directly and patiently with Pyongyang, opposed imposing sanctions on the North Koreans, and publicly supported Pyongyang's attempts to expand the agenda for talks to include larger political issues such as withdrawal of US forces from South Korea and a commitment by Washington not to include South Korea under its 'umbrella' of extended nuclear deterrence. While many in the West believed North Korea was committed to continuing its nuclear weapons programme and was merely stalling for time, the Chinese argued that Pyongyang would trade the bomb for the right package of concessions from the United States. The Chinese therefore praised the Agreed Framework, as it appeared to prove their assessment of the North Koreans was correct (Garrett and Glaser, 1995, p. 535).

Thus, China wields a stabilizing influence in the Korean Peninsula while acting as provocateur in the other two regional 'flashpoints', the South China Sea and the Taiwan Strait, and seeking to repress potential regional leaders such as Japan, India and Vietnam. China's regional relationships reflect a transitory period of Chinese history in which some of the grievances arising from China's weakness of the recent past overlap with Beijing's display of an interest in system 'management' characteristic of great powers.

9

The Future of China's Foreign Relations

The preceding chapters have, it is hoped, provided insight into some of China's particular foreign relationships, each of which involves certain unique circumstances while at the same time tapping into general themes of Chinese foreign policy. It remains now to attempt to draw some general conclusions, while respecting the complexity of the subject.

Chinese foreign policy has three primary and enduring goals: power, wealth and status. 'Power' means Beijing's capacity to influence the policies of other governments and of the international system as a whole toward the outcomes the PRC desires. 'Wealth' means promoting China's economic development and raising the living standards of Chinese citizens. 'Status' means increasing international respect for China.

These three goals are interrelated. Increased power opens new avenues for attaining wealth. A powerful country might, for example, re-shape the rules of international trade to better suit its own comparative advantages. Conversely, economic development provides the basis for strong military forces and other means of getting one's way in international politics. High status follows almost automatically from great power and wealth, as exemplified by the worldwide interest in America's popular culture and economic and political thought during the USA's postwar heyday. Countries with a favourable international reputation in turn enjoy additional political influence and find new business opportunities.

More concrete principles have been deduced by Chinese leaders for applying these broad goals to specific policy issues. A current list of these intermediary principles would include the following: reducing tensions with and among neighbours to facilitate a favourable environment for China's economic development; promoting China's desired international reputation as a responsible and principled power; taking a strong stand on what Beijing has characterized as 'sovereignty' issues, including Taiwan and the Spratly Islands; encouraging other nations to resolve their disputes with China through bilateral negotiations; rallying international support to check what Beijing judges to be excessive US and Japanese political and military influence; encouraging foreign investment in China and foreign purchase of Chinese exports; mollifying foreign fears about the rise of Chinese economic and military power; and minimizing foreign influences that may impact negatively on China's economy, society and political system.

Some specific moves, such as joining the World Trade Organization or normalizing diplomatic relations with South Korea, might contribute at once to all three goals of power, status and wealth. Other specific issues, however, bring the broad goals and intermediary principles into conflict. In the case of the Spratlys, for example, China's desire for international respect of its sovereignty would call for an assertive policy, while its desire to maintain a peaceful political environment would demand a conciliatory posture. In such cases conflicting goals and interests must be traded off. For analytical purposes, these cases are especially interesting because they give insight into the ranking of goals and the hierarchy of principles, inasmuch as a particular policy chosen by the leadership appears to support one interest while undercutting others. Unfortunately, reliably predicting which among the competing considerations will prove dominant is usually difficult and often impossible. One potentially useful analytical key is the suggestion by some analysts that maintaining or increasing national power relative to that of a likely potential adversary would be the overriding goal during periods of high political tension (e.g. the Cold War), but the desire to enhance national wealth and public welfare becomes the most compelling objective of a state's foreign policy during periods of low political tension, such as the post-Cold War era (Miller, 1995; Spirtas, 1996, pp. 419–20). Yet even in the 1990s, when the Chinese government seems committed to pursuing wealth-enhancing policies as long as these policies do not entail a serious compromise of national security, economic gain is clearly not the overwhelming consideration in all Chinese behaviour.

One of the most important contributions a book like this could hope to make is to help reduce the occasions on which outside observers are surprised by Chinese behaviour. This happens when analysts who are familiar with China's basic geopolitical circumstances assume Chinese decision-makers operate in the same way as decision-makers in the other great powers. In fact, to reprise one of my assumptions from Chapter 1, China is much like any other great power, but with a few differences that can sometimes prove critically important. Even if it is correct to assume that China's desire to enhance its national security within the international environment is the single most important consideration in its foreign relations, how Chinese elites interpret the international environment, their alternatives for action therein, and the chances of success of various alternative policies, may be shaped by unique and intangible factors. In the case of Taiwan, for example, Western and other outside analysts who attempted to predict PRC policies based on conventional theories of deterrence without accounting for the .PRC's national self-image would risk underestimating the costs Beijing would pay to prevent 'losing' the island.

Despite its claims that China sets a high moral standard, Beijing generally practises *realpolitik.* Chinese foreign policy throughout the Cold War was highly pragmatic, despite the revolutionary communist rhetoric. In the post-Cold War era, China continues to do what is best for China (or for the CCP) even as it explains how its actions conform to the Five Principles of Peaceful Coexistence. Similarly, China's economic relations remain basically Neo-Mercantilist, with Chinese elites attempting to enjoy the benefits of the world economy while controlling and limiting its impact on Chinese society and its erosion of Chinese sovereignty.

Yet, as we have seen throughout this survey, the PRC's idiosyncrasies have deeply affected most of Beijing's important foreign relationships. These stem largely from two sources: China's historical experience and its political system.

History has left the Chinese with a strong sense of dissonance between China's deserved global position of honour and respect and its recent historical humiliations. PRC relations with ASEAN reveal vestiges of traditional Chinese thinking about its relationship with neighbouring 'barbarian' countries: viewing the subregion as a Chinese sphere of influence (as manifested, for example, in Beijing's claim of ownership over the entire South China Sea), preferring bilateral relationships in which smaller countries show China due deference, and conflating Chinese ethnicity and PRC citizenship. History has also imbued Beijing with a profound sense of insecurity, manifest in the continuous obsession with Chinese 'sovereignty' and Western 'plots', alongside the confidence based on the achievements of Chinese civilization. Most of the present leadership remembers the recent past when China was an impoverished and backward revolutionary state under military threat from one or both superpowers. Before that, of course, things were even worse. Beijing's relations with the United States are strongly coloured by the historical Chinese view of America as the leader of the 'imperialist' powers, while the legacy of the Sino-Japanese and Pacific Wars overshadows PRC relations with Tokyo.

Both the authoritarian character of the regime and the systemic political problem of holding together its vast, multi-ethnic empire contribute to Beijing's comparatively strong tendency to link internal and external security threats. With foreign policy decision-making more centralized than in liberal democracies, China's foreign relations may reflect not only foreign policy goals, but also *domestic* policy goals such as furthering the narrow interests of a particular organization, consolidating a certain leader's position within the Party hierarchy, or discrediting a particular individual or faction. Under some circumstances, internal political considerations might make a critical difference. In some extreme cases, the domestic agenda might overwhelm the foreign policy agenda; it is conceivable that the key decision-makers might choose a policy that, at least in the short term, fails to enhance or perhaps even damages China's international power, wealth and status, but seriously weakens some domestic political rival (e.g. the Cultural Revolution).

The Future: A 'China Threat'?

With rapid economic growth added to its other characteristics, China has the potential to become the superpower of the twenty-first century. This realization has given rise in the 1990s to speculation among analysts and politicians about the possibility of a 'China threat'. Chinese officials have responded with accusations of neo-imperialism and 'Cold War thinking', while busily touring Asia to offer repeated assurances that 'China will never seek hegemony'.

It must be recognized before we go any further that China faces immense internal challenges on the road to superpower status. These include environmental degradation, continued population growth and loss of arable land, rising crime and civil disorder, discontent among peasants who remain in the fields, a wave of uncontrolled migration of other peasants into the cities, widespread corruption among officials, high inflation, the reluctant privatization of un-profitable state-owned industries, separatist pressures in Tibet, Inner Mongolia and Xinjiang, and regionalism in the other provinces. Political instability, an economic slowdown or a devolution of central control into some type of federalism or even a common-wealth of autonomous states might preclude the possibility of a strong China capable of coercing its neighbours. The basis of a 'China threat' might therefore never materialize.

To take another perspective, China could be a threat to East Asian security without being a military superpower. A country does not have to be *dominant* to commit acts that are *destabilizing*. Even relatively weak countries can be trouble-makers if they choose to be. In 1995–6, for example, the Chinese effectually carried out a temporary blockade of parts of the Taiwanese coast by conducting missile tests, which forced the re-routing of ships and aircraft to avoid the danger areas. There is minimal danger of Chinese troops occupying capital cities throughout East Asia the way the Japanese did during the Pacific War. But there is a realistic danger that in a major dispute with its neighbours, the PRC might attempt to gain political leverage by threatening to upset the order upon which this region's prosperity is based. Indeed, if an immensely powerful China entails possible security risks, so does the opposite outcome, a Chinese collapse; these dangers might include refugee outflows, temptation among neighbouring states to enlarge their borders, and loose nuclear weapons.

An important theme that emerges from this survey of China's foreign relations is that China's grand strategy is changing to reflect its position in the hierarchy of the international system. This suggests that if it did indeed become a great power, China would behave differently from the way it did as a weak power. As a great power, China will behave boldly, more inclined to force its will upon others than to consult with them. A powerful China can be expected to use its increased influence to attempt to shape the regional and international political systems more in accordance with Chinese interests. The question is what kind of arrangements the Chinese believe will best facilitate their goals. While great powers are invariably self-interested, history has demonstrated that they may pursue any one of a range of different strategies, and that this choice has profound consequences for neighbouring states. In the twentieth century, for example, East Asia has seen both the relatively benign US hegemony and the relatively malign Japanese hegemony. The worst-case future scenario might involve a Chinese hegemony that sees Beijing acting unilaterally, coercively, and exploitatively under the assumption that China's wealth and security are inversely related to those of other states. Conversely, a powerful future China might determine that its interests are better served through cooperation, consultation, providing public goods, managing stability, and facilitating regional prosperity through peaceful and fair economic competition.

The Chinese would have the world believe they are too poor to pursue an aggressive foreign policy. According to this argument, Beijing must satisfy the demand at home for improved living standards before it could consider a massive commitment of resources to the armed forces, which an adventurist or coercive foreign policy would require. The notion that countries with many poor inhabitants cannot carry out an assertive foreign policy is, however, dubious.

PRC commentators commonly insist that in order to get the correct picture of China's potential power, all the indicators must be averaged per capita, where they are diluted by China's hundreds of millions of poor people. It is not a question of insufficient wealth or economic capacity. One can conceive of a formidable economic Chinese heartland of around 200 million people in the Southeast coastal provinces with productivity and average incomes comparable to the Southeast Asian NICs. The presumption, rather, is that the state's wealth and attention will be absorbed by China's remaining masses of poor, preventing the government from prosecuting an uncooperative or coercive foreign policy.

This presumption is questionable, however, from at least two angles. First, carrying a large number of impoverished citizens does not necessarily prevent a state from pursuing an assertive foreign policy, a principle demonstrated by countries as varied as the United States and North Korea. Second, China's large, mostly poor population may actually be an *impetus* for an assertive foreign policy, as suggested by the PLA Navy's success in employing the potential food and energy resources in the South China Sea as a rationale for naval expansion. In general, going to war is recognized as a tactic some governments employ to rally public support and distract attention from problems at home. In Samuel Kim's assessment, '[A]s China becomes more insecure [due to CCP loss of legitmacy and separatist-fragmentation pressures] and fragmented at home, it feels more compelled to demonstrate its toughness abroad' (Kim, 1996, p. 32).

It also often argued that since Chinese economic development depends on cordial economic relations with other countries, Chinese belligerence towards its neighbours would be counterproductive. But Chinese dependence will fall as the country becomes more powerful and wealthy. Increased relative capabilities make it feasible for a rising great power to exert greater control over its surroundings.

A China that in the words of one analyst seemed 'locked in pre-cold war, almost turn-of-the-century modes of quasi-imperial competition for regional hegemony' (Wortzel, 1994, p. 157) now shows some signs of moderating its outlook. Some Chinese elites have accepted some of the arguments of economic liberalism, as we have seen. Similarly, many Chinese leaders appear to have concluded that multilateral organizations can be as useful as they are troublesome: while they may facilitate other states ganging up on China, they may also assist Chinese efforts to recruit support for the PRC's positions on various issues. While sometimes making ominous gestures, China has also shown considerable patience in its irredentism – insisting on ultimate Chinese sovereignty, but willing to accept the status quo of 'Chinese' territory beyond Beijing's control for decades on end. Often extremely demanding on 'principles' (e.g. using its Security Council position to punish the small, poor Central American country of Guatemala for establishing diplomatic relations with Taiwan), the Chinese have sometimes been surprisingly flexible in practice, even giving away territory in some of their previous border settlements (Hyer, 1995, pp. 42–3).

On balance, however, Chinese foreign relations suggest that if a future China became the dominant Asia-Pacific power under a government like that in Beijing today, the region would face uncomfortable changes. At present, the Chinese leadership seems generally to eschew the liberal values many theorists believe contribute to peace: it has an authoritarian government that represses its people's political freedoms; it forcibly maintains an empire of captive peoples even after other empires have broken up; it threatens to retake Taiwan by force and resorts to crude tactics of military intimidation; it demonstrates resistance to multilateralism in security issues; it often breaks agreements designed to control the proliferation of weapons of mass destruction; and in the opinion

222 Chine's Foreign Relations

of many observers, it seeks to enjoy the benefits of the rules of international trade without itself honouring these rules. Furthermore, the Chinese harbour a deep-seated historical conviction that China is the natural and proper leader of East Asia, a predisposition that could make the PRC prone to pursuing an assertive political agenda and to disregarding the objections of its neighbours.

China is undertaking a major rejuvenation of its military forces at a time when even Chinese analysts say China's environment is more peaceful and secure than at any other time in the PRC's history. Some observers take this as evidence of a hidden intent to launch an aggressive foreign policy; the Chinese and their supporters say the PRC's current military renovation is limited, overdue, and reasonable for a country of China's size. China's decision to build up its military today does not tell us how the PLA will be employed tomorrow. It does indicate, however, that future Chinese leaders will have additional assets to rely on in pursuit of their interests. A powerful military is a necessary if not a sufficient qualification for an aspiring hegemon. When such a capability exists, the temptation to use it is strong.

Key Issues for Chinese Foreign Relations into the Next Century

Before the question of China's impact upon the future security of the region is completely answered, several important issues are likely to make an impact on Asia-Pacific affairs in the near term. How the PRC conducts itself in resolving the Taiwan and South China Sea disputes (see Chapter 7) are certainly among these issues. Another formerly 'lost' piece of Chinese territory, Hong Kong, may prove similarly significant. Although Hong Kong reverted to PRC control on 1 July 1997 as the Hong Kong Special Administrative Region (SAR), Hong Kong retains strong links with the West developed under 155 years of British rule. At the same time, however, Hong Kong embodies intense feelings of Chinese nationalism. Because British administration of Hong Kong was a legacy of China's subjugation by the nineteenth-century imperial powers, Beijing was especially sensitive to any British moves during the handover negotiations that might be perceived as disregard for PRC sovereignty. Britain was frequently accused of priming Hong Kong as a 'time bomb' to subvert China's political system. Based on the principle of 'one country, two systems', the Chinese promised not to change Hong Kong for at least 50 years after assuming administrative control. Beijing would take charge only of Hong Kong's defence and foreign policies.

After Tiananmen, however, Sino-British relations deteriorated, and negotiations over Hong Kong became more adversarial. Hong Kong Governor Chris Patten undertook several acts Beijing considered provocative, including the establishment of an elected Legislative Council in 1995 (prior to this, even under British rule, Hong Kong's leaders were appointed, not elected). The Chinese argued that by attempting to institutionalize democracy at the last minute, Britain was violating the spirit of the mutual agreement not to change Hong Kong's system. Patten's act also revived the 'time bomb' charge among Chinese observers. In March 1996, Beijing announced that the elected Legislative Council would be annulled immediately upon the transfer of Hong Kong to PRC rule, and that a provisional government selected by the Chinese would take its place.

Washington has served notice that it will be closely monitoring the new Chinese administration in Hong Kong, where some 37,000 American expatriates live. In accordance with the 1992 United States–Hong Kong Policy Act, which is non-binding but could be invoked to put policy pressure on the White House, the US government pledges to verify China's promise not to interfere with Hong Kong's socioeconomic system. The Act declares that Hong Kong remains 'fully autonomous' from the PRC and is to be considered by the US government 'as a separate territory in economic and trade matters'. In addition, the Act says 'The human rights of the people of Hong Kong are of great importance to the United States and are directly relevant to United States interests in Hong Kong'. If the US government finds that Chinese authorities have abused human rights in Hong Kong or infringed upon the SAR's autonomy, the PRC would be subject to American sanctions. These might include a denial of MFN trading status to Hong Kong, even if MFN is granted to the rest of China.

Some moves by Beijing-appointed Hong Kong politicians even before the handover took place caused many observers to fear that civil and political rights would be curtailed. In any case, as Chinese authorities settle in to govern people of a divergent culture and tackle a myriad unfamiliar issues, mistakes and over-reactions are probably unavoidable. Responses from observers in Congress and elsewhere are likely to be sharp and impatient. Beijing will interpret

American criticism or sanctions over Hong Kong as foreign intrusion into the PRC's internal affairs, and probably also as an effort by China's enemies to protect and nurture an anti-CCP movement in Hong Kong in the hope that it will spread into and eventually subvert the entire mainland. A strong and angry counter-reaction from the PRC would be inevitable. Thus, Hong Kong might well become the focal point of the next crisis in Sino-US relations.

A second key issue for China's future relations is whether or not the Chinese will fully appreciate other countries' fears of growing Chinese power and assertiveness. The issue is especially crucial in Sino-Japanese relations. If the Chinese live in fear of a revival of Japanese militarism, the Japanese live under the shadow of Chinese nuclear weapons. Japan's advocacy of nuclear arms control has made little impact on PRC policy. In a departure from Tokyo's usual policy of 'separating politics from economics', Japan suspended its overseas direct assistance (ODA) programme in 1995 in a protest against Chinese nuclear testing. This prompted a predictable response: Beijing flashed the war guilt card and warned that Tokyo's action jeopardized the long-term health of the bilateral relationship. After reports emerged that Washington and Tokyo planned to cooperate on a proposed theatre anti-ballistic missile defence system (TMD), the Chinese asserted the TMD was designed to neutralize China's nuclear retaliatory capability and warned that its deployment would jeopardize Chinese participation in a comprehensive ban on nuclear testing.

The Japanese are seriously concerned about the possible spillover from instability within China, such as independent action by rogue military units or large numbers of Chinese refugees sailing to the Japanese islands. Some Japanese commentators have also expressed some of the same fears of an emerging 'China threat' discussed in the West. Aside from the occasional indiscreet public statements by individual politicians, the Japanese government rarely makes strong statements on foreign affairs; it was therefore significant that in 1992 the Japanese government publicly warned the Chinese not to purchase an aircraft carrier, which Beijing was reportedly then considering, because this would undermine regional security. The Japanese are disturbed by jingoist Chinese sentiments, which often appear in Chinese discussions of issues such as the Spratly Islands, in much the same way as statements by some Japanese right-wingers alarm the Chinese. Yet even if China refrains from overtly threatening acts or statements, Chinese economic growth expands China's capabilities, and therefore increases the potential damage a hostile China could do to Japan's interests, which is the contingency for which Japanese defence planners must prepare.

There appears to be a real danger that China's strong historical sense of victimization at the hands of Japan has left the Chinese under-sensitive to Japanese insecurity resulting from PRC policies. From the Chinese perspective, it is Japan that must reassure China, not the other way around. This attitude is reinforced by the PRC's continual references to imperial Japan's war crimes and Tokyo's moral (if not financial) indebtedness to China. If Beijing fails to understand that some of its policies may make the Japanese feel insecure, it may inadvertently push Japan toward a military buildup and encourage those Japanese who believe their country should take greater control of its external political environment to protect Japanese interests. This scenario could easily lead to a disruption of regional trade and investment flows, or even a Sino-Japanese cold war.

The influence of Chinese domestic politics on Chinese foreign policy has been one of this book's most important themes. As David Bachman notes, 'Because foreign policy is likely to be the product of many of the same decision-making structures as domestic policy, Chinese foreign policy is an extension of Chinese domestic politics' (Bachman, 1994, p. 44). The relationship between China's domestic and international politics will not change in the near future; domestic politics will continue to be one of the critical determinants of the PRC's external behaviour in the coming century. As noted earlier, either stability or instability in Chinese domestic politics might contribute to an assertive foreign policy. The containment of potentially serious social and economic problems would facilitate China's continued growth into a superpower that might then attempt to dominate the region's political and economic affairs. Conversely, unchecked discontent or disunity might push the regime or one of its factions to promote Chinese hypernationalism as a solution to domestic problems, with negative spillover effects on foreign policy.

But these scenarios assume the persistence of a one-party dictatorship. What if China converted to a democratic political system at about the same time as it became Asia's strongest power? Some observers see signs of gradual democratization in China: elections being implemented at the municipal level, the Chinese legal system shifting toward the rule of law, and the Chinese media becoming freer in at least certain kinds of reporting. Based on these trends and on the experiences of other authoritarian states that converted to democracies after their annual per capita gross domestic product rose to an annual level of $5,000–$7,000, one analyst predicts that China will be a democracy by 2015, when China is expected to reach the $7,000 mark (Rowen, 1996, p. 68). The consequences of such a development in Chinese foreign relations might be dramatic. Peaceful reunification with Taiwan would become a serious possibility, as the chief obstacle, incompatible sociopolitical systems, would have been removed. More broadly, if the theory of a 'democractic zone of peace' (i.e., democracies do not fight each other) is correct, the region might look forward to the end of any possibility of military conflict between China and most of its neighbours, including all the major states. As a caveat, however, one reputable study distinguishes between 'mature, stable' democracies and new, 'transitional' democracies, arguing that the latter are highly prone to get involved in wars, even with other democracies (Mansfield and Snyder, 1995, pp. 5–38). This suggests that China's war-proneness might actually increase in the short term if the PRC became a democratic state.

Finally, and most important, is the question of whether China will accommodate itself to the present international system or seek to supplant it. With its various proclamations of diplomatic 'principles', Beijing has already shown an interest in formulating an international order with a Chinese imprimatur. The United States and other foreign governments, seeing China as a rising power, are rushing to socialize or 'enmesh' China so that the international system will survive the admission of a Chinese superpower – getting China to fit the system, rather than the reverse. Thus far the Chinese have submitted, albeit sometimes reluctantly, to most of the important aspects of the system. China's present policies – including peace offensives in every direction (except Taiwan's), willingness to conform to World Trade Organization guidelines, and limiting threats to use force to cases of disputed territory that the Chinese have traditionally considered their own – might indicate an acceptance of the status quo and continuing socialization to international norms. It is also possible, however, that these are temporary strategies to be abandoned after a decade or two of economic buildup, and that Beijing will have less patience with the demands of foreigners after China's improved relative capabilities have greatly lowered the costs of establishing a regional sphere of influence.

10

Chinese Foreign Policy and International Relations Theory

In the foregoing chapters, we discerned several patterns in China's foreign relations, and formulated a few basic principles that may help us interpret and understand present and future Chinese foreign policy. The final task of this book is to relate these findings to some of the larger theoretical issues discussed in the literature of international politics, especially the level of analysis problem, and rationality, to which they are particularly relevant

One of the great, and still unsettled, research questions in the field of political science is whether the driving forces of foreign policy decision-making are to be found inside or outside of states. The 'inside' refers to a particular state's unique domestic characteristics. The 'outside' is the international system, the set of all the world's states plus the patterns of interaction among them. This question invokes what international relations scholars call the 'level of analysis problem'. The 'problem' is where to look for the phenomena that cause states to act in the ways they choose. Explanations for a given country's foreign policy may be placed in one of several 'levels' or theoretical categories. While scholars have disagreed about the number of such categories, the most important distinction is that between the *system level* of analysis and the *state level* (sometimes called *unit level*) of analysis. The system level focuses on the international structure: the distribution and interactions of states as parts of a group. Explanations that take a system-level approach presume foreign policy is a reaction to the dangers and opportunities in the state's external environment. The cause of a particular state's actions, in other words, is to be found in the placement and activities of the other states around it. The state-level approach, on the other hand, looks for explanations of a state's foreign policy within the state itself. Each country is considered unique, and its external behaviour is presumed to grow out of a complex interaction of internal factors. The implications of this theoretical distinction are far-reaching. The system-level approach suggests the international system largely determines the behaviour of states, regardless of their internal characteristics. If this is the case, students of China's (and other countries') foreign policy should focus their attention on the powerful systemic forces that operate outside individual countries. The state-level approach, however, suggests a state's foreign policy cannot be understood without a specific knowledge of that state's history, political system, culture, and leaders.

The System Level of Analysis

The international relations literature includes three grand systemic theories, each of which provides a distinctive framework for interpreting China's foreign relations: Neo-Realism, Liberalism, and Neo-Marxism. Each of these theories helps to explain some aspects of Chinese foreign policy.

Neo-Realism

As we saw in Chapter 1, Neo-Realism maintains that while states may be concerned with raising the population's standard of living and promoting national moral values internationally, these goals must ultimately remain subordinate to ensuring the state's survival, without which all aspirations are doomed anyway. To guard against the worst-case scenario of national enslavement or destruction, states tend to see each other as potential enemies. States may rely on powerful friends for help, but only at the risk of abandonment or exploitation. Friendly inter-state relationships, moreover, are often transitory. The few states powerful enough to dominate their environment do so, for this is the surest means of attaining security (and, once this is assured, other goals as well).

In the Neo-Realist view, international cooperation is restricted by two phenomena. The first is every state's fear of leaving itself vulnerable to the control of foreigners. The second is the relative gains problem: even if, in absolute terms, two states would gain by cooperating, one would be likely to gain more than the other. Thus, relative to each other, one state would gain and the other would lose. Facing this prospect, the expected loser would probably refuse to cooperate, forgoing an absolute gain in order to deny its rival a relative gain. Neo-realists also assume that states are rational, unitary actors in their external behaviour because when it comes to foreign policy, all factions and organizations agree on the common goal of making the state as secure as possible.

My survey of China's foreign relations demonstrates that there is merit in the Realist assumption that moral and ideological concerns are secondary to the desire of states to maintain and increase their power relative to other governments (for other, corroborating opinions, see Christensen, 1996, pp. 37–52; Tow, 1994, pp. 120, 124; Ng-Quinn, 1984; and Robinson, 1994a, p. 563). While Chinese officials emphasize that their actions are motivated chiefly by a desire to assist fellow communists in other countries, to promote world peace and prosperity, or to further the cause of international justice, Chinese policies are generally self-serving, and often ruthless. The PRC changed alliance partners from the socialist Soviet Union to the capitalist United States in response to shifting geopolitical conditions, and even during its more avowedly ideological stage, China's record of political and military support for Third World countries suggested simple self-interest was a stronger consideration than Beijing's stated interest in promoting worldwide socialist revolution (Nelson, 1981, pp. 200–1; Klein, 1989, p. 144). In the post-Cold War era, as well, Beijing remains 'the high church of realpolitik' (Christensen, 1996, p. 37).

As Neo-Realists would expect, international regimes tend to infringe upon Beijing's sense of sovereignty and its fear of vulnerability to outside nations. China's heavy involvement in international trade and global regimes in recent years is mostly because the Chinese saw no other means of redressing their economic and diplomatic weakness, not because they are committed to the principle of political and economic integration among nations. Beijing remains fearful of penetration of the Chinese state by outside forces and organizations, and these fears place limits on how much perceived vulnerability the government will tolerate. Also in line with Neo-Realist thinking, China continues to view the other powerful states in the Asia-Pacific region, including 'pacified' Japan, as potential enemies, a perception that sometimes restricts cooperation that appears mutually beneficial in purely economic terms.

Finally, Neo-Realists expect China's external behaviour to follow its relative capabilities and position in the international distribution of power. This assumption appears well-grounded: while the relatively weak China of the 1980s was forced to make significant concessions to international regimes, world public opinion and superpower pressure, the more confident China of the present, emboldened by its rapid economic growth, has been more demanding and less cooperative with its neighbours on some political and economic issues.

Liberalism

What I call 'Liberalism' here is a collage of the principal assertions of several schools of thought, including interdependence theory, complex interdependence, and liberal institutionalism. These various theories have different emphases and disagree on some issues, but collectively they offer a thorough and coherent alternative to Realism.

According to the Liberal theory of international trade, as we saw in Chapter 4, states find it cost-effective to pursue their developmental objectives through economic cooperation, which creates disincentives for inter-state conflict. Through trade, all the participating parties get richer without having to fight. Since war would upset this trade, each party also has an incentive to prevent war. Economic interdependence makes states more responsive to international laws and norms, because a state knows that if it misbehaves, other states may cut off its access to the markets and suppliers upon which it has become dependent.

As a more general theory of international politics, Liberalism rejects most of Neo-Realism's basic assumptions. While states may indeed be self-interested and prone to disputes, Liberals believe governments can learn to settle their disputes peacefully and 'unlearn' destructive behaviour, including war. Instead of accepting anarchy and conflicting national interests as eternal features of international relations, Liberals promote the construction of a new system based on moral and legal principles. Liberals see Neo-Realist thinking itself as a major part of the problem. The main task is getting states to realize that practices such as war, coercion and arms buildups are counterproductive, and that all states would be better off in a world of cooperation, free international commerce and respect for international law. Liberals maintain that in the modern world, international norms are increasing in importance, so the political and economic costs to states that violate these norms have become high. States value international institutions and regimes and may modify their behaviour to retain their membership. In addition, military force is less useful than in the past as a means of achieving state goals. Liberals also believe the realist assumption that international relations are mostly about national governments struggling for security is greatly overdrawn. First, states are not the only important actors in international relations, but must share the stage with non-government organizations, international institutions, and multinational corporations. States are increasingly unable to control their own people's affairs, as inexorable economic, social and cultural forces freely permeate national borders. Second, national governments are just as concerned about the economic welfare of their populations as about military security. Even dictatorships cannot ignore the public's demands for improvements in standards of living.

In accordance with the expectations of Liberalism, Chinese leaders feel strong pressure from their citizens to raise living standards. The Chinese leadership has also come to accept the Liberal premise that international trade and investment are the most promising means of economic development (at least for the time being), as expressed in innumerable statements along these lines: 'The only viable way for a nation to seek survival and development is to engage in economic construction, improve people's livelihood and enhance international mutually-beneficial co-operation. China needs a long-lasting peaceful international environment for its development' (Jiang, 1995, p. 4). Liberals would be quicker than Neo-Realists to take such statements as proof that China is unlikely to use force except in self-defence.

Liberal theorists would emphasize that having joined the international community to partake of the irresistible benefits, China is gradually being socialized. Beijing is unable to conceal policies that violate international norms, and often finds itself under great pressure to mollify world public opinion, as evidenced by its recent media campaigns to defend itself against accusations of human rights abuses and failure to protect intellectual copyrights.

Beside these developments, worldwide trends such as the weakening power of central governments, the dependence of modern economies on the free flow of information, the decreasing value of territorial conquest as a means of economic growth, and the tendency of political liberalization to follow economic growth all provide reason for Liberals to believe that China's 'engagement' with the international economic and diplomatic community will significantly shape China's foreign relations in ways that are generally positive for both the outside world and the Chinese themselves.

Even if the Liberals are correct about the general direction of global trends, however, many Chinese elites do not appear ready to submit without a fight, and their capacity to resist should not be underestimated. The Tiananmen Massacre was a dramatic rebuff to the 1980s optimism of many Western observers who believed China was striding boldly toward political liberalization. Liberal theory may extol values such as multilateralism, upholding universal human rights, adherence to written rules for fair international trade, and renunciation of military force as a means of settling disputes, but the extent to which Beijing shares these values appears limited.

Neo-Marxism

The Neo-Marxist outlook on international trade discussed in Chapter 5 stems from a view of international relations that includes the basic Marxist assumptions about the role of capitalism in world history. The struggle between economic classes, presently between the capitalist and the working class, is the prime mover of history and politics. The international capitalist system has economically developed the world with unprecedented efficiency, although it has also brought massive injustice, conflict, and misery. Capitalism is also inherently unsustainable. To sustain their profits, the capitalist classes must continually increase the surplus they extract from the working classes. Eventually this becomes intolerable and the working classes overthrow their masters, instituting a more equitable system. Socialism breaks out in individual states and eventually encompasses the whole world, moving history into its final phase before social and economic utopia.

In the Marxist-inspired dependency theory or World System Theory propounded by scholars such as Immanuel Wallerstein, international relations are a macrocosm of the same exploitative system that exists in individual capitalist societies. Capitalist classes in the major powers use foreign policy as a means of maximizing their access to the world's markets, resources and labour under favourable terms. During the colonial period, rapacious European imperialism warped the political and economic development of the Third World. Although most of these countries would achieve independence after the Second World War, many were poorly prepared to function as nation-states. They therefore remained effectual semi-colonies of their former masters, politically and militarily weak relative to the major powers, and unable to sell anything on the world markets except raw materials, for which markets are unpredictable and profit margins low.

Countries that participate in the international economy fall into a worldwide division of labour that maintains dynamic growth in the developed states, but leaves most of the Third World stagnant and poor. The division has three major components: the core, the periphery, and the semi-periphery. The core states specialize in capital-intensive, high-technology goods and services. Since the system pays the greatest rewards to accumulations of capital, the core states reap an inordinate share of the world's surplus, and consume a disproportionate amount of the earth's resources. To sustain their position, they rely on cheap raw materials and labour from the poorer countries, which compose the periphery. Peripheral countries, comparatively lacking in capital, education and skills, find it difficult to bridge the gulf between themselves and the core. Worse, the core nations may even collude to keep the periphery underdeveloped and politically weak, an arrangement that benefits the rich countries. Between the core and periphery are the semi-peripheral states, intermediaries that provide cheap manufactures to both sides and exchange their low-cost labour for the core's higher technology. There is, nevertheless, some long-term mobility within the structure; a fortunate few may move up from the periphery into the semi-periphery.

The capitalist-oriented governments of the developed states strive to perpetuate this system by co-opting the elites of peripheral countries. In exchange for economic and military aid, these cooperative regimes keep their territory and populations locked into a relationship that is beneficial for a few but debilitating for the rest. The capitalist powers move swiftly to crush alternative systems, which if allowed to flourish might lure away members of the capitalist system.

Neo-Marxist theory merits consideration as an explanatory framework for Chinese foreign policy for two reasons. First, Marxism has had a major impact on the CCP's interpretation of international affairs. The language and themes of political discourse in China remain largely Marxist, even if China's domestic economic system is moving from the socialist model toward capitalism. For example, many Chinese commentaries maintain that China's tensions with the major powers are rooted in the desire of their capitalist classes to overthrow the CCP and replace it with a government that would facilitate the economic exploitation of China by outsiders. In the early decades of the regime, China also said its hostility toward some Third World regimes was based on their alliances with capitalists in the developed world. To a certain extent, then, we could expect that Marxist assumptions act as guidelines for Chinese foreign policy-makers – not because policy serves ideological goals in contravention of the national interest, but rather because Marxist ideology influences policy-makers' interpretation of what the national interest is.

Secondly, the core–semiperiphery–periphery model described by World System Theory offers an enlightening perspective on the economic aspects of China's interaction with the outside world. In the terms of the theory, China is a semi-peripheral state. It is an efficient producer of many manufactured goods for export to both core and peripheral countries. Its low labour costs and tightly controlled workforce make it an attractive base for foreign investors. At the same time, it remains dependent on the developed countries for high-technology products and expertise. World System Theory can also help illuminate the differences in economic development among various regions within China (Cumings, 1994, p. 402). China's development strategies can be explained in relation to the global capitalist economy: Beijing first competed with this global economy, then withdrew from it, and finally embraced it. Immediately after assuming power, the CCP regime supported the establishment of a rival, socialist economy. When relations soured with the Soviet Union, its chief partner in this enterprise, China attempted autarky. The results were poor, convincing the post-Mao leadership that tying China into the capitalist world system offered the best hope of economic development.

Beyond this, the Neo-Marxist approach has clear limitations. Like Marxism in general, it overemphasizes transnational class interests as the main determinant of foreign policy in the major powers. It is also less well-equipped than Realism or even Liberalism to make forecasts about future Chinese foreign policy. Indeed, the point of dependency and World System Theory is that the international capitalist economy works to keep the underdeveloped countries impoverished and to widen the economic gulf between them and the developed nations. Yet post-Mao China voluntarily entered this system in the hope of using it to accelerate Chinese economic development, and even to allow China to catch up with the core nations. The strategy is working; China's belated participation in the system has brought it unprecedented wealth and, by the early 1990s, the world's highest economic growth rate. China 'seems to have turned dependency theory on its head', gaining more out of the capitalist world system than the system's supposed managers (Robinson, 1994a, p. 29).

Realism is a parsimonious theory with significant, if not comprehensive, explanatory power. Pound for pound, it is probably the single most useful tool for analyzing foreign policy. Yet Neo-Realism is too simple to explain everything. While it serves as a fruitful starting point, it must be qualified by the realization that the case of China challenges some of Neo-Realism's basic assumptions, including the unity and power of central governments, the weakness of international norms and institutions, the utility of military force and virtual uselessness of other types of 'power', and the invariable preference of states for military security over wealth. The assumptions provided by Liberalism can step in to explain many of the situations Neo-Realism cannot. The scope of Neo-Marxism's usefulness is somewhat smaller; its strongest point is its elucidation of the global division of labour, and how China fits into the world economic system.

The State-Level of Analysis

Among Sinologists, or people who specialize in the study of China, most explanations of Chinese foreign policy take the state-level approach. There are two reasons for this. First, Sinologists are experts in Chinese history, culture, and language. They are naturally drawn to the approach that presumes these things matter, and repulsed by the approach that implies these things do not matter. Second, their case has some merit. The history of unexpected twists and variations through several decades of PRC foreign policy indicates that internal factors are an important consideration for anyone trying to grasp the total picture of Chinese policy-making.

The state-level approach to explaining Chinese foreign policy rejects the idea that the outside world dictates China's behaviour. Internal forces are crucially important – especially, it might be argued, in China's case. Military threats are unprecedentedly low, giving Beijing great latitude in determining how many and what sort of resources are allocated to the armed forces, and minimizing any possibility of outside military coercion. In the economic realm, as well, the influence of the outside world is constrained by many layers of insulation (e.g., the nonconvertibilty of the Chinese currency, the *renminbi*) and by the strength of the Chinese state. Consequently, the international system has comparatively little effect on China's actions (Bachman, 1989, pp. 32–4). This would suggest that the primary sources of Chinese foreign policy are to be found within China, not in China's external environment.

For state-level theorists, the simple elegance of the system-level approach is appealing, but illusory; the real story is found in the details. The sources of Chinese external behaviour reside within China, and are uniquely Chinese. The foreign policy-making processes of other states do not necessarily explain those in China, and vice-versa. Hence, to a great degree, one must be a Sinologist to take the state-level approach.

This approach, of course, opens up an almost limitless number of causal factors. One possible focus of study is a key individual leader, such as Mao Zedong or Deng Xiaoping. There is considerable evidence that Mao dominated the making of China's major foreign-policy decisions during his tenure (Barnett, 1985, p. 7). If so, Mao's unique character, life experiences, ideological orientation, educational background, and perceptions of the outside world might have proved critically important on certain occasions. The focus on a single, dominant leader bears out the value of the state-level approach if we assume that this leader, as a product of his or her domestic environment, made different decisions from those you or I might have made under the same circumstances. Many analysts caution, however, that because of Deng Xiaoping's efforts to institutionalize decision-making and to seek assent from other powerful groups on important policy changes, the dominant-leader assumption is probably outmoded (Kim, 1994c, p. 24).

Another possible determinant of foreign policy behaviour unique to the particular country under study is its political structure. One of the characteristics of China's authoritarian political system is that it gives the public relatively little input into foreign policy-making.

This allows the Chinese leadership to tolerate a comparatively high number of casualties among its soldiers in pursuit of the state's political goals. Thus, the CCP was able to absorb some 900,000 casualties to maintain the status quo ante in the Korean War. A decade later, Beijing decided to withdraw voluntarily from territory on the Sino-Indian border it had just captured from Indian troops. (Chinese estimates of Korean War casualties tend to be lower. Xu [1993, p. 56] used PLA archives to arrive at the figures of 152,000 Chinese combat deaths and 230,000 wounded. The point remains valid: Chinese casualties were high, and could have been higher without seriously threatening the CCP's grip on power.) Of the Chinese withdrawal after the clash with India, then-US Assistant Secretary of State Roger Hilsman observed, 'Could you imagine the difficulty we would have with the Pentagon in pulling back from territory that had cost that many casualties, no matter the political end it served?' (quoted in Whiting, 1975a, p. 165). Indeed, in the United States, with its multiparty electoral politics and free press, the perception of wasteful or unjustified US military involvement in Korea and Indochina has been a major factor in bringing down governments, even though American casualty levels were far lower than those that the Chinese suffered in Korea (some 33,600 US soldiers died in Korea, and 56,000 in Indochina).

Of the many other possible examples of the state-level approach, we might examine one such theory in a little more depth to get an idea of the approach's strengths and weaknesses. Let us take the argument that modern Chinese defence policy is shaped by Chinese culture and history. Military historians see continuity in the emphasis on psychological warfare and deception in ancient Chinese military classics such as Sun Zi's *Art of War* and the *Romance of the Three Kingdoms,* and in such modern examples of Chinese military thinking as Mao's Zedong's principles of guerrilla warfare. Gerald Segal, for example, concludes that 'tricks and stealth . . . appear to be a relatively special focus in the Chinese case' (Segal, 1985, p. 40). Other scholars postulate that this tradition of military deception accounts for China's lack of enthusiasm for multilateral security cooperation (Garrett and Glaser, 1994, p. 28). China's 'century of shame', a period of humiliation at the hands of foreign nations beginning with the Opium War defeat in 1842 and lasting until the establishment of the People's Republic, is commonly accepted as a major influence on PRC policies, from general tendencies such as China's frequent demand for 'respect' and recognition as a great power by the international community, to specific issues such as China's approach to solving the Spratly Islands dispute (You, 1994, p. 396).

The challenge of cultural/historical theories is in demonstrating that they are better than conventional explanations which are simpler and thus preferable, *ceteris paribus*. Along these lines, some scholars have argued that China's use of military force against other states, particularly in the pre-modern period, was distinctly different from the pattern demonstrated by the Western powers, and that China's behaviour stemmed from traditional Chinese philosophy. While the powerful states of the West used their military might to acquire additional territory, resources and riches, China showed little interest in employing its power for commercial gain, even where it enjoyed military superiority. Instead, the Chinese leadership used force to defend against invasion or to remind weaker neighbours to treat Beijing with respect (Adelman and Shih, 1993, pp. 4, 28–33; Chen Jian, 1993, pp. 193–4).

This argument is harder to sustain for post-1949 China. One reason is that the behaviour patterns of ancient China might not apply to a modern state in a modern international system that 'punishes' states that have the wherewithal to take greater control of their external environment but decline to develop this potential (Layne, 1993, p. 9). Ancient China might have imagined itself as 'a vast and self-sufficient empire with no need for anything beyond its long borders' and with the luxury of 'ignoring the existence of an external threat' (Adelman and Shih, 1993, p. 30); modern China has abandoned this myth forever.

Furthermore, while the foreign policy of ancient China might appear dramatically different from that of other large states, the behaviour of the People's Republic of China does not. Consequently, many cultural/historical theories of PRC foreign policy merely rationalize selected aspects of Chinese philosophy with Chinese behaviour that appears suspiciously similar to that of other states in similar circumstances. In one such effort, Rosita Dellios (1994) argues that the Chinese attack on Vietnam in 1979 'illustrated China's endeavours to maintain what was perceived to be the proper hierarchy of relations', a concept embodied in traditional Chinese political philosophy. This episode, however, is equally comprehensible as typical hegemonic enforcement of the regional status quo. Indeed, Western analysts with little or no understanding of Chinese culture immediately understood the attack as a 'punitive invasion'.

Similarly, after discussing the cultural basis of Mao's 'people's war' strategy, Dellios admits that the concept is not unique to China, but 'may be found among many cultures and throughout history'. Dellios concludes that uniquely Chinese thinking drives Chinese foreign policy 'although Chinese behaviour may display the symptoms of classical realist calculations' (Dellios, 1994, pp. 8–11). But if Chinese behaviour conforms to the parsimonious and broadly applicable realist model, many would ask, what additional insight is gained through a focus on Chinese culture?

Is China a Rational, Unitary Actor?

Along with the level of analysis problem, another important and fundamental theoretical question is whether the Chinese government should be considered a rational, unitary actor. If so, the study of China's (or any other country's) foreign policy is greatly simplified. Unfortunately, the real world tends to be inconveniently complicated, seriously challenging the rational, unitary actor presumption. In no case are these challenges stronger than with China.

A government is a *unitary* actor when decisions are made by a single powerful individual or by a small group of like-minded individuals with a single point of view and pursuing a single agenda. By contrast, a unitary actor does not prevail when different groups or individuals with dissimilar agenda have decisive input into some or all foreign policy choices, steering a country's foreign relations in several directions at once.

The criteria for 'rationality' most commonly employed by international relations theorists are fulfilled if: (1) the decision-maker has a set of values in ranked order; (2) the ranking of values remains consistent; (3) the decision-maker calculates the costs and benefits of the available policy alternatives in terms of his or her values; and (4) chooses the alternative that offers the best hope of fulfilling the highest-ranked value. This definition of rationality allows for the possibilities that decision-makers may miscalculate, may not have complete or accurate information at the time they make their decisions, and may not invest the time and effort to study the consequences of every possible alternative. Furthermore, the particular values the decision-makers hold, or the order in which certain values are ranked, may not match the expectations of outside analysts. Thus, strictly speaking, policy decisions such as the Great Leap Forward and the Tiananmen Massacre were not necessarily 'irrational', although from some people's point of view they may seem mistaken, wasteful or immoral.

Lenient though this definition is, some types of policy-making would still fail to meet its criteria for rationality. If decision-making is rational, cost–benefit calculations are made from an ordered list of values that is consistently followed. This would not be the case if decision-making power is constantly moving among different organizations or political factions, each with its own unique list of ordered values. Similarly, suboptimal policy-making based on the narrow self-interests of a group that had temporarily gained control of foreign policy could also be considered irrational.

Suboptimality occurs when a unit (e.g., one branch or agency of the government) makes policies that benefit itself but are detrimental to the larger whole of which the unit is a part (e.g., the national interest).

Chinese policies have often been characterized as 'irrational' by Western politicians, analysts and media commentators. To the extent that this argument refers to the frequent shifting of decision-making power among several groups of elites with differing agenda, it may be an appropriate characterization. One suspects, however, that most of the people who call Beijing's behaviour 'irrational' really mean they find a certain policy morally offensive or poorly suited to the apparent goal. Neither of these are legitimate grounds for inferring irrationality. Sadly, morality has little to do with achieving most political goals. More important, we are wrong to assume that a given decision-maker's ordered list of values is the same as *our* list, or that we can always accurately deduce an actor's goals simply by observing his or her behaviour.

The prevalence of factional or bureaucratic infighting within the Chinese government constitutes the main challenge to employing the unitary and rational actor assumption in the study of Chinese foreign policy. Many scholars believe the process of policy-making in China 'depend[s] more on chance conjunctions of factions, interests, issues, and events than on causal logic' (Kim, 1994c, p. 24). According to this view, no single group or individual in China is strong enough to consistently dominate important decision-making. Therefore, all the groups seeking to influence foreign policy must find partners with which to form coalitions and make a united push for a preferred policy option. Debate and bargaining are central to the process. Although a coalition's policy preference may be based on individual or organization self-interests, the coalition argues that what it wants is what best serves the national interest. A major policy shift occurs when the sponsoring coalition is powerful enough to force it through. The 'open door' economic policy of the 1980s, for example, was chosen because it served the domestic needs of several powerful organizations (Bachman, 1989, pp. 46–7).

Similarly, Allen Whiting notes that while China consistently faced challenges from the United States throughout the period 1989–94, 'responses to these challenges vary depending on the relative strength of Deng Xiaoping and two sources of assertive nationalism: the "leftist" ideological faction and components of the People's Liberation Army'. Deng and his protégés favoured the 'open door' development strategy and a conciliatory approach toward the United States, while the military and 'leftist' conservatives emphasized the danger of capitalist subversion and demanded stronger Chinese responses to American pressure on a variety of issues. The specific policies over these five years reflected developments in the policy-making tug-of-war between these two coalitions (Whiting, 1995b, p. 315). Perhaps the clearest and most dramatic example of irrationality in Chinese foreign policy-making resulting from factional and organizational infighting occurred during the Cultural Revolution. In May 1967, authorities in the British-administered port of Hong Kong were suffering through a wave of demonstrations and violence by communist militants protesting against British 'imperialism' and demanding that administration of the territory be surrendered to the local communist party. On 15 May, the Chinese Ministry of Foreign Affairs suddenly released a statement calling upon the British government to 'immediately accept all the just demands' of the militants, and to release and compensate the rioters who had been arrested – in effect, the statement called upon the British to turn Hong Kong over to the control of radical Maoists.

This was a shocking departure from Beijing's previous policy toward Hong Kong. While reserving China's ultimate ownership of the British colony, Beijing had been careful to preserve Hong Kong's status as one of the capitalist world's great financial and trade centres, an arrangement from which China benefited handsomely. The explanation was that a radical clique had temporarily seized control of the Foreign Ministry and began issuing policy pronouncements without authorization from Mao or Zhou Enlai. Zhou later personally apologized for the incident, and the leader of the clique was reportedly executed. This episode constituted irrationality because the values and preferences of decision-makers were not 'consistent' – one faction won control over another, and the standard agenda was abruptly replaced by a radically different one. Yet this was such an unusual case that it is probably best understood as the exception that proves the rule; in contrast, most Chinese foreign policy reflects a single agenda that changes only gradually over long periods of time.

Another challenge to the notion that Chinese foreign policy is rational is the argument that cultural differences make the rationality model inappropriate for China. Jonathan R. Adelman and Chih-yu Shih argue that the concept of rationality employed in the English-language international relations literature is a 'traditional Western' idea that is 'not totally transferable to another culture'. Indeed, attempting to apply it to Chinese behaviour is 'a form of ethnocentrism'. As proof, they offer several examples of Chinese policies that 'Western rationality' cannot explain: the Empress Dowager's declaration of war on the Western powers in 1900; the Guomindang's passivity toward and even talk of rapprochement with invading Japanese forces in the first half of the Pacific War; the shelling of the Taiwanese-occupied island of Quemoy on alternate days according to an announced schedule in 1958; the unilateral withdrawal of victorious Chinese forces from Indian territory in 1962; and the announcement by Beijing of its intention to punish Vietnam, followed shortly thereafter by a Chinese incursion (Adelman and Shih, 1993, pp. 9–10).

Adelman and Shih are correct in pointing out that many Chinese policies have puzzled Western analysts. But while they attribute this to the inapplicability of the 'Western' rationality assumption to China, there is an alternative explanation. Westerners have often failed to comprehend the values, preferences and perceptions that prevail in Beijing.The rationality model describes a logical process, but does not fill in the blanks; this is up to the analyst. Thus, the process described by the rationality model may well apply to China (and, indeed, to all governments universally), but this assumption alone does not guarantee accurate forecasting of Chinese policies.

Instances of suboptimality and changes in the controlling agenda can be found amidst strategies that span decades. The most serious question, therefore, is which represents the essence of Chinese foreign policy; whether culture and factional politics preclude any real predictability, or whether the overall picture is generally consistent, with occasional lurches arising from internal sources.

Conclusions

Since proponents of the system-level approach and the state-level approach each make a strong case, it is most reasonable to accept that China's national leaders base their foreign policy decisions on *both* domestic and external considerations.

External considerations are critical because foreign countries have the potential power either to destroy China or to facilitate the achievement of China's main goals. Furthermore, the various powerful groups in China often agree on how to best deal with external threats and opportunities – all Chinese elites have a common interest in China's security. To this extent, focusing on the external environment may serve as a relatively simple analytical key for explaining much of China's foreign relations. Domestic considerations must be accounted for because foreign policy-making power is not highly centralized, factions and organizations tend to exhibit suboptimal behaviour, and it is often debatable what specific policies will be best for China in the long run.

It is clear that Chinese elites themselves view internal and international politics as closely connected, a theme that recurs throughout this book. Many of the leading scholars of Chinese foreign policy now conclude that to focus on either external or internal sources of foreign policy alone is insufficient (Whiting, 1975a, p. xiv; Bachman, 1989, p. 44; Cumings, 1989, p. 220). Each comprehends only part of the whole tapestry. Rather, as Samuel Kim writes, '[B]oth domestic and foreign policies and objectives are interwoven in terms of cause and effect', and consequently foreign policy is 'the outcome of an ongoing encounter between decision makers' perceptions of needs, interests, and beliefs and their perceptions of the international situation' (Kim, 1989b, p. 21). Thus, there are really *three* important areas of concern: international imperatives, domestic imperatives, and the *interaction* between them as perceived by Chinese elites. Taking both system-level and state-level approaches seriously and seeking to understand the interaction between the two greatly complicates the study of Chinese foreign policy, but probably brings us closer to the truth – which, it appears, is highly complex.

To a greater degree than many governments, Beijing tries to make comprehensive policy on issues that are seen to have both international and domestic aspects, rather than distinguishing between 'foreign' and 'domestic' issues as separate realms of policy-making. Domestic power struggles may have critical implications for Chinese foreign relations. As Bruce Cumings observes, the emergence of a new movement in Chinese domestic politics signals the ascendance of a new governing coalition and 'entails a foreign policy corollary' (Cumings, 1989, p. 220). The process also works in reverse. To one degree or another, the international system shapes the domestic structure and politics of its member states (Gourevitch, 1978, pp. 881–912; Katzenstein, 1976, pp. 4–13). International conditions may favour the ascendance of some organizations or factions over others within the Chinese government. Enmeshment in international networks and regimes may also help China's ruling elites to 'learn' and incorporate global norms. As an example of this, Samuel Kim cites Beijing's repudiation of the notion that war between China and the capitalist powers is inevitable (Kim, 1989c, p. 165; see also Kim, 1994c, p. 31).

If Chinese foreign policy-makers worry about both international and domestic imperatives, the two sets of considerations may on occasion come into conflict, forcing a choice between one or the other. The violent suppression of demonstrators in Tiananmen Square was such an occasion: extensive foreign media coverage ensured there would be an international backlash that would reduce China's prestige and economic opportunities, but the large-scale challenge to the Party's authority put the regime's immediate survival in jeopardy. As this episode illustrated, in the trade-off between international and domestic considerations, the latter may win out. To say that Beijing bases its foreign policy decisions on internal as well as external developments implies that individual leaders want to maintain their personal status in the government as much as they want to see China's national goals fulfilled; when forced, they would sacrifice the latter objective for the former.

Chinese foreign policy decision-makers are each 'rational' in the sense that they have consistent, ordered preferences and choose alternatives they believe will support their highest-ranked values at an acceptable cost. China, however, is not always a rational, unitary actor in international politics. Different groups with conflicting outlooks and preferences share influence over foreign policy.

Narrow organizational self-interest is one source of disagreement. Even where elites are legitimately concerned with protecting 'national security', perceptions of what this means and what specific policies it implies may vary greatly. Consequently, some issues find these groups unanimous in their policy recommendation, but others generate debate that can only be settled through bargaining and coalition building. Since the same faction or coalition does not win every battle, the overall policy picture may be inconsistent. Taken as a whole, the process is technically 'irrational' because a single list of ordered preferences is not consistently followed over a long time period.

In sum, China is not a pawn of the forces and constraints of international politics, but its actions show considerable predictability and conformity with some mainstream theoretical constructs. While the PRC often behaves as a typical great power, its peculiar characteristics can be crucially important. To fully comprehend Chinese foreign relations, one should seek to understand both China and general international political theory. China remains an inescapably complex actor, befitting its mostly venerable attributes.

Bibliography

Adelman, Jonathan R. and Chih-yu Shih (1993) *Symbolic War: The Chinese Use of Force, 1840–1980* (Taipei, Taiwan: Institute of International Relations).

Allen, Kenneth W., Glenn Krumel and Jonathan D. Pollack (1995) *China's Air Force Enters the 21st Century* (Santa Monica, CA: RAND).

Allison, Graham T. (1971) *Essence of Decision: Explaining the Cuban Missile Crisis* (Boston: Little, Brown).

Austin, Greg (1995) 'The Strategic Implications of China's Public Order Crisis', *Survival*, vol. 37, no. 2 (Summer).

Bachman, David (1989) 'Domestic Sources of Chinese Foreign Policy', in Kim (1989a).

Bachman, David (1994) 'Domestic Sources of Chinese Foreign Policy', in Kim (1994a).

Bachman, David (1995) 'China in 1994: Marking Time, Making Money', *Asian Survey*, vol. 35, no. 1 (January).

Barnett, A. Doak (1985) *The Making of Foreign Policy in China: Structure and Process* (Boulder, CO: Westview Press).

Barnett, A. Doak *et al.* (1996) 'Developing a Peaceful, Stable and Co-operative Relationship with China', National Committee on American Foreign Policy, New York, July.

Baum, Julian (1995) 'A Case of Nerves', *Far Eastern Economic Review*, 20 July.

Baum, Julian (1996) 'Bargaining for Position', *Far Eastern Economic Review*, 5 September.

Bedeski, Robert E. (1995) 'Sino-Korean Relations: Triangle of Tension, or Balancing a Divided Peninsula?', *International Journal*, vol. 50, no. 3 (Summer).

Beijing Review (1964a) 10 July; cited in Whiting (1975a, p. 174).

Beijing Review (1964b) 24 July; cited in Whiting (1975a, p. 174).

Beijing Review (1979) 30 March.

Beijing Review (1982) 21 June.

Beijing Review (1986) 21 April.

Beijing Review (1989) 'On Quelling Rebellion in Beijing', 10–16 July.

Beijing Review (1992a) 'Tibetans on Human Rights in Tibet', 5–11 October.

Beijing Review (1992b) 'Tibetans Enjoy All Human Rights', 13–19 April.

Beijing Review (1992c) 18–24 October.

Beijing Review (1995) 'Lee's Cornell Speech Rapped on Chinese Press', 14–20 August.

Betts, Richard K. (1995) 'Vietnam's Strategic Predicament', *Survival*, vol. 37, no. 3 (Autumn).

246

Bickers, Robert A. and Jeffrey N. Wasserstrom (1995) 'Shanghai's "Dogs and Chinese Not Admitted" Sign: Legend, History and Contemporary Symbol', *China Quarterly*, no. 142 (June).

Bitzinger, Richard and Bates Gill (1996) 'Gearing Up for High-Tech Warfare? Chinese and Taiwanese Defense Modernization and Implications for Military Confrontation Across the Taiwan Strait', CAPS Papers No. 11 (Taipei: Chinese Council of Advanced Policy Studies), September.

Bodansky, Yossef (1997), 'Why Beijing "eventually expects war with the United States"', *Defense and Affairs Strategic Policy* (May–June).

British Broadcasting Corporation (BBC) (1994) *Summary of world broadcasts: Asia-Pacific*, FE/2054, 22 July.

BBC, (1994) *Summary of world broadcasts: Asia-Pacific*, FE/2133, 22 October.

BBC (1995) *Summary of world broadcasts: Asia-Pacific*, FE/2402, 7 September.

Cabestan, Jean-Pierre (1995) 'The Cross-Strait Relationship in the Post-Cold War Era: Neither Reunification Nor "Win-Win" Game', *Issues & Studies*, vol. 31, no. 1 (January).

Camilleri, Joseph (1980) *Chinese Foreign Policy: The Maoist Era and its Aftermath* (Oxford: Martin Robertson).

Chan, Gerald (1996, 'Towards an IR Theory with Chinese Characteristics', paper presented at a conference on 'Globalism, Regionalism and Nationalism: Asia in Search of its Role in the 21st Century', Makuhari, Japan, 20–2 September.

Chanda, Nayan (1996), 'No-Cash Carrier', *Far Eastern Economic Review*, 10 October.

Chang, Gordon H. (1988) 'To the Nuclear Brink: Eisenhower, Dulles, and the Quemoy-Matsu Crisis', *International Security*, vol. 12, no. 4 (Spring).

Chassin, Lionel (1965) *The Communist Conquest of China: A History of the Civil War, 1945–1949*, trans. Timothy Osato and Louis Gelas (Cambridge, MA: Harvard University Press).

Chen Jian (1993) 'Will China's Development Threaten Asia-Pacific Security? A Rejoinder', *Security Dialogue*, vol. 24, no. 2 (June).

Chen Jian (1996) 'Understanding the Logic of Beijing's Taiwan Policy', *Security Dialogue*, vol. 27, no. 4 (December).

Chen Jie (1994) 'China's Spratly Policy', *Asian Survey*, vol. 34, no. 10 (October).

Chen Qimao (1993) 'New Approaches in China's Foreign Policy', *Asian Survey*, vol. 33, no. 3 (March) p. 244.

Cheng Chu-yuan (1964) *Economic Relations Between Peking and Moscow, 1949–1962* (New York: Praeger).

Cheung Tai Ming (1992) 'Smoke Signals', *Far Eastern Economic Review*, 12 November.

Choudhury, Golam W. (1982) *China in World Affairs: The Foreign Policy of the PRC Since 1970* (Boulder, CO: Westview Press).

Christensen, Thomas J. (1992) 'Threats, Assurances, and the Last Chance for Peace: The Lessons of Mao's Korean War Telegrams', *International Security*, vol. 17, no. 1 (Summer).

Christensen, Thomas J. (1996) 'Chinese Realpolitik', *Foreign Affairs*, vol. 75, no. 5 (September/October).

'Chronicle' (1978) *China Quarterly*, no. 73 (March).

Chu Shulong (1994), 'The PRC Girds for Limited, High-Tech War', *Orbis*, vol. 38, no. 2 (Spring).

Chu Shulong (1996a) 'Sino-US Relations: The Necessity for Change and a New Strategy', *Contemporary International Relations* (Beijing), vol. 6, no. 11 (November).

Chu Shulong (1996b) 'National Unity, Sovereignty and Territorial Integration', *The China Journal*, no. 36 (July).

Committee on Foreign Affairs (1993) United States House of Representatives, 'The Future of United States–China Policy', US Government Printing Office, 20 May.

Cossa, Ralph A. (1994) 'The PRC's National Security Objectives in the Post-Cold War Era and the Role of the PLA', *Issues & Studies*, vol. 30, no. 9 (September).

Cossa, Ralph A. (1996) 'The Major Powers in Northeast Asian Security', McNair Paper 51, Institute for National Strategic Studies, National Defense University, Washington DC, August.

Craig, Mary (1992) *Tears of blood: A Cry for Tibet* (London: HarperCollins).

Cranston, Senator Alan (1992), in United States Senate Committee on Foreign Relations, *US and Chinese Policies Toward Occupied Tibet* (Washington: US Government Printing Office).

Cumings, Bruce (1989) 'The Political Economy of China's Turn Outward', in Kim (1989a).

Cumings, Bruce (1994) 'What Is a Pacific Century – and How Will We Know When It Begins?', *Current History*, vol. 93, no. 587 (December).

Cumings, Bruce (1996) 'The World Shakes China', *The National Interest*, no. 43 (Spring).

Da Jun (1995) 'Where Will Japan Go?', *Xinhua* news report, 7 December. 1995, in FBIS, *Daily Report: China*, 7 December.

Dawnay, Ivo (1997), 'Beijing launches computer virus war on the west', *The Age* (Melbourne) 16 June.

Dellios, Rosita (1994) 'Chinese Strategic Culture: Part 1 – The Heritage from the Past', Research Paper No. 1, Centre for East-West Cultural and Economic Studies, Bond University, Gold Coast, Australia, April.

Deng Xiaoping (1980) 'Why China Has Opened Its Doors', Foreign Broadcast Information Service, *Daily Report: China*, 12 February.

Denoon, David B. H. and Wendy Frieman (1996) 'China's Security Strategy: The View from Beijing, ASEAN and Washington', *Asian Survey*, vol. 36, no. 4 (April).

Ding Kuisong (1996) 'ARF: Successes Amid Challenges', *Contemporary International Relations*, vol. 6, no. 8 (August).

Dittmer, Lowell (1994), 'China and Russia: New Beginnings', in Kim (1994a).

Donnet, Pierre-Antoine (1994) *Tibet: Survival in Question*, trans. Tica Broch (Delhi: Oxford University Press).

Dreyer, June Teufel (1996a) 'Regionalism in the PLA', *China Quarterly*, no. 146 (June).

Dreyer, June Teufel (1996b) 'China's Strategic View: The Role of the People's Liberation Army', Strategic Studies Institute, US Army War College, Carlisle Barracks, PA, April.

Du Gong (1991) 'Some Perceptions of a Changing Pattern of International Relations', *International Studies* (Beijing), no. 4 (October).

Dupont, Alan (1996) 'Is There An "Asian Way"?', *Survival*, vol. 38, no. 2 (Summer).

East Asian Analytical Unit (EEAU) (1996) *Asia's Global Powers: China–Japan Relations in the 21st Century* (Canberra, Australia: East Asian Analytical Unit).

Economist, The (1995) 'Shrinking the Chinese State', 10 June.

Elegant, Robert (1996) 'Foreign Illusions About Influencing China Lead to Kowtows', *International Herald Tribune*, 18 July.

Fan, K. (ed.) (1972) *Mao Tse-Tung and Lin Piao: Post Revolutionary Writings* (Garden City, NY: Anchor Books).

Feeney, William R. (1994) 'China and the Multilateral Economic Institutions', in Kim (1994a).

Foot, Rosemary J. (1988/89) 'Nuclear Coercion and the Ending of the Korean Conflict', *International Security*, vol. 13, no. 3 (Winter).

Foot, Rosemary (1996) 'Chinese–Indian Relations and the Process of Building Confidence: Implications for the Asia-Pacific', *Pacific Review*, vol. 9, no. 1.

Forney, Matt and Nigel Holloway (1996) 'Out of Synch', *Far Eastern Economic Review,* 5 December.

Forney, Matt and Nayan Chanda (1996) 'Comrades in Arms', *Far Eastern Economic Review*, 2 May.

Friedman, Thomas L. (1995) 'American Business Is Seeing the Light About Rule of Law in China', *International Herald Tribune*, 9 January.

Frieman, Wendy (1996) 'New Members of the Club: Chinese Participation in Arms Control Regimes 1980–1995', *The Nonproliferation Review*, vol. 3, no. 3 (Spring/Summer).

Gao Yi (1992) 'Deng Xiaoping Lun Kexue Jishu Shi Diyi Shengchanli', *Liaowang*, no. 17.

Garrett, Banning and Bonnie Glaser (1994) 'Multilateral Security in the Asia-Pacific Region and its Impact on Chinese Interests: Views from Beijing', *Contemporary Southeast Asia*, vol. 16, no. 1 (June).

Garrett, Banning and Bonnie Glaser (1995) 'Looking Across the Yalu: Chinese Assessments of North Korea', *Asian Survey*, vol. 35, no. 6 (June).

Garrett, Banning N. and Bonnie S. Glaser (1995/96) 'Chinese Perspectives on Nuclear Arms Control', *International Security*, vol. 20, no. 3 (Winter).

Garver, John W. (1996) 'Sino-Indian Rapprochement and the Sino-Pakistan Entente', *Political Science Quarterly*, vol. 111, no. 2 (Summer).

Garver, John W. (1993) *Foreign Relations of the People's Republic of China* (Englewood Cliffs, NJ: Prentice Hall).

Garver, John W. (1992) 'China's Push Through the South China Sea: The Interaction of Bureaucratic and National Interests', *China Quarterly*, no. 132 (December).

Geng Huichang (1992) 'Multi-National Coordination: Feasibility in Asia-Pacific', *Contemporary International Relations*, vol. 2, no. 11 (November).

Gladney, Dru C. (1995) 'China's Ethnic Reawakening', *Asia Pacific Issues No. 18*, East-West Center, Honolulu, January.

Glaser, Bonnie S. (1993) 'China's Security Perceptions: Interests and Ambitions', *Asian Survey*, vol. 33, no. 3 (March).

Godwin, Paul H. B. (1996) 'From Continent to Periphery: PLA Doctrine, Strategy and Capabilities Towards 2000', *China Quarterly*, no. 146 (June).

Godwin, Paul H. B. (1991) 'Chinese Defense Policy and Military Strategy in the 1990s', in US Congress Joint Economic Committee, *China's Economic Dilemmas in the 1990s: The Problems of Reform, Modernization, and Interdependence* (Washington, DC: US Government Printing Office, April).

Goh Chok Tong (1993) 'Drop the Stick, Grow with the Chinese', *International Herald Tribune*, 21 May.

Goh, Sunny (1994) 'Chinese Academics Dismiss Study as "Baseless, Malicious"', *The Straits Times* (Singapore), 9 March.

Gourevitch, Peter (1978) 'The Second Image Reversed: The International Sources of Domestic Politics', *International Organization*, vol. 32, no. 4 (Autumn).

Gilpin, Robert (1987) *The Political Economy of International Relations* (Princeton, NJ: Princeton University Press).

Guojia Jigou Bianzhi Weiyuanhui (1991) *Zhongguo Zhengfu Jigou* (Beijing: Zhongguo Renshi Chubanshe).

Gurtov, Melvin and Byong-Moo Hwang (1980) *China Under Threat: The Politics of Strategy and Diplomacy* (Baltimore: Johns Hopkins University Press).

Gyari, Lodi G. (1992), in United States Senate Committee on Foreign Relations, *US and Chinese Policies Toward Occupied Tibet* (Washington: US Government Printing Office).

Gyatso, Tenzin (1983) *My Land and My People* (New York: Portala Press).

Halperin, Morton H. (1974) *Bureaucratic Politics and Foreign Policy* (Washington: Brookings Institution).

Hamrin, Carol Lee (1994) 'Elite Politics and the Development of China's Foreign Relations', in Robinson and Shambaugh (1994).

Harding, Harry (1994) ' "On the Four Great Relationships": The Prospects for China', *Survival*, vol. 36, no. 2 (Summer).

Harding, Harry (1987), *China's Second Revolution* (Washington, DC: Brookings Institution).

Harris, Stuart (1995) 'The Economic Aspects of Security in the Asia-Pacific Region', *Journal of Strategic Studies*, vol. 18, no. 3 (September).

Harris, Stuart (1996), 'China, Economics and Security', paper presented at a conference on 'China and the Asia-Pacific Economy', University of Queensland, Brisbane, Australia, July.

Harris, Stuart and Heather Smith (1996) 'Economic Relations Across the Strait: Interdependence or Dependency?', conference on 'Political and Strategic Foundations of Taiwan's Future', Australian National University, 7–8 May.

Healy, Tim and Laurence Eyton (1996) 'Perils of Money Diplomacy', *Asiaweek*, 20 Dec.

Heping (Beijing) (1992) December.

Hiebert, Murray and Adam Schwarz (1995) 'But Can They Sing Karaoke?', *Far Eastern Economic Review*, 3 August.
Hinton, Harold C. (1994) 'China as an Asian Power', in Robinson and Shambaugh (1994).
Hollingworth, Clare (1994/95) 'PLA Fears Japan', *Asia-Pacific Defence Reporter*, 1995 Annual Reference Edition (December 1994/January 1995).
Hsiung, James C. and Steven I. Levine (eds) (1992) *China's Bitter Victory: The War with Japan, 1937–1945* (Armonk, NY: M. E. Sharpe).
Huang Caihong (1992) 'The Chinese Navy Escorts the Reform', *Liaowang*, no. 16, 20 April.
Huang Cisheng and Wang Lincong (1992) 'Shilun Mao Zedong de Hezhanlue Sixiang', in *Quan Jun Mao Zedong Junshi Sixiang Xueshu Taolun Wen Jing Xuan*, Vol. I (Beijing: Academy of Military Sciences Press).
Hyer, Eric (1995) 'The South China Sea Disputes: Implications of China's Earlier Territorial Settlements', *Pacific Affairs*, vol. 68, no. 1 (Spring).
Ijiri Hidenori (1990) 'Sino-Japanese Controversy Since the 1972 Diplomatic Normalization', *China Quarterly*, no. 124 (December).
International Institute for Strategic Studies (IISS) (1996/97) *The Military Balance 1996/97* (Oxford: Oxford University Press).
Jacobson, Harold K. and Michel Oksenberg (1990) *China's Participation in the IMF, the World Bank and GATT: Toward a Global Economic Order* (Ann Arbor, MI: University of Michigan Press).
Jane's Defence Weekly (1994) 'Making a Modern Industry', 19 February.
Jencks, Harlan W. (1994) 'The PRC's Military and Security Policy in the Post-Cold War Era', *Issues & Studies*, vol. 30, no. 11 (November).
Ji Guoxing (1994) 'The Diaoyudao (Senkaku) Disputes and Prospects for Settlement', *Korean Journal of Defense Analysis*, vol. 6, no. 2 (Winter).
Jiang Zemin (1995) 'China's Policy Toward East Asia', *Heping* (Peace), no. 36–7 (March).
Jiao Wu and Xiao Hui (1988) 'Modern Limited War Call for Reform of Traditional Military Principles', *Guofang Daxue Xuebao*, no. 11, 1 Nov. 1987; Joint Periodicals Research Service, China, No. 37, 12 July.
Jin Dexiang (1991) 'The World in [the] 1990s: More Unrest, More Turmoil Ahead?', *Contemporary International Relations*, no. 6 (February).
Jin Junhui (1995) *International Studies* (Beijing), nos 4–5.
Joffe, Ellis (1995) 'The PLA and the Chinese Economy: The Effect of Involvement', *Survival*, vol. 37, no. 2 (Summer).
Joffe, Ellis (1996) 'Party–Army Relations in China: Retrospect and Prospect', *China Quarterly*, no. 146 (June).
Johnston, Alastair Iain (1995/96) 'China's New "Old Thinking": The Concept of Limited Deterrence', *International Security*, vol. 20, no. 3 (Winter).
Johnston, Alastair Iain (1996) 'Realism Versus Realpolitik: Explaining Chinese Security Policy in the Post Cold War Period', paper prepared for International Studies Association-Japan Association of International Relations Joint Convention, Makuhari, Japan, 20–22 Sept.
Jun Zhan (1994) 'China Goes to the Blue Waters: The Navy, Seapower Mentality and the South China Sea', *Journal of Strategic Studies*, vol. 17, no. 3 (September).

Kao Shaw-Fawn (1990), China and ASEAN: Strategic Interests and Policy Prospects', Ph.D. dissertation, Department of Government, University of Virginia, January.

Karniol, Robert (1996) 'China and Tajikistan in Bilateral Pact on Military Cooperation', *Jane's Defence Weekly*, 9 Oct.

Katzenstein, Peter (1976) 'International Relations and Domestic Structures: Foreign Economic Policies of Advanced Industrial States', *International Organization*, vol. 30, no.1 (Winter).

Kaye, Lincoln (1995a) 'The Grip Slips', *Far Eastern Economic Review*, 11 May.

Kaye, Lincoln (1995b) 'Local Hero', *Far Eastern Economic Review*, 11 May.

Kent, Ann E. (1993) *Between Freedom and Subsistence: China and Human Rights* (Hong Kong: Oxford University Press).

Khrushchev, Nikita (1970) *Khrushchev Remembers*, trans. S. Talbott (Boston: Little, Brown).

Kim Ilpyong (1995) 'The Sino-Soviet Alliance and the Korean War', *Korea and World Affairs*, vol. 19, no. 2 (Summer).

Kim, Samuel S. (ed.) (1989a), *China and the World: New Directions in Chinese Foreign Relations*, 2nd edition (Boulder, CO: Westview Press).

Kim, Samuel S. (1989b) 'New Directions and Old Puzzles in Chinese Foreign Policy', in Kim, (1989a).

Kim, Samuel S. (1989c) 'China and the Third World: In Search of a Peace and Development Line', in Kim (1989a).

Kim, Samuel S. (1991) *China In and Out of the Changing World Order* (Princeton, NJ: Center for International Studies, Princeton University).

Kim, Samuel S. (1994a) *China and the World: Chinese Foreign Relations in the Post-Cold War World* (Boulder, CO: Westview Press).

Kim, Samuel S. (1994b) 'China's International Organizational Behaviour', in Robinson and Shambaugh (1994).

Kim, Samuel S. (1994c) 'China and the World in Theory and Practice', in Kim (1994a).

Kim, Samuel S. (1994d) 'Mainland China in a Changing Asia-Pacific Regional Order', *Issues & Studies*, vol. 30, no. 10 (October).

Kim, Samuel S. (1995) 'China's Pacific Policy: Reconciling the Irreconcilable', *International Journal* (Canada), vol. 50, no. 3 (Summer).

Kim, Samuel S. (1996) *China; Quest for Security in the Post-Cold War World* (Carlisle Barracks, PA: Strategic Studies Institute, US Army War College).

Klein, Donald W. (1989) 'China and the Second World', in Kim, (1989a).

Klintworth, Gary (1995) 'China's Evolving Relationship with APEC', *International Journal*, vol. 50, no. 3 (Summer).

Lampton, David M. (1995) 'China and the Strategic Quadrangle: Foreign Policy Continuity in an Age of Discontinuity', in Michael Mandelbaum (ed.), *The Strategic Quadrangle: Russia, China, Japan and the United States in East Asia* (New York: Council on Foreign Relations Press).

Lardy, Nicholas R. (1994) *China and the World Economy* (Washington, DC: Institute for International Economics).

Layne, Christopher (1993) 'The Unipolar Illusion: Why New Great Powers Will Rise', *International Security*, vol. 17, no. 4 (Spring).

Lee Aekyung (1996) 'Taiwan's Mainland Policies: Causes of Change', *Journal of East Asian Affairs*, vol. 10, no. 2 (Summer/Fall).

Lee Chong-sik and Hyuk-sang Sohn (1995) 'South Korea in 1994: A Year of Trial', *Asian Survey*, vol. 35, no. 1 (January).

Lee Hong Yung (1994) 'China and the Two Koreas: New Emerging Triangle', in Young Whan Kihl (ed.), *Korea and the World: Beyond the Cold War* (Boulder, CO: Westview).

Lee Lai To (1995) 'ASEAN and the South China Sea Conflicts', *The Pacific Review*, vol. 8, no. 3.

Leifer, Michael (1996) *The ASEAN Regional Forum*, Adelphi Paper No. 302 (London: Oxford University Press).

Leo Suryadinata (1985) *China and the ASEAN States: The Ethnic Chinese Dimension* (Singapore: Singapore University Press).

Lewis, John W., Hua Di and Xue Litai (1991) 'Beijing's Defense Establishment: Solving the Arms-Export Enigma', *International Security*, vol. 15, no. 4 (Spring).

Lewis, John W. and Xue Li-tai (1988) *China Builds the Bomb* (Stanford, CA: Stanford University Press).

Li Peng (1990) 'Li Peng Addresses National Conference on Nationalities Affairs', Xinhua broadcast, 20 Feb. 1990, in British Broadcasting Corporation, *Summary of World Broadcasts*, FE/0696, 23 Feb.

Li Peng (1994) 'Li P'eng's (Li Peng's) Speech at the National Conference on Judicial Work (December 24, 1993)', *Issues & Studies*, vol. 30, no. 8 (August).

Li, Rex (1996) 'The Taiwan Strait Crisis and the Future of China–Taiwan Relations', *Security Dialogue*, vol. 27, no. 4 (December).

Li Weiguo (1992) 'Tiaozheng Zhong de Hei Zhanlue yu Hei Caijun Zhong de Xin Wenti', *Guoji Wenti Yanjiu*, no. 8, July.

Li Xiaobing, Chen Jian and David L. Wilson (1995/96), 'Mao Zedong's Handling of the Taiwan Straits Crisis of 1958: Chinese Recollections and Documents', Woodrow Wilson International Center for Scholars, Washington, DC, *Cold War International History Project Bulletin*, nos. 6–7.

Liu Huaqing (1986) 'Talents are the Key to Building a Powerful Modern Navy', *Hong Qi*, no. 486.

Liu Hauqing (1993), 'Unswervingly Advance Along the Road of Building a Modern Army of Chinese Characteristics', *Jiefangjun Bao*, 6 August.

Liu Jiangyong (1994) 'On the Establishment of [an] Asia-Pacific Multilateral Security Dialogue Mechanism', *Contemporary International Relations*, vol. 4, no. 2 (February).

Lu Ning (1997) *The Dynamics of Foreign-Policy Decisionmaking in China* (Boulder, CO: Westview Press).

Lu Zhongwei (1992) 'Security of Northeast Asia and Prospects for Multilateral Consultation', *Contemporary International Relations*, vol. 2, no. 11 (November).

Lu Zhongwei (1995) 'Post-War Japan at Fifty', *Contemporary International Relations* (Beijing), vol. 5, no. 7 (July).

Lym, Robyn (1996) 'Beijing's realpolitik', *Trends*, ISEAS, *Business Times*, 27–8 July.

Ma Zongshi (1994) 'China Dream in the Global 1990s and Beyond', *Strategic Digest* (New Delhi), vol. 24, no. 1 (January).

Mahbubani, Kishore (1994) 'You May Not Like It, Europe, But This Asian Medicine Could Help', *International Herald Tribune*, 1 Oct.

Malik, J. Mohan (1995a) 'China-India Relations in the Post-Soviet Era: The Continuuing Rivalry', *China Quarterly*, no. 142 (June), p. 320.

Malik, J. Mohan (1995b) 'China's Policy Towards Nuclear Arms Control', *Contemporary Security Policy*, vol. 16, no. 2 (August).

Malik, J. Mohan (1995c), 'Mongolia's Policy Options in the Post-Soviet World', *The Korean Journal of Defense Analysis*, vol. 7, no. 1 (Summer).

Mansfield, Edward D. and Jack Snyder (1995) 'Democratization and the Danger of War', *International Security*, vol. 20, no. 1 (Summer).

Mansingh, Surjit and Steven I. Levine (1989) 'China and India: Moving Beyond Confrontation', *Problems of Communism*, no. 38.

Mao Zedong (1969) *Selected Works*, vol. 4 (Beijing: Foreign Languages Press).

Mapes, Timothy (1996) 'Nervous Neighbours', *Far Eastern Economic Review*, 12 Dec.

McBeth, John (1995) 'Oil-Rich Diet', *Far Eastern Economic Review*, 27 April.

McGregor, Richard (1996)' 'Chinese Professor Backs US Asia Role', *The Australian*, 2 Dec.

Mearsheimer, John J. (1994/95) 'The False Promise of International Institutions', *International Security*, vol. 19, no. 3 (Winter).

Menon, Rajan (1997) 'The Strategic Convergence Between Russia and China', *Survival*, vol. 39, no. 2 (Summer).

Michael, Franz (1988) 'Non-Chinese Nationalities and Religious Communities', in Yuan-li Wu, *et al.* (1988).

Miller, Benjamin (1995) *When Opponents Cooperate: Great Power, Conflict and Collaboration in World Politics* (Ann Arbor, MI: University of Michigan Press).

Moltz, James Clay (1995) 'From Military Adversaries to Economic Partners: Russia and China in the New Asia', *Journal of East Asian Affairs*, vol. 9, no. 1 (Winter/Spring).

Montinola, Gabriella, Yingyi Qian and Barry Weingast (1995) 'Federalism Chinese Style: The Political Basis for Economic Success in China', *World Politics*, vol. 48, no. 1 (October).

Nan Li (1996) 'The PLA's Evolving Warfighting Doctrine, Strategy and Tactics, 1985–95: A Chinese Perspective', *China Quarterly*, no. 146 (June).

Nathan, Andrew J. (1996) 'China's Goals in the Taiwan Strait', *The China Journal*, no. 36 (July).

Naughton, Barry (1994) 'The Foreign Policy Implications of China's Economic Development Strategy', in Robinson and Shambaugh (1994).

Nelson, Harvey W. (1981) *The Chinese Military System: An Organizational Study of the Chinese People's Liberation Army* (Boulder CO: Westview Press).

Ng-Quinn, Michael (1984) 'International Systemic Constraints on Chinese Foreign Policy', in Samuel S. Kim (ed.), *China and the World*, 1st edition (Boulder, CO: Westview Press).

Norbu, Jamyang (no date) *Horseman in the Snow: The Story of Aten, an Old Khampa Warrior* (Dharamsala, India: Dharamṣala Press).

Ono Shuichi (1992) *Sino-Japanese Economic Relationships: Trade, Direct Investment, and Future Strategy*, World Bank Discussion Paper No. 146 (Washington DC: The World Bank).

Pan Shiying (1993) *Reflections on Modern Strategy: Post-Cold War Strategic Theory* (Beijing: Shijie Zhishi Chubanshe).

Panikkar, K. M. (1955) *In Two Chinas* (London: Allen & Unwin).

Park Choon-ho (1972) 'Continental Shelf Issues in the Yellow Sea and the East China Sea', Law of the Sea Institute, Occasional Paper No. 15 (University of Rhode Island).

Peng Dehuai (1981) *Peng Dehuai Zishu* (Shanghai: Renmin Chubanshe).

Pillsbury, Michel (ed.) (1997) *Chinese Views of Future Warfare* (Washington, DC: National Defense University Press).

Qian Qichen (1990) 'China's Important Role in World Affairs', *Beijing Review*, 15–21 Oct.

Qian Qichen (1992), Speech to the United Nations General Assembly, in Foreign Broadcast Information Service, *Daily Report: China*, 1 October.

Qian Qichen (1994) 'Ch'ien Ch'i-ch'en's Report on the International Situation (September 5, 1992)', *Issues & Studies*, vol. 30, no. 1 (January).

Qian Qichen (1995a) 'Unswervingly Follow the Independent Foreign Policy of Peace', *Quishi* (Beijing), no. 12, 16 June.

Qian Qichen (1995b) Speech to UN General Assembly, 28 Sept. 1994; text of speech in 'China Proposes Nuclear Package', *Heping*, [n.v.], no. 36–7 (March).

Qiang Zhai (1995/96) 'Mao Zedong and Dulles' "Peaceful Evolution" Strategy: Revelations from Bo Yibo's Memoirs', Woodrow Wilson International Center for Scholars, Washington DC, *Cold War International History Project Bulletin*, nos 6–7 (Winter).

Qiao Shi (1994) 'Ch'iao Shih's (Qiao Shi's) Speech at the Commencement of the Central Party School (January 6, 1993)', *Issues & Studies*, vol. 30, no. 3 (March).

Quinn-Judge, Sophie (1997) 'Common Cause', *Far Eastern Economic Review*, 8 May.

Ren Jianxin (1995) 'Ren Jianxin's Speech at the National Conference on Political-Legal Work (December 21, 1993)', *Issues & Studies*, vol. 31, no. 1 (January).

Renmin Ribao (1965) 10 January.

Renmin Ribao (1979) 21 November; cited in Shambaugh (1994a).

Robinson, Thomas W. (1994a) 'Chinese Foreign Policy from the 1940s to the 1990s', in Robinson and Shambaugh (1994).

Robinson, Thomas W. (1994b) 'Interdependence in China's Foreign Relations', in Kim (1994a).

Robinson, Thomas W. and David Shambaugh (eds) (1994) *Chinese Foreign Policy: Theory and Practice* (New York: Oxford University Press).

Ross, Madelyn C. (1994) 'China's International Economic Behaviour', in Robinson and Shambaugh (1994).

Rôss, Robert S. (1988) 'China and the Ethnic Chinese: Political Liability/ Economic Asset', in Joyce K. Kallgren, Noordin Sopiee and Soedjati

Djiwandono (eds), *ASEAN and China: An Evolving Relationship* (Berkeley: Institute of East Asian Studies, University of California).

Ross, Robert S. (1996) 'Enter the Dragon', *Foreign Policy*, no. 104 (104).

Rowen, Henry S. (1996) 'The Short March: China's Road to Democracy', *The National Interest*, no. 45 (Fall).

Salameh, Mamdouh G. (1995–6) 'China, Oil and the Risk of Regional Conflict', *Survival*, vol. 37, no. 4 (Winter 1995–6).

Schultz, Clifford II and William J. Ardrey IV (1995) 'The Future Prospects of Sino-Vietnamese Relations: Are Trade and Commerce the Critical Factors for Sustainable Peace?', *Contemporary Southeast Asia*, vol. 17, no. 2 (September).

Segal, Gerald (1985) *Defending China* (London: Oxford University Press).

Segal, Gerald (1994a) 'China Changes Shape: Regionalism and Foreign Policy', Adelphi Paper No. 287, International Institute for Strategic Studies, March.

Segal, Gerald (1994b) 'China's Central Government Losing Grip on Provinces', *The Straits Times* (Singapore), 8 March.

Segal, Gerald (1994c) 'China: Arms Transfer Policies and Practices', *Contemporary Security Policy*, vol. 15, no. 2 (August).

Segal, Gerald (1995) 'Tying China into the International System', *Survival*, vol. 37, no. 2 (Summer).

Segal, Gerald (1996) 'East Asia and the "Constrainment" of China', *International Security*, vol. 20, no. 4 (Spring).

Selth, Andrew (1996) 'Burma and the Strategic Competition between India and China', *Journal of Strategic Studies*, vol. 19, no. 2 (June).

Sha Zukang (1995) 'China and the NPT', *Disarmament*, vol. 18, no. 1.

Shambaugh, David (1994a) 'Patterns of Interaction in Sino-American Relations', in Robinson and Shambaugh (1994).

Shambaugh, David (1994b) 'Growing Strong: China's Challenge to Asian Security', *Survival*, vol. 36, no. 2 (Summer).

Shambaugh, David (1996a) 'China's Military in Transition: Politics, Professionalism, Procurement and Power Projection', *China Quarterly*, no. 146 (June).

Shambaugh, David (1996b) 'China's Military: Real or Paper Tiger?', *The Washington Quarterly*, vol. 19, no. 2 (Spring).

Shen Qurong (1992) '[The] Security Environment in Northeast Asia: Its Characteristics and Sensitivities', *Contemporary International Relations,* vol. 2, no. 12 (December).

Sheng Lijun (1995a) 'China's Foreign Policy Under Status Discrepancy, Status Enhancement', *Contemporary Southeast Asia*, vol. 17, no. 2 (September).

Sheng Lijun, (1995b) 'China's Policy Towards the Spratly Islands in the 1990s', Strategic and Defence Studies Centre, Working paper No. 287 (Australian National University, June).

Shi Ze (1995) Changes in Russia's Strategic Position in 'the Asia-Pacific Region and its Impact', *International Studies* (Beijing), nos 4–5.

Shi Ze (1996) 'Perceptions on the [sic] Sino-Russian Relations in the New Era', *International Studies* (Beijing), no. 5.

Shichor, Yitzhak (1995) 'China's Defence Capability: The Impact of Military-to-Civilian Conversion', CAPS Papers No. 8, Taipei: Chinese Council of Advanced Policy Studies, April.

Shinn, James (ed.) (1996) *Weaving the Net: Conditional Engagement with China* (New York: Council on Foreign Relations).

Shuja, Sharif M. (1995) 'Russian and Chinese Diplomacy in Korea: Continuity and Change', *Issues & Studies*, vol. 31, no. 8 (August).

Si Cheng (1996) 'Chinese Say "No" to the United States', *Beijing Review*, 21–7 Oct.

Si Mu (1981) 'Dangqian Guoji Xingshi he Wuoguo Shehui Zhuyi Xiandaihua Jianshe', *Sixiang Zhanxian*, no. 4 (September).

Singh, Udai Bhanu (1996) 'Recent Trends in Sino-Vietnamese Relations', *Strategic Analysis* (India), vol. 19, no. 2 (May).

Smil, Vaclav (1996) 'Environmental Problems in China: Estimates of Economic Costs', East-West Center Special Report No. 5 (April).

Snyder, Scott (1996) 'The South China Sea Dispute: Prospects for Preventive Diplomacy', Special Report, United States Institute of Peace, Washington DC, August.

South China Morning Post (1995) 'Army Wants Tougher Stance on US, Taiwan', 17 July, 1995; FBIS, *Daily Report: China*, 17 July.

Spence, Jonathan D. (1990) *The Search for Modern China* (New York: W.W. Norton & Co.).

Spirtas, Michel (1996) 'A House Divided: Tragedy and Evil in Realist Theory', *Security Studies*, vol. 5, no. 3 (Spring).

Spurr, Russell (1988) *Enter the Dragon: China's Undeclared War Against the US in Korea, 1950–51* (New York: Newmarket Press).

Starr, John Bryan (1996) 'China in 1995: Mounting Problems, Waning Capacity', *Asian Survey*, vol. 36, no. 1 (January).

Straits Times (1993) 'Push for Democracy in Asia by Clinton Would Be a Mistake, Says SM Lee', 20 January.

Straits Times (1994) 'Li: Westerner Who Thinks He Can Do Better Welcome to Lead China', *Straits Times*, 7 July.

Straits Times (Singapore) (1997a) 'Beijing Seals Off Town in Xinjiang After Riots', 12 February.

Straits Times (1997b) 'Jakarta's Chinese Told: Tone Down New Year Joy', 4 February.

Straits Times (1997c) 'Taiwan "to Open Door to Mainland Tourists"', 5 February.

Strasser, Steven (1995) 'A New "Anti-China Club"?', *Newsweek*, 17 July.

Su Qianming (1992) 'Shilun Changgui Liliang yu Zhanlue Heweishe Liliang Xiang Jiehe', in *Quan Jun Mao Zedong Junshi Sixiang Xueshu Taolun Wen Jing Xuan*, Vol. I (Beijing: Academy of Military Sciences Press).

Sukma, Rizal (1994) 'Recent Developments in Sino-Indonesian Relations: An Indonesian View', *Contemporary Southeast Asia*, vol. 16, no. 1 (June).

Sullivan, Roger W. (1992) 'Discarding the China Card', *Foreign Policy*, no. 86 (Spring).

Sun Yat-sen (1928) *San Min Chu I: The Three Principles of the People* (Shanghai: The Commercial Press).

Sutter, Robert G. (1996) *Shaping China's Future in World Affairs: The Role of the United States* (Boulder, CO: Westview Press).

Swaine, Michael D. (1995) *China: Domestic Change and Foreign Policy* (Santa Monica, CA: RAND).

Swaine, Michael D. (1996) 'The PLA and Chinese National Security Policy: Leaderships, Structures, Processes', *China Quarterly*, no. 146 (June).

Tang Tai (Hong Kong) (1992) 'CCP Takes Offensive on Human Rights Issue', 15 July, 1992, p. 41; US Foreign Broadcast Information Service, *Daily Report: China*, 22 July.

Thornton, Richard C. (1982) *China: A Political History, 1917–1980* (Boulder, CO: Westview Press).

Tibetan Bulletin (1990) 'A Child Prisoner Tells His Experience', May–June.

Tibetan Bulletin (1992), "The ABCs of Discrimination in Tibet," January–February.

Tiglao, Rigoberto (1995) 'Remote Control', *Far Eastern Economic Review*, 1 June.

Tow, William T. (1994) 'China and the International Strategic System', in Robinson and Shambaugh, (1994).

Tyler, Patrick E. (1996) 'Chinese Seek Atom Options to Fend Off Asteroids', *The New York Times*, 27 April.

Tyler, Patrick E. (1997) 'China Sends a Message to Taiwan by Vetoing UN Peacekeeping Force', *International Herald Tribune*, 13 January.

Valencia, Mark J. (1995) *China and the South China Sea Disputes*, Adelphi Paper No. 298 (Oxford: Oxford University Press).

Van Ness, Peter (1970) *Revolution and Chinese Foreign Policy: Peking's Support for Wars of National Liberation* (Berkeley: University of California Press).

Wallerstein, Mitchel B. (1996) 'China and Proliferation: A Path Not Taken?', *Survival*, vol. 38, no. 3 (Autumn).

Walt, Stephen M. (1992) 'Revolution and War', *World Politics*, vol. 44, no. 3 (April).

Waltz, Kenneth N. (1979) *Theory of International Politics* (New York: McGraw-Hill).

Wanandi, Jusuf (1996) 'ASEAN's China Strategy: Towards Deeper Engagement', *Survival*, vol. 38, no. 3 (Autumn).

Wang Fei-Ling (1997) *Tacit Acceptance and Watchful Eyes: Beijing's Views about the U.S.-ROK Alliance* (Carlisle Barracks, PA: Strategic Studies Institute, US Army War College).

Wang, James C. F. (1992) *Contemporary Chinese Politics: An Introduction* (Englewood Cliffs, NJ: Prentice-Hall.

Wang Jianwei (1996) 'Coping With China as a Rising Power', in Shinn (1996).

Wang Jisi (1990) 'International Relations Theory and the Study of Chinese Foreign Policy from a Chinese Perspective', paper delivered at the conference on 'Ideas and Interpretations in Chinese Foreign Policy', Aspen/Snowmass, Colorado, USA, 8–13 August.

Wang Renzhi (1990) 'On Opposing the Tendency of Bourgeois Liberalization', *Renmin Ribao* (overseas edition), 23 February.

Wang Shu-shin (1994) 'Military Developments of the People's Republic of China After the 1989 Tiananmen Massacre', CAPS Papers No. 5 (Taipei: Chinese Council of Advanced Policy Studies, June).

Wang Yunlang (1995) 'Zhoubian Guojia Haijun Liliangde Fazhan ji Duiwoguode Yingxiang', *Junshi Xueshu*, no. 10.

Wei Liang-ts'ai (1985) 'The Foreign Policy of the PRC Since 1949: A Critical Analysis', in Yu-ming Shaw (ed.), *Power and Policy in the PRC* (Boulder, CO: Westview Press).

Whiting, Allen S. (1975a) *The Chinese Calculus of Deterrence: India and Indochina* (Ann Arbor, MI: University of Michigan Press).

Whiting, Allen S. (1975b) 'New Light on Mao: 3. Quemoy 1958: Mao's Miscalculations', *China Quarterly*, no. 62 (June).

Whiting, Allen S. (1995a) *East Asian Military Security Dynamics* (Stanford, CA: Asia-Pacific Research Center).

Whiting, Allen S. (1995b) 'Chinese Nationalism and Foreign Policy After Deng', *China Quarterly*, no. 142 (June).

Wilson, Ian (1993) 'China and the New World Order', in Richard Leaver and James L. Richardson, *The Post-Cold War Order: Diagnoses and Prognoses* (St. Leonards, NSW, Australia: Allen & Unwin).

Winterford, David (1993) 'Chinese Naval Planning and Maritime Interests in the South China Sea: Implications for US and Regional Security Policies', *Journal of American East Asian Relations*, vol. 2, no. 4 (Winter).

Wortzel, Larry M. (1994) 'China Pursues Traditional Great-Power Status', *Orbis*, vol. 38, no. 2 (Spring).

Wu Yuan-li *et al.* (1988) *Human Rights in the People's Republic of China* (Boulder, CO: Westview).

Wye, R. F. (1995–96), Book Review Section, *Survival*, vol. 37, no. 4 (Winter).

Xi Runchang (1991) 'Struggle Among Big Powers for Leading Role in Establishing New World Order', *Liaowang*, overseas edition, no. 19, May 13, 1991; Foreign Broadcast Information Service, *Daily Report: China*, 22 May.

Xie Guang *et al.* (eds) (1992) *Dangdai Zhongguo de Guofang Keji Shiye*, vol. 1 (Beijing: Dangdai Zhongguo Chubanshe).

Xie Yixian (1989) 'Bashi Niandai Zhongguo Duiwai Zhence de Zhongda Tiaozheng Jiqi Yiyi', *Qiushi*, no. 1.

Xinhua News Service (1996) 'Ninth Five-Year Plan, Long-Term Target', Foreign Broadcast Information Service, *Daily Report: China*, 96-070, 10 April.

Xinhua News Service (1990) 'Li Peng Speaks on Market, Industrial Production', FBIS, *Daily Report: China*, 9 October.

Xu Xiaojun (1994) 'China's Grand Strategy for the 21st Century', National Defense University (Beijing) seminar, 15–16 February.

Xu Yan (1993) 'Chinese Forces and their Casualties in the Korean War', *Chinese Historians*, vol. 6, no. 2 (Fall).

Yan Xuetong (1993) 'China's Security After the Cold War', *Contemporary International Relations*, vol. 3, no. 5 (May).

Yan Xuetong (1995) 'China's Post-Cold War Security Strategy', *Contemporary International Relations*, vol. 5, no. 5 (May).

260   *Bibliography*

Yang Bojiang (1996) 'Why US-Japan Joint Declaration on Security Alliance?', *Contemporary International Relations*, vol. 6, no. 5 (May).

Yang Chunchang (1989) *Deng Xiaoping Xinshiqi Jianjun Sixiang Yanjiu* (Beijing: People's Liberation Army Press).

Yen Hua (1996) 'Jiangsu, Shandong Factions Carve Up Military Power – Inside Story of Unusual PLA Top-Level Changes', *Chien Shao*, 1 Feb. 1996, pp. 38–40; Foreign Broadcast Information Service, *Daily Report: China*, 22 Feb.

You Ji (1994) 'A Test Case for China's Defense and Foreign Policies', *Contemporary Southeast Asia*, vol. 16, no. 4 (March).

Yu Ming-shan (1996) 'Transforming into a World Security System', *Wen Wei Po*, 18 April.

Yuan Jing-Dong (1995) 'China's Defence Modernization: Implications for Asia-Pacific Security', *Contemporary Southeast Asia*, vol. 17, no. 1 (June).

Yuan Qitong (1994) 'Yuan Ch'i-t'ung's (Yuan Qitong's) Address at the Conference of United Front Work Department Directors of Fukien Province (September 26, 1991)', *Issues & Studies*, vol. 30, no. 7 (July).

Zhang Guocheng (1996) 'Japan's Constitution is Facing a Test', *Renmin Ribao*, 23 April, 1996, in FBIS, *Daily Report: China*, 29 April.

Zhang Jianzhi (1987) 'Dui Caijun Jiben Lilun Wenti de Tantao', in *Guiji Caijun Duozheng yu Zhongguo* (Beijing: Current Affairs Press).

Zhao Quansheng (1996) *Interpreting Chinese Foreign Policy: The Micro–Macro Linkage Approach* (Hong Kong: Oxford University Press).

Index